Suffolk County Council

Libraries & Heritage /ρ ɜⁿ

You may keep this title until the last date stamped below or the date given on your receipt.
Providing it has not been reserved by another library user, you may renew it by visiting any Suffolk library, via the world wide web or by telephone. To renew your loans by web use **http://libcat.suffolkcc.gov.uk**
To renew your loans by telephone, please dial **0901 888 8989** and have your **library card** and (numeric) **PIN** ready. Calls are charged at a **premium** rate.

Any overdue charges on this title will be made at the current ADULT rate.

http://www.suffolkcc.gov.uk/libraries_and_heritage

GW00703178

30127 05918229 0

SCENES FROM YESTERDAY

SCENES FROM YESTERDAY

Susan Tolman

The Book Guild Ltd
Sussex, England

First published in Great Britain in 2002 by
The Book Guild Ltd
25 High Street
Lewes, East Sussex
BN7 2LU

Typesetting in Times by
SetSystems Ltd, Saffron Walden, Essex

Printed in Great Britain by
Antony Rowe Ltd, Chippenham, Wiltshire

A catalogue record for this book is
available from the British Library

ISBN 1 85776 683 0

TEMPORA MUTANTUR ET MUTAMUR IN ILLIS

Times change and we change in them

CONTENTS

FOREWORD

It may justifiably be asked why I should have wanted to write about the early life of an insignificant girl, hardly out of her childhood, spent in a country of little interest to an English reader whose knowledge of little Austria is taken from holiday advertisements, travel brochures and *The Sound of Music*. The great Austrian composers and the Vienna schools of music and painting belong to the wider culture of Europe as a whole much beyond the scope of these notes.

The reason for setting these memoirs down is not self-importance, nor a sentimental and self-indulgent looking back through the benevolent mists of time. The reason lies in my life-long fascination with the past. Again and again, when reading a well-researched historical work I have become aware of the complete reliance by the writer on official documents and state papers, and how little is available and quoted from records made by the ordinary men and women of any age until the advent of the tape recorder and its refinements. Perhaps these earlier records don't exist except to a very limited extent. Eye-witness accounts, where they do exist, conjure up a picture of daily life as it was lived by the vast majority of ordinary people according to their station in society. That, not unnaturally, is bound to be biased, for each of us can only see, know and experience a fraction of the events and happenings amongst which we live. This is vividly demonstrated when comparing the accounts given by two independent witnesses to a traffic accident.

What I have endeavoured to do is to describe a little of a way of life that has not only physically completely disappeared, but will soon do so also from the minds of those present at the time and now facing the end of life's journey within the very near future.

PART ONE

1

Beginnings – 1920

15 January was bleak indeed. Midwinter, the darkest month of the year in a country which had not only lost a disastrous war but, as a consequence of that cataclysmic event, had lost its very identity. Revolution had swept across its many lands, the Emperor, heir of a tradition going back over a thousand years, had been deposed and sent into exile in Switzerland, the refuge of the dispossessed. Into this turmoil and utter depression I was born on that day, long and thin, with a head full of dark brown hair and a long scratch on my nose, weighing all of five pounds. It was not a question of prematurity but simply a case of an undernourished, very young mother.

Vienna, my native city, until 15 months earlier the capital of a large empire which had grown over many centuries until it housed 14 different nationalities within its borders, was facing a grim future as the swollen head of a diminutive rump. Nearly one third of the population of the newly created republic of Austria lived within its circumference, and naked starvation stalked its streets. One of the well-remembered sights of my young days was the multitude of short, bowlegged persons, the result of childhood rickets, from which I, too, was to suffer severely. It was commonly called the 'English Disease' for it was generally accepted that it had been Great Britain which had inflicted the sea blockade to try and starve the Central Powers into submission. Bread consisted of the stalks of the maize plant ground into a kind of flour with the addition of a little rye. It fell to pieces on being cut. Fresh vegetables were unobtainable and people had to make do, when they could get it, with *Dörrgemüse*, an early form of dried roots. The hatred engendered by this state of affairs expressed itself in the way most letters ended with the slogan '*Gott strafe England!*' (May God punish England!)

That my legs did not take on the bowlegged appearance associated with this often fatal deficiency disease is entirely due to the attention they received from my mother and nurse, aided by a general physical weakness which prevented any early attempts at walking. Daily hour-long massage coupled with large doses of cod liver oil in its most obnoxious unrefined form eventually showed results. So it came about that I could not walk until the age of 17 months – but with straight legs.

A much worse effect of this dreadful disease of semi-starvation was the inability of the soft spot, the fontanelle, on the top of my head to close, as it normally does, by the age of two. A baby's head at birth being very large in relation to the rest of its body, the various seams joining the bones are flexible to make its passage through the birth canal possible and only slowly harden into the firm skull of an adult. With the soft spot still open at the age of two, an early death was to be my lot unless a prolonged stay at the seaside could be arranged.

Mother, fortunately, had an aunt married to a rich Berlin shoe manufacturer who generously paid for her, my sister, younger by a year, and myself to spend the months of July and August at Arendsee, a Baltic seaside resort. The miracle happened. I took to the water like a fish, although only two and a half and my skull healed up. It further brought my one and only visit to Berlin and gave me one of my earliest memories, that of throwing pots of pelargoniums from my great-aunt's second-floor balcony onto the heads of the passers-by down below! The well-deserved punishment which must have followed such an act I cannot recall. Another vivid snapshot remaining with me is that of my mother climbing into the top bunk of our second-class sleeper.

Arendsee, too, has left its imprint. The wide blue sea was just the other side of the road from the guesthouse at which we were staying, and both it and the sea have remained with me. Water from that moment onward became my passion. It never held any terror, I never knew what it is to be afraid of it. Father was anxious not to lose his children in a drowning accident on the many long walking tours we were a little later to undertake, but he need not have worried. Being somewhat clumsy, I have always felt safer in water than on land.

I was the first-born of a couple very much in love. My father had met my mother under most romantic circumstances, in spite of the oppressive war atmosphere. He was a 36-year-old bachelor, a Doctor of Law with an upper-middle-class background. His grandparents on his mother's side were rich landowners in Bohemia. His father also came from Bohemia, but from its capital Prague. One of my grandfather's brothers was a publisher of dubious romances, one of which became a family joke, since it bore the title *The Popess Joanna* and came in 23 volumes. It made a lot of money. Another owned a large draper's shop in Meran in the South Tyrol. Their mother tongue was German, as it was, at that time, of most members of the educated classes in Bohemia. Of course, they also spoke Czech, often calling it their first language since they were, in the main, nursed by wet-nurses who were healthy young countrywomen with enough milk for their own and a stranger's child. Later on

5

in life we often bought shoes from my father's old nurse who had married a shoemaker and cobbler and lived within easy walking distance from us.

Father had qualified as a lawyer to please his mother, but had no intentions of ever sitting over dusty briefs. He was a born writer and story teller, and the inward urge to engage in creative writing already manifested itself at school, when he managed to fail a test by treating the essay topic of 'The Circulation of Water' in poetic form, which did not find favour with his science teacher. By the time he set eyes on mother he was a man of the world and a famous writer. His renown rested at that time on his gift of mirroring his life and times in a satirical manner expressed through the mouths of a number of characters. One of his pseudonyms was 'Poldi Huber' under which he published, in the juiciest of Viennese dialects, the thoughts and comments from a fourth-form primary schoolboy from one of the roughest quarters of town. The odd thing was that he never spoke in dialect but only in the elegant German of the well-bred Viennese. His school days had brought him into contact with boys from a working-class background clever enough to pass the entrance examination into grammar school, whose vocabulary constituted almost a separate language. One of the few consolations we had after the occupation of Austria by Germany in 1938 was the inability of the German troops, mainly originating from East Prussia, to understand their Viennese 'brothers'.

Mother, at what turned out to be the decisive moment of her life, was aged 20 and a stunning beauty. How it used to rile me as a teenager to be told by honest male friends that I was indeed quite good-looking, but not a patch on mother! Her background was utterly different from father's. Her father had trained as an artist and was earning a precarious living from portrait painting and Pointillist landscapes which hardly ever sold. His family was lower-class Viennese. He must have been very good-looking and possessed of a lot of charm, for he managed to marry the daughter of a successful merchant – very much against her parents' wishes – which took considerable courage on her part. Poor woman, her happiness was not to endure. When Mother was two and a half her mother gave birth to twins, contracted childbed fever and died at the age of 24. The boy followed his mother within a week, and the girl was put up for adoption. Grandfather, who was anything but domesticated, and did not have the means of employing somebody to look after his oldest orphaned child, had to ask various relations to come to the rescue by, in turn, giving her shelter. The effect of this unsettled childhood was what one might expect when a sensitive, very artistic child is involved. Her instability of temperament had unwelcome consequences for us children.

However, in August 1917 all that was apparent was her dark beauty. It was customary to hold a fête on the Emperor's birthday on 17 August, and since it was wartime the theme was war charities. Father who, although in the army, had not been able to serve in the field, being an asthmatic, had been detailed to join a group of entertainers to the forces, travelling through the Balkans to cheer up the troops. On that day he, being on leave, was manning a stall in the Türkenschanzpark, one of the many large parks within the city's boundaries, for the sale of his books with the profits devoted to charitable causes. Mother had won a large number of picture postcards in the tombola and was walking past his stall, clutching them without knowing what to do with her winnings. That was his clue!

'Miss, would you like to exchange some of your postcards for some of my books?' was his opening gambit. A bargain was struck, and after a further five minutes of conversation he asked her in all seriousness: 'Miss, will you marry me?'

'Doctor, you must be crazy!' was the not unnatural reply from Mother, who knew who he was and considered him, quite rightly, to be trying to make a pick-up. Well, it took five months for Father to convince her of his commitment. They were married on 30 January 1918 in Vienna's Protestant garrison church, with two passers-by for witnesses and Mother's father to give her away. This marriage, entered into on such short acquaintance and in such unsettled times, was a true love match surviving many vicissitudes, including the traumatic upheaval of having to leave a beloved home and country and making a fresh start across the ocean. It only ended after 42 years with Father's death.

Perhaps it worked so well because they were so different and, in this way, complemented each other. Father, highly talented, highly educated, a writer, a wit, a humorist, a composer of songs and excellent pianist, a linguist fluent, apart from German, in Czech, French and Italian, a classicist with a profound knowledge of the Greek and Roman languages and civilisations, was, at the same time, a dreamer, unwordly in business and a strong believer in human goodness. Mother, having left school at 14 without ever having learnt to spell properly, was extremely practical and understood instinctively human nature. She could only write in the Gothic script, was an innate artist, highly musical, though untrained, who sang beautifully to Father's accompaniment. Her artistry manifested itself in the way she furnished our flat from very little, painting chairs and cupboards whenever their colour started to offend her. She loved clothes and was deeply unhappy if she could not dress in the latest fashion. She, I am sure, saw herself as presenting a picture.

Her taste in clothes was also forced on us children. My sister and I do not resemble each other in any way, apart from having reached approximately the same height. As a teenager I was dark and thin, and she was auburn and plump. But still, we had to wear identical dresses made to measure by a dressmaker and designed to the last button by Mother, whose greatest concession to our wishes was that I wore red to set off my dark hair, and my sister green to match her reddish curls. No wonder neither of us developed a great interest in fashion, my sister going so far as to wear her grown-up daughters' cast-offs as long as they more or less fit.

My sister was born only 14 months after me, but she could very well have been much younger, so much had circumstances changed in that short period. Father, having lost a fortune by investing in war bonds of the now defunct double monarchy, had by then had to start battling with the terrible inflation following in the aftermath of a lost war.

At the time of my birth only the best had been considered good enough for the first-born, and the Sanatorium Löw the only maternity clinic fit for a new member of the Weil family. So I was born amid all the trappings of luxury and delivered by a top-flight obstetrician. Only it was a pity that the midwife working with him did not know the correct length of navel cord to be left with the infant, to ensure a satisfactory healing of the hole in the lining securing the intestines through which the baby had been fed in its mother's tummy. The cord was cut off too short, resulting in a hernia to be added to the rickets and the low birth weight. Not exactly a propitious start to life. Having exhausted all external means to correct the hernia, which threatened an extrusion of the bowels with every tumble I took, a quite serious operation at the age of seven at last closed the hole in the abdominal sac, leaving a long and ugly scar. Belly dancing quite obviously would not be one of my accomplishments.

My sister was given quite a different entry into the world. Father, having had to retrench his expenses, arranged for her to be born at the Rudolfiner Heim, a maternity home patronised by the middle-income group. The trappings were simple but the staff were very competent and offered excellent care. Her birth weight was normal and she knew nothing of rickets, an open spot on the top of her head and a hernia. She had red hair, a disgrace in the Vienna of those days always to be hidden under a bonnet, blue eyes which later on always corresponded in colour with that of her hair, and was lovely and chubby with dimples in all the right places, while I was dark, had blue eyes which gradually turned brown, and was very thin with spindly legs. 'Sparrow legs' Mother called me.

We were each given one first name only. My parents had hoped for a boy as their first-born and had his names all ready but, alas, it was not to be. Since it was a girl, Susanne had to do. Mother, completely ignorant of a word of English beyond 'yes', greatly admired everything originating from the country that, until so very recently, had been numbered amongst Austria's enemies. When it came to choosing a name for my sister, she somehow alighted on the title of Dickens' *Little Dorrit*, and Dorrit it was and still is. Fortunately, my sister does not read Dickens or, to her great distress, she would have learnt that hers is a man's surname. Untutored enthusiasm can lead to strange results.

Although we are so close in age, we had and still have little in common. My interests from babyhood on were of the intellectual kind, reading one of my greatest pleasures, music part of life. My sister being practically tone-deaf – the story went that she only recognised the National Anthem when everybody else stood up – must have had a hard time in our musical household. She loved playing with her dolls, lodged on the top of the two large wardrobes in our room, of which she had at least 20, while my one and only, called Liesel, peacefully and undisturbed slept in her pram. My cousin's small but beautifully made working model of a steam engine was of much greater interest to me.

There is nothing coherent I remember of my pre-school days. Snapshots remain of the people mother hired to help to look after us. There was Fräulein Käthe from Berlin, specially brought to Vienna to prevent us from picking up the 'terrible' Viennese dialect which Mother spoke to perfection when she wanted to and Father employed so cleverly in his satirical writings. No doubt, she was efficient and we spoke clear and acceptable German, but her moral character must have been somewhat below the standard expected for she made a rapid exit with Mother muttering something about 'love bites on her neck'. At the time this meant nothing to us, of course. She was followed by Fräulein Mizzi (the Viennese form of 'Maria' and also the term bestowed upon pussies, to which they are supposed to answer) who always wore national costume, came every weekday afternoon, and whose main task was to take us for the obligatory walk in the park.

The most lasting impression of those early years was the contracting by both of us girls of the endemic whooping cough, which was literally sweetened by a delicious-tasting cough syrup liberally dispensed from a large soup spoon. Once able to resume our visits to the park, we were made to keep well away from other children, making us feel like the out-casts we were. The cough being still troublesome by the summer of 1924, Mother took us and Fräulein Mizzi off to the Adriatic, where the warm sun and sea did what was desired of them. It also gave me my first sight of a seaplane. Along the waterfront of the small Istrian town of Porto Rose, at that period a part of Italy although with an entirely Croatian population, were parked several hydroplanes, which I studied with very great interest while clambering over the rocks on the fore-shore. One in particular intrigued me. Its pilot was sitting on the floor of the biplane with his feet dangling in the water and a fishing rod in his hand, making a peaceful impression. It seems hardly possible that we should have progressed in less than a lifetime from such primitiveness to the jumbo jet which transported my husband, myself and another 300-odd passengers over 8000 miles in nine hours from Vancouver to London in 1990.

The whooping cough, having departed, was immediately replaced by an attack of a dangerous strain of dysentry. The hotel where we were staying had a small stream running through its grounds, whose water was contaminated and out of bounds to all children. Of course a few of us had to find out why, myself included. The resulting illness was so severe that Mother packed up and transferred her family to Seeboden on Lake Millstatt in Carinthia to allow her child to die on native soil. Father joined us there. The illness was fought with the skinless breast of boiled, not roasted, chicken and, horror upon horrors, powdered medicinal charcoal. Several times a day this had to be administered dry from a large teaspoon. How Mother kept her temper when I blew into the hated loose powder, evenly distributing it over myself, her and much else I do not know.

Recovery came only slowly, and I retain a vivid picture of reclining in a pushchair, being unable to walk through weakness in spite of my advanced age of four years and seven months. It was early autumn, and children were playing the traditional games of that season, longingly watched by me. It was a first taste of an often recurring situation in my subsequent life, that of the outsider watching from a distance and unable to become involved.

2

Schooldays

In spite of everything I grew thin, with little appetite and difficult about the eternal spinach which was considered essential to a child's well-being – today we know better – and the question of schooling had to be dealt with.

Compulsory schooling started with the autumn semester after one's sixth birthday, but children born before or on 15 January of the following year could, after a medical test, be admitted earlier. I took the test, consisting in walking up and down before a doctor, having the usual checks as to the functioning of one's faculties and a conversation with him to ascertain the state of my mental maturity, and I was passed as fit to go to school.

But the nearest state school, and we all had to go to our nearest school, was too rough for Mother. Father had friends who ran a small, private, expensive primary school in the Palace of Schönbrunn's old servants' quarter, and there I went in September 1925. Our class teacher was a man who, I discovered years later, must have been at the beginning of his career. To us he was a figure of great awe and fear. We, 20 little boys and girls, had to sit with our hands laid on the desk in front of us, palm downwards, unless engaged in some lawful activity. Absolute silence reigned, only punctuated by questions and answers in the course of a lesson. But how well we were taught.

We all learnt to read and write within a few months. The

method used was quite ingenious. From a box of cut-out letters with which each child had been equipped, the twin of the one written on the blackboard by our teacher had to be picked out and arranged inside a strip of transparent paper fixed to the upper half of the box. Then we copied it into our notebooks, first in pencil but soon in ink, with steel nibs dipped into the inkwell fitted to each desk. The battle against inkblots, spillage from the well and general untidiness was never-ending.

There was little time for play. My teacher and I did not hit it off, possibly on account of my inclination of walking round the classroom in the middle of a lesson, and I got punished for things I had not done, like throwing a pot of ink against the classroom wall. While looking in surprise at the spreading stain and the boy who had perpetrated the deed, I was taken hold of, wrongly accused of committing the felony and condemned to spending a whole lesson standing in a corner of the room facing a cupboard. Oh, what a long time 50 minutes is to a child of five! The consequences were unforeseen. I started to walk in my sleep and was terrified of the patterns made at night by the street lights on the floor of our bedroom. At the end of the academic year a change of school seemed advisable.

Mother somehow managed to get me into a state primary school on the other side of the park of Schönbrunn, outside our catchment area, and happiness was the result. We were all girls, and our teacher was Fräulein Klara Werner. Nothing could have been more old-fashioned than both her and the school. The buildings were old, well hidden behind a very high, solid wooden gate, the interior plain, with large windows letting in a lot of light. There was gaslight and a coal stove giving out some warmth in winter. The desks of solid oak were arranged in rows, each with a lid under which to place our books. They were allocated to us, and no moving around was allowed.

Fräulein Werner was tall and plump, very plump indeed, and wore shapeless brown dresses summer and winter, and her long plaited hair in a large bun over each ear. We wondered how she could hear anything, but she did and we loved her. There being no school uniform, we could wear whatever our mothers considered to be a reasonable outfit or, more to the point, what could be afforded, times being hard. National costume was the usual garb. It consisted of a white blouse with a lacy frill round the high neck, made from cotton for summer and something warmer in winter, a dirndl dress made from a flowered material, and a matching but plain half-apron tied round the waist with a bow at the back. This obviated the desire to compete with the other girls in one's dress, and with a change to a clean apron one's appearance was once more fresh and attractive.

Fräulein Werner not only insisted on the highest possible standards in one's work – I once lost a mark for not placing two figures to be added up exactly below each other – but inspected our overall neatness, extending her scrutiny to our personal cleanliness. Once a week we had to assemble on the stairs leading from the front hall to our classroom on the first floor, one girl to a stair, to have our fingernails examined. 'Mourning black' was not allowed, and shoes had to be as clean as the hands. Poverty was no excuse for being dirty and uncared for.

Somehow it did not seem difficult to progress in accordance with the teaching schedule laid down by the Ministry of Education. By the end of the second year we had mastered the cursive script, and by the end of the fourth, which also meant the end of primary school, we could, in addition, write in the spiky awkward German script. We had learnt our multiplication tables progressively one at a time by reciting each in chorus at the beginning of the school day for the whole of the six-day week until we knew them by heart, up to and including twelve times twelve.

Simple fractions had been tackled as a necessary prerequisite for those who wanted to go on to grammar school, which most did. When we left school Fräulein Werner presented each girl with a framed etching of St Stephen's Cathedral, executed and signed by her. I have it still.

1928 stands out like a beacon in my memory. It was the centenary of the death of Franz Schubert, Vienna's very own, nicknamed 'Schwammerl' (little mushroom) by his affectionate friends on account of his figure, and the whole of Vienna was celebrating the life of one of its greatest sons. At school the authorities decided to hold a concert at which we pupils would be performing some of his best-known songs. For weeks we learned and practised. On the 'Day' we were to wear Viennese dress of the period and, if possible, the long curls fashionable at that time. The dress posed no difficulty, since it was a loose confection made from flowered cotton and trimmed with braid. But the curls! I had short hair with a fringe across the forehead. Mother, inventive as always, had an answer.

Some years earlier, when the post-war craze for short skirts was matched by that for short hair, she had had her beautiful thick long hair cut off, and entombed it in a long, decorated cardboard box. As she and I shared the same hair colour, her discarded tress was taken to the hairdresser in the shop down below and six corkscrew curls were fashioned from it. These were then, three on either side, sewn to the bonnet which went with the costume. When it had been put on my head nobody could have told that I was wearing false hair. How proud I was of my long hair! As to the songs, well, I sing them still and only have to hear one of them to be back on the stage in our little school, aged eight, remembering the glory of what had once been.

Even at that early age, when time seems to pass so very slowly as almost to be standing still, the years went by, and so it came about that I found myself applying for a place at a grammar school (Gymnasium) at the uncommonly early age of nine years and five months. The choice had fallen on the one nearest to us, which was my father's old school. It was a classical school of the strictest order, and exclusively male. Until the advent of a socialist city administration after the war the provision of higher education for girls was almost nonexistent. The very few all-girls schools were privately run, expensive and snobbish. Women were not meant to have trained minds, a quite unnecessary accomplishment for good housewives and mothers. They went to household schools, learned to manage servants and how to supervise the cook. Only there were not all that many servants left, and women tried to spread their wings. To alleviate the shortage of places for girls, most boys' grammar schools were forced by law to open their doors a crack to the other sex. Of course the composition of the staff remained as before, with the addition of female Physical Education and Needlework teachers. The syllabuses were laid down by the Ministry of Education just as in the primary schools, and one had to pick one's school in accordance with the subjects one wished to study, for deviation from the rigid teaching plan was impossible.

There were three types of grammar school: classical, classical and modern, and just modern. At the classical or humanistic Gymnasium, the emphasis lay on the study of the classical languages, Latin for seven years, ancient Greek for four, and all the arts subjects with mathematics and the sciences of secondary importance. It was considered the most difficult option.

At the 'Realgymnasium' the arts and sciences were in balance, and its teaching plan was designed to equip its students for any type of higher education to be undertaken later on. There were still seven years of Latin but no Greek, with English or French taking its place, a considerable amount of mathematics, and all three sciences. In the last two years philosophy, logic and technical drawing were added to the basic core subjects.

The third option, the technical 'Realschule' cut away from the classical tradition, taught French and English and a great deal of mathematics and science, and prepared budding scientists and engineers for their future professions. The course of study in all three kinds of school lasted eight years and finished with the 'Matura', the leaving exam, non-obligatory but hardly ever not attempted, for without it progress up the higher educational ladder was firmly barred. If none of these schools was suitable one went to the 'Haupt-schule', comparable to a secondary modern school, up to the age of 14, which was then the leaving age, or to one of a variety of vocational schools which, besides teaching the core subjects, prepared for a career in commerce or a trade.

Having injudiciously fallen ill at the time of the obligatory entrance examination without which one could not enter grammar school, I had to sit it in splendid isolation in a spartan classroom supervised by an extremely bored young master who had been made to attend in his own time in the afternoon, which was normally free and unencumbered. The subject of the German composition was 'A Dream'. With considerable difficulty I managed to write six lines and presented my *oeuvre* to my superior with the question whether I had written enough. He, obviously anxious to get away, glanced at his watch, then my effort and took it.

A few days later my father was informed that, incredible as it may seem, I had passed, and in the middle of September I went off with my new satchel under my arm, the insignia of my now more grown-up status, to attend the school around the corner. No longer did I carry all my belongings in a leather knapsack on my back, no longer was there the long walk through the whole length of the park of the Palace of Schönbrunn in all weathers in the company of my father and sister, who had joined me two years later at the primary school; no longer were we all girls together.

The school building, in solid grey granite, was imposing, and the overwhelming majority of my fellows were male. Not having any brothers, it was quite a shock, as were the male teachers, who bore the title 'Professor' and were university graduates to a man. Gone was the intimate way of being addressed by one's first name, our surname had to do. We girls sat together in a little group surrounded by a sea of masculinity, making 40 in all. Our parallel form was boys only. There was the consolation of frequenting a school bearing the illustrious name of the Chancellor Ignaz Seipel, who had been to school with Father and had saved Austria from the inflationary abyss into which it threatened to disappear in 1924. For a long time after that fateful year a cupro-nickel coin worth ten groschen – approximately one old farthing – circulated bearing the inscription 1000 kronen (crowns). It was a wholesome reminder of the debasement of money.

The ethos of the school was strictly Catholic, even though state schools were officially non denominational. Religious instruction was a firmly embedded subject on the timetable – it headed the list of subjects on the twice-yearly report forms – and pupils who were not of the prevailing persuasion experienced certain disadvantages. Catholic religious instruction was given twice a week in lesson time when those of us, myself included, who professed a different belief had to find a corner somewhere outside the classroom for its duration. I often ended up, by kind permission of the relevant professor, in the history lesson of the year above mine.

However, religious instruction we non-Catholics could not escape. School started at 8 a.m. and finished either at 12 or 1 p.m. from Monday till Friday, and at 12 p.m. on Saturdays, but for us Friday afternoon meant two hours

19

with our spiritual mentor. Religious education was entirely denominational and taken by clergymen of many faiths. There were Protestants who followed Luther's teachings, to whom my family belonged, known by the initials A.B. (Augsburger Bekenntnis) after the word 'Protestant'; there were Protestants of the Calvin and Zwingli schools, indicated by the initials H.B. (Helvetisches Bekenntnis), there were Old Catholics, whose grandfathers had refused to recognise the Pope's infallibility in religious matters pronounced as a doctrine in the 1880s, and there were members of the Jewish faith. I cannot recall anybody belonging to the Mohammedan religion but, no doubt, there were some somewhere in Vienna. These details were carefully recorded on our school reports next to our name, and a mark entered against the subject at the top of the list.

The quality of instruction varied enormously. For one, being so few in number we could not be taught as a year group, but the four years of the lower and again the four years of the upper school were put together, which must have made the task of drawing up a teaching plan almost impossible. While I find it difficult to recall which pastor studied what part of the Bible with us, I vividly remember a dear old man who, having spent nearly a lifetime preaching the faith to bored youngsters, had decided to desist and to substitute readings from his favourite author instead. In the second half of the 19th century, before the Romantic movement had run its course, Rudolf Baumbach, a native of Thuringia, had produced the most charming rural tales full of romantic love, fairies, living trees and murmuring water. The small cupboard-like room lined with books expanded as we listened enthralled, transported into a world of sheer delight. Our lessons had become worthwhile and, with hindsight, we surely learned more about ethical truth and behaviour in this way than from the ponderous and, to the young, often quite incomprehensible words of the Good

Book. Only a lifetime of experience has taught me the meaning of the Parable of the Prodigal Son.

However, more serious religious studies had to be undergone with the approach of my 14th birthday. Catholics went to their first communion at the age of seven, and were much envied by us for the trappings that accompanied that event. It always took place, as it still does today, in the period between Easter and Whitsun, May being the month most favoured by nature and man. The *Firmpate* or *Firmpatin* (according to the sex of the child to be confirmed) was a second godfather or godmother to the *Firmling* and was most carefully chosen by the child's parents with an eye to the state of his or her wallet and social status, which might prove of help to their offspring in the future. This was, of course, often the same person who had been put in charge of its spiritual welfare at its baptism.

On the great day it was their pleasant duty to defray all the expenses accruing from the customary activities following the religious ceremony in the morning, and they were not inconsiderable. There was the hire of the fiacre, the two-horse open carriage with its jaunty driver, usually the owner, dressed in his well-cut suit and always with a brown or black bowler hat on his head. For this special occasion the vehicle almost disappeared under a sea of white paper flowers, which not only covered its sides but hung down over the back almost to the ground. The horses were not immune either and had to bear their share of the floral display, while the driver, high up on his bench seat, wore a large white buttonhole. Into this eye-catching apparition climbed the *Firmling* all dressed in white, the girls with veils like miniature brides, the boys in white sailor suits, the parents and godparents in their best finery. The latter had already done half their duty by presenting the customary gifts to their charges. These consisted of a watch, the metal being in accordance with the giver's means, and a copy of

21

the Bible bound as expensively as the godparents' pocket could stand.

Then there came the slap-up lunch for the newly sanctified child and his parents, followed, joy upon joy, by the subsequent visit to Vienna's ancient amusement park, known as the 'Wurstelprater'. It took its name from the 'Hanswurst', the *Pulcinello* of Neapolitan origin, which eventually became Punch and Judy in English and acquired the diminutive '-el' in Austrian. *'Prater'*, the Latin for meadow, was applied to the whole extensive area adjoining the Danube east of the city centre, of which one corner was given over to the people's enjoyment and was and still is located in that vast parkland stretching down to the river. It was the gift to his subjects from the Emperor Josef II, 'the people's emperor', who had liked nothing better than to walk through this domain of his accompanied by his large family, 'at one with his people'.

What an odd and yet typically Austrian character this man of the Enlightenment possessed. Eldest son of the great Empress Maria Theresia, eldest brother of the ill-fated Marie Antoinette, Queen of France, whom he abandoned in her need, he became Emperor of the Holy Roman Empire of the German Nation on the death of his otherwise completely insignificant father, the Emperor Francis I of Lorraine, in 1770, and co-regent of his mother for the last ten years of her life.

Having been brought up at a court where his mother ruled over her inheritance, the Austrian Crownlands and Bohemia and Moravia as Archduchess of Austria, and was Queen of Hungary, in intermittent conflict with the magnates of that country, as well as presiding over an ever-increasing family numbering eventually 13, he turned against almost everything she had stood and fought for. Frederick II of Prussia, arch-enemy of Austria and instigator of the Seven Years War between the two powers over possession of Silesia, which he finally won, became Josef's shining example, to be followed and imitated as far as possible.

Voltaire, who had been so much admired by Frederick, became his guide and mentor. Frederick's founding of the first compulsory primary schools for the whole of the population under his rule was shortly followed by a similar act in the Austrian lands. Frederick's simple way of life had to be copied down to Josef's interment in a plain copper coffin without the adornments commonly put on Imperial tombs. How very Austrian to consider home-grown values inferior to those imported from abroad, to absorb them into the fabric of society and to adjust accordingly. It was enlightened – for, after all, it was the Age of the Enlightenment – graciously to mingle with the populace and to throw open to all and sundry parkland previously the province of the ruling families. When the dispossessed aristocrats grumbled about the loss of the Prater game reserve, saying that they could no longer be among their equals, Josef answered ironically:

'If I always wished to be among my equals, I should be forced to take my walks in the Capuchin Crypt among the deceased Habsburgs.'

The attractions of the Wurstelprater were many and great. There was the ancient Chinese statue at its entrance called the 'Kalifati' to welcome one to the thrills of the ghost train, with its skeletons popping up from nowhere, the shooting galleries, with their array of wonderful prizes, bumper cars and coconut shies. But the apex of one's enjoyment was a ride on the 'Riesenrad', the giant ferris wheel erected at the time of the great international exhibition in the 1880s and a landmark ever since. The carriages, each the size of a small railway coach, rose slowly from the ground, coming to frequent stops to allow a good view of the town and its surrounding countryside from varying heights.

Very tired small children dressed in, by now, grubby white, the girls' veils if still in place no longer resembling those of brides, the boy's trousers bearing witness to the consumption of quantities of multi-coloured ice-cream, returned home in the evening to sleep the sleep of the exhausted just.

Now we, the Protestants of the Lutheran persuasion, approached the first Communion in a somewhat different style. I, too, was to be confirmed in the May following my 14th birthday. But to prepare for this grave step, the affirmation of the faith into which I had been christened, I had to undergo spiritual training. This was given by our pastor at weekly seminars in the church hall attached to our church. Protestants were rare creatures in Catholic Austria, and the confirmation classes, which ran from September until May, brought together young people from a considerable area. The boy with whom I shared a bench was the grandson of the pastor who had baptised me, and the pastor, the current incumbent, who instructed us, had married my parents.

My sister and I began to attend church regularly on Sunday mornings. Our parents hardly ever came with us. Mother was too busy with her household duties, and Father, I later came to realise, had shed his religious beliefs long ago, although he never explained what, if anything, had taken their place.

Eventually the great day came. It was Thursday, 10 May in that momentous year of 1934, after the Socialist uprising in February and before the murder of the Catholic Chancellor Engelbert Dollfuss in July. My godmother, my father's sister, had died most terribly of cancer when I was two and

24

had to be replaced with someone else. No-one could be found to take on the duties of a confirmation godmother and, as a last resort and at the last minute, Mother took over the role.

The day dawned overcast and warm. I dressed in my new white dress and, to my great satisfaction, put on my first pair of court shoes with 'a heel'. Not that I could properly walk in them, being suddenly elevated by a good inch and a half at the back, but no matter, I was grown-up. Mother gave me a watch which looked quite nice, although it was only made from silver and not the traditional gold, but at least it had gold-coloured numerals and hands, and it did go for about a month. Then we set off for church, this time the whole family including Father, but it was by tram and not the fiacre considered every child's due.

Having partaken in the Communion and been confirmed as a member of the church, we were each presented with a certificate bearing witness to that momentous event. Mine had a picture of a large cross rising from a stormy sea covering the top third of the document. Its symbolism was to be made clear within a very short time. On leaving the church we made our way to the Prater. The sky had turned an ominous black, and as soon as we got off the tram at our destination thunder and lightning rent the air, and we were in for a drenching. A bedraggled little party, including a very disappointed me, had to take shelter where it could and, eventually, return home without much sampling of what had been anticipated for many months.

My sister, who followed in my footsteps a year later, fared quite differently. Her godmother, a dear friend of the family, did her proud. She was given a beautiful gold necklace with a diamond-studded gold cross, the weather was perfect, and her day out at the Wurstelprater exactly what it should have been. She has her necklace still, while my watch, after having been to the repairers so often that the bills exceeded its original cost, had to be discarded. But it had been a dramatic entry into adulthood!

Schooldays are the happiest days of your life, it is said, and so they were for me, but not entirely. My father's old school, the classical Gymnasium situated a short walk from our flat, was even in the early 1930s old-fashioned. Apart from the curriculum prescribed by the state through the Ministry of Education, with its heavy bias towards the classical world and its nod towards the sciences, it was run on the most restrictive lines. The forced entry of a few girls into an all-male society hardly changed anything. Our teachers, the *'Herren Professor'*, were all men, with the exception of the Physical Education and Needlework ladies.

Three of these men remain indelibly etched in my memory. One was a young good-looking, bronzed geographer called Professor Nusser, who went on polar expeditions and had accompanied Alfred Wegener, whose brand-new and, as yet, not really accepted theory of continental drift he taught with great aplomb. We hung on every word he said. He was our hero, for had we not all been brought up on the heroic feats of the Norwegian Fridtjof Nansen and his good ship the *Fram* in which he had tried to reach the North Pole, the ultimate goal for any explorer of those days.

Our Latin master, Latin being compulsory from the second year onwards, on the other hand, was a man who had been greatly disappointed by life and who took his revenge in terrorising his poor defenceless pupils. We were 40 at the beginning of the year, and we were 20 who went up into the third form, the rest having failed the subject, and were thus condemned to repeat the year. The system, and it is the same to this day, requires a pass in all the major subjects before removal to the next higher class is granted. Failure in one means an exam in it after the summer holidays before the start of the first semester. A repeat failure means repeating the year. Failure in more than one subject means automatic repetition of the year, and yet another failure results in expulsion from grammar school and transfer to the Hauptschule until school-leaving age is reached.

Latin became a dreaded subject, and when the same teacher was put in charge of our Greek lessons in the fourth form, I could not cope with any degree of success. My unhappiness was greatly aggravated by the man who taught us German that year. Being my father's daughter, I had always been ambitious to do well in that subject, cared for words and style and endeavoured to write acceptable essays which, up to that time, I appeared to be able to do, gaining good marks and the approval of my teachers. Suddenly, Professor Sengsbratel started to find fault with everything I did. My marks were barely pass ones, my efforts slackened, I became inattentive and dropped behind. The last straw came when my mother was commanded to see the Head-master, an Olympian figure whom we only saw from a distance but who, in my opinion, had one redeeming feature. He was the possessor in the school garden, stretching out behind his study, of a wonderful cherry tree which bore the most juicy, sweet white cherries, of a kind I have never encountered since. It was considered a daring game to steal a few of them, a feat undertaken with a wildly beating heart. However, the bidding of Mother had nothing to do with cherries but was a matter so grave that it might have ended in my expulsion from the school.

Professor Sengsbratel was a qualified teacher of not only German but also Latin, and on account of his somewhat eccentric demeanour was a topic of conversation among his pupils. It transpired that in the circle of what I had considered to be my friends at school I had indulged in making fun of him by suggesting that he, on getting home, put on a

Roman toga and in front of a full-length mirror recited Latin poetry. Somebody, wanting to ingratiate himself had told him about it, and the silly man had carried the tale to the Head. In the event I was neither expelled nor even given a mark for bad conduct.

Father, good classicist that he was, had watched my struggle with Ancient Greek, a language he loved and much preferred to Latin. After the incident with Professor Sengs-bratel and his Roman toga he finally made up his mind on a point which had exercised him since I had first started on this course of study. It surely would be much more profitable for me to learn English instead of a dead language, however beautiful and poetic. After all, it was the language of commerce, and a knowledge of it could become quite a useful asset. Since the end of the fourth year saw the conclusion of Lower School studies as well as that of compulsory education, it would be the most suitable time for transfer to another type of grammar school for the long haul to the much-desired 'Matura'.

A quarter of an hour's walk from our flat, and nowhere near as comfortably housed, was a Realgymnasium bearing the proud name of Austria's greatest writer and poet Franz Grillparzer. The accommodation consisted of two floors of a building originally used by a Hauptschule and just big enough for the eight forms of the Upper School. The Lower School had to make do with classrooms located in a primary school building a little further down on the other side of the road. The teachers had to be good sprinters in order to get to their lessons on time, although these were separated by a five-minute break. Lessons lasted 50 minutes, the mid-morning break a quarter of an hour. School, as usual, began on the dot of 8 a.m., and it was the schoolkeeper's job to stand by the front door and catch the late-comers. Even one minute beyond the bell resulted in having to be at school for a whole six-day week by 7.30 a.m. seated on the long bench hugging the wall outside the staffroom, in full view of the passing traffic. Once caught was usually enough, the lesson learnt.

The syllabus, as one knew, differed in certain respects from that of the Seipelgymnasium which I had just left. Instead of Ancient Greek, English was the second foreign language after Latin, and a start with it was made in the fifth year, the first year of the Upper School. It was a compulsory subject in the leaving examination, the 'Matura', the 'open sesame' to university. The sciences were favoured much more strongly than I had encountered heretofore and, in particular, I was lacking in certain mathematical skills. Before my transfer could be confirmed, proof of competence had to be brought. The normally gloriously carefree summer months had to be spent swotting up the solution to algebraic problems, and geometry became the hunting ground for a less than enthusiastic mind. September came and with it the obligatory examination, the passing of which opened the door to a world of learning utterly different from the one I had left behind. Nobody could have enjoyed school more than I did from then on.

Our form master, Professor Dr Emil Nack, who stayed with us right up to the end of our schooldays, took us for German and Latin – every teacher had to be able to teach two often quite unconnected subjects. He cared little for the latter and immensely for the former. Latin lessons took all kinds of form. We did the minimum laid down, for it, too, was compulsory at 'A' level, and read our way through parts of all the great Roman authors. Tacitus, whose style was difficult but at least not as turgid as Livy, whose sentences were never-ending, became the one on whom we had to focus most attention in the last year, for was he not the 'German' author giving an extended account of the Romans' encounters with the various Tutonic tribes across the Alps? The defeat of Varus in AD 9 particularly sticks in my mind. How boring it all was! On the other hand, Cicero, with his lively mind, his almost modern approach when trying to alert his fellow senators to the dangers posed by the city state of Cartage in North Africa, became my favourite whom I managed to read without much difficulty.

But there was enough time left in Latin lessons for other things. We discussed architectural styles, with visits to buildings in towns featuring them, and were introduced to interior design which, at that time, was dominated by the Scandinavians. It became the rage to paint one wall of one's sitting room a different colour from the other three, wallpaper was considered old-fashioned, decorative tablecloths and doilies were discarded, and furniture took on the stark functional lines propagated by the Norsemen. I have forgotten most of the Latin acquired in many weary hours of study, but my love and appreciation of the plastic arts, first kindled by 'Uncle Emil' have remained with me all through life.

His real obsession, though, was German literature. He prided himself on teaching it literally from its earliest beginnings to the present day, and made us work like the devil. Here was the water to which this duck took joyously. Father spent many a lunchtime examining me to see whether I really managed to retain the four disparate books I was in the habit of reading all at the same time, and was astonished to find that I did. Oh, what it was to 'discover' literature, although as I came to realise later on in middle age, there was much the head had understood but not the heart. And how wonderful it was to have the time to read for hours, untroubled by the cares of daily living. No chores, no money worries, no obligations beyond keeping one's neck clean and doing one's homework.

Boys did not intrude on my consciousness, as they did not seem to do with most of the girls at school. They were in my class of course, for it was again a school of about 500 with 50 girls wedged like a sandwich filling into three years, the years of a Socialist city government in favour of mixing the sexes and offering equal educational opportunities to all. The boys were our comrades, even brothers, but only seldom objects of one's fancy. In the rare cases where an innocent affection manifested itself and a couple paired off, an amused toleration was displayed by the others.

The other great relevation of lasting effect of my years in the Upper School was learning English. French being regarded as the language of polite society, my mother had decided that an early start should be made with its acquisition. She found a young woman to act as governess on two afternoons a week, and so my sister, aged five, and I, a year older, duly took the first faltering steps towards becoming civilised. They were very faltering indeed, as our young teacher was desperately in love with a, to us, unknown person, and made us sit endlessly in her flat at one side of her desk while she wrote long letters to him on the other. Here it was that I first encountered the symbolic 'xxx's at the end of a letter, racking my brain as to their meaning but much too shy to ask. Only many years later did I learn their significance.

Having become aware of the shortcomings in employing this lovesick creature, Mother went to the other extreme and engaged a widow of about 70, whose main concerns were her aching stomach and her only son, who seemed to be spending more time in prison than out of it. She herself was the scion of a rich family who had had her educated in France for several years, and who had married a good-for-nothing charmer in whose footsteps the son had chosen to walk. This meant little to us while trying to read Alphonse Daudet's *Lettres de mon Moulin*, gradually absorbing the beautiful language and the seemingly effortless artistry of his style. But French grammar being very different from that of German and, badly taught, proving difficult, my spelling of it only improved after a stay at a French convent school on Lake Geneva years later.

How differently did I fare with English. Our first teacher, Professor Krieger, had spent a year at Oxford, and we were firmly convinced that he spoke German with an English accent! He always dressed impeccably in well-cut suits of English cloth, had a well-kept small moustache and exuded 'Englishness'. No matter the difficult pronounciation, no matter the impossible spelling: I had to master this language. At the end of the first year's tuition I triumphantly went off on holiday with a Tauchnitz edition of Edgar Wallace's *The Feathered Serpent*. I did not know who Edgar Wallace was, nor could I understand the title apart from the article 'the', but read the book I would. While my parents took their afternoon siesta I lay in a deckchair under a tall fir tree in the garden of a small hotel at Velden on the Wörthersee in the county of Carinthia, with a dictionary in one hand and the book in the other. Slowly and painfully looking up practically every word, I worked my way through its 250-odd pages. Did I get the sense of it? I doubt it, but the glow of achievement acted as a spur.

For the following three years English was taught by Professor Hübner, a solid and sensible Viennese whom we, for very dubious reasons, considered, of all things, to look Japanese. The following jingle was thought to encapsulate the essence of his teaching:

> Mr Japsy teaches English
> But there are no happy ends
> For he asks everybody:
> 'Please give quickly the contents.'

I cannot judge how good his English really was, but his teaching inspired us all. When we complained about having to learn grammar his reply was that, as an alternative, we would have to read 20 English books a year! He knew only too well that the acquisition of a language is mainly a feat of memory, and that accuracy has to be worked for even in one's mother tongue.

We soon read books by well-known authors, like Robert Louis Stevenson's *The Rajah's Diamond*, Dickens' *A Christmas Carol* and John Galsworthy's *The Apple Tree*. Only Shakespeare we did not touch, and what a wise thing that was! I loved the language, the people whose way of expressing themselves it was, even London in November fog, about which we learnt a poem by heart. We sang 'Clementine', 'My Bonny Lies over the Ocean' and 'Loch Lomond' with great gusto and less musicality. It certainly was much better than mathematics or, the bugbear of my last two years at school, technical drawing. With my clumsiness and slightly defective eyesight it was a nightmare to cope with Indian ink, a T-square and a drawing board. My mother, to encourage me, had given me a precision set of draughtman's instruments with which to perform on the white and very expensive cartridge paper. It remained a nightmare having to draw cubes in a variety of planes, seen from all angles, demonstrate differently slanting cuts through cylinders turning on their axes, rotate spheres through several dimensions – there seemed to be a new problem to be dealt with every week.

Professor Frisch could not understand the difficulties experienced, with one notable exception, by all the girls. Quietly and calmly, a stately and extremely neat figure dressed in an immaculate white coat, he would stand in front of the large blackboard covered in meticulous drawings and express his utter astonishment. How was it that women were able to visualise a hat from all sides and angles, back, front, any old how, and yet appeared unable to do so with a simple cylinder? I still don't know the answer to that, except perhaps that it may be question of interest. If cylinders were the headgear of the day, women very likely would be able to make themselves a complete picture of them. However, as this dreadful subject was compulsory to 'A'-level, many hours had to be spent in coming to terms with it. And to what purpose? To be able to read the ground plan of a house, maybe. It did teach us, though, persistence and application, even when it meant foregoing much more pleasurable pursuits.

There are still mysteries from my schooldays haunting me today. Physics, another compulsory subject like all three sciences, had to include practical work. This meant returning to school by 2.30 p.m. on one afternoon a week after a morning lasting from 8 a.m. to 1 p.m. for 'physical exercises'. None of these except one has remained in my memory, since their sense and purpose escaped me at the time. For quite the wrong reasons, the one exception lives on in my mind's eye.

From the school's entrance hall the staircase led to the two upper floors alongside the right-hand wall, leaving the stairwell empty. Down this vertical shaft we were told to suspend a small weight on a long string from the second floor, no doubt, as I have come to understand, to demonstrate the action of the pendulum and the relation of its speed to the length of the means of its suspension. That we never saw or learned this was entirely the case of good intentions going wrong. Every youngster moving up or down the stairs felt compelled to put out a hand, catch the string and give it a good jerk. Still, I do remember that particular afternoon.

In spite, or perhaps because of, the severity of the discipline ruling our behaviour not only in school but also outside it, and the great respect we had for our teachers, who exerted their authority wherever we came in contact with each other, my years at school certainly were some of the happiest of my life. The strong thirst for knowledge of all kinds among the young was slaked by the diet put before us, with the preparation for life in those days a prime object of what went on in the classroom.

Shorthand was compulsory in the fourth form and could be continued for a further year on an optional basis. Already my father had been taught it at the end of the last century as an aid to note-taking when attending university lectures, and wrote all the drafts and ideas of his literary work in it. Unfortunately for him, for he had hoped to have my help in typing a clean copy from his shorthand notes, the system we were following differed from his, although it was based on it. Like him, I not only became quite proficient but later managed to adapt it to English until its use was superseded by more modern tools.

This being the Vienna of Sigmund Freud, psychology was included in the timetable in the penultimate year. Our teacher, Professor Fritz Redl, had been a student of Freud and introduced us to some of his theories and findings much in advance of the times. Into the normally extremely formal classroom atmosphere intruded a spirit which, if it had been known to the Headmaster, must surely have led to an early retirement of our mentor. We had to call him 'Uncle' and his girlfriend 'Aunt', we had to address him in the familiar '*Du*' rather than the '*Sie*' which was accorded to us by our teachers and, of course, by us to anybody not of the family or intimate circle of friends, which made us feel uncomfortable. We went on most informal class outings with the two of them and carried out psychological tests considered quite unsuitable for young people in mixed company. Soon after, however, he obtained a teaching post at a prestigious American university where, I am sure, he prospered. His legacy has been an abiding interest in the working of the human mind and the causation of people's emotions and actions. It has enabled me to cope with the avalanche which overtook my country and family by teaching me that human beings are made neither good nor bad, but are capable of being either when driven by impulses of which they are not consciously aware.

These formative and fruitful days ended in June 1937 when, at the age of 17 years and four months, I passed the 'Matura', the Higher School Leaving Examination, with distinction.

3

Sport

Although I was never afraid of water, Father considered it essential for reasons of safety, in case we were to fall into a pond or river on the many walking tours we undertook, to have my sister and myself taught to swim properly as soon as possible, having learnt to do so himself at the age of four.

Vienna enjoys a continental climate with hot summers, cold winters and short springs and autumns. To make the most of the warm weather the town is dotted with open-air public swimming pools, while the 'Old Danube' offers delightfully calm waters for every conceivable kind of water sport. The 'Old Danube' owes its origin to the decision of the city fathers in the middle of 19th century to regulate the heavy spring flow of the Danube when carrying the melt waters from the mountain rivers running into it, with its consequential, often quite disastrous, flooding of the river's left bank, by building a new and secure bed for its course along the old city. The branches now cut off from the main water course were dubbed 'The Old Danube' and while maintaining a subterranean connection with its progenitor, resulting in a corresponding raising and lowering of the water level, became the playground of the Viennese. A visit to it involved a long journey by tram from our flat and meant a day's outing.

We were, however, lucky to be living within a short walking distance from Schönbrunn, the park and palace begun by the Emperor Charles VI and completed his daughter, the Empress Maria Theresia, as an Imperial summer residence in the Vienna woods. The Emperor Franz Josef, the second longest reigning monarch in the history of Europe, eventually made it his all-the-year-round residence. To please his wife, this beautiful but oh, so tragic wife, the Empress Elisabeth, a boating lake was laid out at the top of the hill facing the palace across the 'parterre' with its wide sweeping paths, baroque flower beds and sculpted trees. It was completely hidden away among trees and the path leading to it hardly visible, rising behind an Egyptian obelisk. Such precautions were made necessary by the fact that the park, apart from a minute section on either side of the palace set aside for the Emperor's private use, was open to all and sundry and was a favourite weekend destination for the local population.

By the time I had reached the age of five and was ready to be initiated into the art of moving through water without swallowing any of it, Austria had become a republic and the Empress's boating lake a public swimming pool. In the wake of the collapse of the Austro-Hungarian Empire and the lost war, ex-regular army officers in particular had a hard time to keep themselves and their families from starving to death. They could be found in any and every kind of occupation, and so it came about that I was handed over to an army disciplinarian who had little patience with a dreamy child only too easily distracted from what should have been of the utmost interest to her.

The first lesson on dry land, when the basic movements of the breast stroke were demonstrated and learned, passed without much trouble. But once I was suspended from a rope fastened at one end to a thick webbing belt round my chest and at the other to a wheel running along an overhead rail round the pool, matters were not quite so satisfactory.

'You swim like a bent front door key!' exclaimed my

instructor in utter despair. Nevertheless, the bent front door key learned to do the breast stroke, learned to dive off the high and low diving boards and became a certificated 'free' swimmer by covering three lengths of the pool in one go, and all this by the age of seven.

Having once started, swimming became an obsession. Every known stroke was added to the repertoire within a few years and once, in my early teens, serious training for competitions lasting hours at a time became a regular indulgence. Not that competitions saw much of me, who could only train in the summer, but it was excellent exercise and quite safe, since there seemed no conceivable way in which one could be injured even while suffering from a rupture.

Over the years the bathing facilities in Schönbrunn were rebuilt, the pool was enlarged and the sunbathing area was improved, but the stately trees surrounding it still gave one the feeling of intimacy with the water. Once the season had started on 15 May, much of my learning homework was done lying in the sun after a work-out, and most of the revision of German literature, from notes neatly typed and bound by me, took place in the boiling hot early summer hunched over them with my back to the sun in a bathing costume of solid wool.

This addiction to swimming involved my sister and myself in a curious incident. With our much older cousin George, we, aged 14 and 15, had been to one of the bathing establishments along the Old Danube on a day hot even by Viennese standards. We were wearing identical, apart from the colour, halter-neck sundresses well covered in front but with low-cut backs over which fitted short matching bolero jackets. On account of the searing heat and with some trepidation, we decided on the way home to take the risk of walking through the deserted streets to the nearest tramstop carrying the jackets instead of wearing them. As was, I suppose, inevitable, a policeman in full summer uniform, including white cotton gloves, in a temperature of over 40°C, stopped us and, to my cousin's immense embarrassment, accused us of being indecently dressed.

Nothing we could say assuaged his legal indignation, not the scorching heat, not our youth, not our very proper cousin, a student of the classics at the University of Vienna, which he proved himself to be by producing his visiting card on which it was clearly stated. We were hauled off to the local police station and fined the statutory amount of two shillings each on the spot. It was lucky that cousin George had some money on him to bail us out for we were penniless, and there is no knowing what would have happened otherwise. After all, two shillings were far more than our weekly pocket money. As it was, our parents were quite taken aback when presented with the receipt for a fine paid on behalf of their two most carefully protected and brought-up daughters for being indecently dressed. I only hope that policeman did not live long enough to see what is permissible today.

In a sense we were both fortunate and unfortunate to have a police station accommodated in one of the ground-floor premises of our very large block of flats let out to various enterprises. This meant being protected by the eye of the law when it came to being burgled, although Mother lived in constant dread of an intruder. This, at the time, did not seem odd, even though we did not know of anybody who had suffered that fate, and our flat was located on the second floor with the only access through the front door. This was festooned with three mortice locks, which all had to be locked whether the family was in or out, and its solid oak interior surface had been made secure with a criss-cross arrangement of thick iron bars. Once the front door was shut and locked with us securely behind it, we were safe from the outside world!

But apart from any sense of security bestowed by the ever-present police force, it brought with it certain hazards and led to my only brush with the law, when I was guilty of a misdemeanour. Exactly opposite to our house the tram No. 63 stopped, which was the one I had to take on my way to school when walking would have taken too long to get me there on time. The method employed by me was to look out of the window for the approaching tram, rush down the two flights of stairs and catch it, usually just as it was starting to move off. This convenient activity, however, came to an abrupt end when arriving home from school one day my mother confronted me with the words: 'I have had to pay a fine for you today.'

What had happened was really quite simple. One of 'our' policemen, who knew me by sight, had seen me jump on a moving tram, a heinous offence punishable by law. Instead of charging me in person as he should have done, he had gone straight to my mother, who promptly deducted the, to me, considerable sum of the two-shilling spot fine from my pocket money over three weeks. This meant no cinema visits for a whole month. I certainly never offended again – unless quite certain of not being observed.

4

Health Matters

The body of the rickets-afflicted child gradually outgrew the debilitating effects, but could not overcome the handicap of the rupture inflicted at birth, with its constant threat of intestinal strangulation. All physical activity like running and jumping had to be closely watched, and finally, every other means having failed, it was decided that in the spring after my seventh birthday I would have to be operated on, in spite of being underweight. The hospital I entered just before Easter was run by Catholic nuns who had dedicated their lives to the care of the sick.

In the operating theatre, after I had been strapped down by the wrists and ankles, stark naked, to the operating table, a thick wire mesh mask was put over my face onto which pure ether was dripped while I was asked to show how well I could count. I awoke in a small ward with three beds in it, one of which was occupied by an old lady and the other by a young girl who had just had her appendix removed. With regaining consciousness I became aware of an almost unbearable pain. The large wound right across the front of my tummy, measuring about 15cm, had been closed with large staple-like metal clips. In order to prevent their popping out a heavy sandbag had been put on top of them. This I bore for a couple of days before begging for its removal, which was grudgingly granted. No painkillers were administered nor, I suppose, were any known suitable for such a young child. No food was allowed for three days, with cold black unsweetened tea the only drink. On the fourth day a frankfurter sausage in gravy broke the involuntary fast! No wonder I grew up physically tough and inclined to ignore the everyday aches and pains which are one's lot in life. However, apart from the disfigurement of the large scar running vertical across my belly, the operation was a tribute to the surgeon and confirmation of the, at that time, worldwide reputation of the Viennese school of medicine, whose ministrations I was to sample on several more occasions later on.

My second encounter came at the age of 13, when it was diagnosed as being necessary to remove the adenoids which were held responsible for the breathing difficulties under which I laboured, especially at night. This operation was carried out in a somewhat crude fashion with my sitting on a simple plain wooden chair. A piece of cotton wool soaked in ether was momentarily pressed against my face to make me lose consciousness, but not long enough, only to come round during the removal of the second adenoid. The aftercare was nil except that I was given ice-cream to eat – considered a great luxury in winter and only obtainable from the leading patisserie in the centre of the town.

This operation, unfortunately, did not cure what it was meant to, and on my reaching 16 it became expedient to remove a bone from my left nostril. This again was carried out under a local anaesthetic, which made it possible for me to watch in admiration the great skill of the surgeon and taught me to make the best of a difficult situation. After being given a plate of tomato soup to eat, I was discharged from hospital with an absorbent plug in each nostril. Accompanied by Father, I travelled home by underground.

My last encounter of a serious nature with the world of medicine before leaving home was the consequence of a skiing accident. Every February our school closed its doors for a week while its pupils, suitably guarded and guided, went off into the mountains to explore the white wonder world. The sexes were, of course strictly separated, so much so, that we went to different places. The most vivid of these trips remains the first one.

The accommodation was primitive, even by the less demanding standards of the thirties. The dormitory, a large oblong room, was furnished along each of its long walls with a wooden structure onto which were put a number of individual mattresses filled with straw. For cover we were each given a grey woollen blanket. The stove at the end of the room spat out heat provided it was assidously fed with logs. As soon as everybody had bedded down the stove went out and the cold settled down with us. We never undressed, which saved trouble in the morning. Although it was bitterly cold it was dry with little snow on the ground. To reach a suitable patch of it an hour's trudge with the heavy hickory skis over one's shoulder had to be undertaken, but there was quite a stunning compensation for all this effort. The wood we had to cross was covered, as far as the eye could see, with a carpet of Christmas roses in full bloom, growing so densely together that only with the greatest care was it possible to avoid stepping on one. Every hardship endured during this week, including the blisters nicely covering one's heels, became as nothing, and the memory of that incredible sight has lightened many a dark moment for me.

Christmas 1937 saw my sister and myself given into the care of a friend of Mother's who took us, with her son of a similar age, high up to a mountain hut for some 'real' skiing. It was a glorious situation facing the Dachstein, one of Austria's best-known mountains outside the Tyrol, the snow conditions were excellent, the hut comfortable and well-run, even though all provisions had to be laboriously brought up on the backs of local lads. Those were the days when one walked or skiied but did not ride. It could have been the holiday of a lifetime, but the fates decreed otherwise.

On the second of our ten days' vacation I was appointed sweeper-upper of a small party, which meant my bringing up the rear to make sure nobody got lost or left behind. Coming down the slope at the back of the hut in single file after a morning's outing, I did not notice that the weight of about ten persons all following each other in the same track had exposed the roots of a small fir tree growing across it. Busily keeping my eyes fixed on my charges and travelling at a fair pace, I caught the tip of my right ski in the tree's roots. The result was a sudden violent wrenching of the knee, a hideous noise, a terrific pain and an inability to stand up and put any weight on that leg.

Fortunately, somebody had noticed my non-arrival at the hut and came to help me down. There was no way in which medical assistance could be summoned, and the rest of the party would not have appreciated having their holiday ruined by having to carry me down the mountain.

The knee swelled up like a balloon, and the thigh and calf bones would not balance on top of each other. I borrowed a good stout bandage, bound the offending joint very tightly and went on skiing, although I could only manage it within the vicinity of the hut. Without aid I skiied down the mountain at the end of our stay. At home, after a couple of days without any improvement in mobility, I had to confess to Father that my knee was troublesome. He blew his top, then sent me to the Orthopaedic Hospital to the best and rudest consultant surgeon in the Vienna of that period, who bore the rather appropriate name of Professor Spitzy (*spitz*=pointed like a needle). A small test, and I was whisked into hospital for three days to have the whole of my right leg, from the hip to the toes, put in plaster of Paris, where it stayed for five weeks. I had torn the ligaments in the knee and badly injured the ankle. Professor Spitzy caused my temperature, which had not risen even when passing through the common childhood diseases like mumps and measles, to climb alarmingly by telling me quite bluntly that, due to the long delay in seeking treatment, there was a 50/50 possibility of no healing taking place and my being left a cripple for life.

Youth, however, is resilient. I quickly learned to manoeuvre my leg up and down stairs by swinging it from the hip, went to my university course on the underground with it sticking straight out in front when seated, and even went dancing. The after-effects of the plaster caused far more pain and discomfort than ever did the initial treatment. Of course, it was nothing unusual to have a limb in plaster in Vienna in the winter. Public transport was full of people sporting their injuries, not exactly like trophies but as part of the price to be paid for being a member of the snow-loving fraternity.

Professor Spitzy deserved his reputation. He saved my knee, although it took many years for it to resume its original shape and to stop acting as an indicator of a change to wet weather. It still will not bend as far or as easily as its twin, but that is hardly a necessity in daily life.

5

Holidays

From an early age, travel was part of life. It was customary to leave Vienna during the hottest months of the year, and since the schools broke up very early in June, it was not until I arrived in Vienna many years later as a visitor from another country that I spent a July or August in that city.

Travelling by car was only for the rich and not something one ever considered possible. In any case, neither of my parents would have made a competent driver – Father on account of being lost in a world of creative thoughts to be noted down in shorthand on the back of old envelopes on his long daily walks, and Mother on account of her temperament and a certain lack of co-ordination. She was, for instance, quite unable to take part in ballroom dancing, her motions resembling those of a bird hopping along, which was all the more surprising in view of her great musicality. Any attempt at driving a car could only have ended in instant disaster.

When very young our holidays were spent in Austria. One hot summer we travelled by train, third class of course, on hard wooden benches, to the Waldviertel (the wooded quarter) in Upper Austria, a province little known to the outside world even today. There, aged six, I watched the owner of 'our' inn extract the honey from the waxen combs of his many beehives by turning the handle of an extractor for hours, and for the first time tasted the delicious product

47

of his bees and their industry. In the little village square I stood and watched, and sometimes was allowed to try my hand at drawing water from the village pump, the only source of supply for most of the houses around.

With the air temperature at its hottest, the river Kemp promised welcome relief, except that its width and slight current were deceptive, and even at my tender age the water only reached to my waist when I stood up in it. It required some skill not to hit the bottom with one's knees when trying to swim.

The way back up the steep hill to the village and midday dinner was tedious and wearying, but had its pleasant surprises. Where the trees had been felled for timber and the area reforested with hundreds of tiny pines straight from the tree nursery, thousands of wild strawberries ripened in the boiling sun. They asked to be picked and enticed us to dawdle and eat and eat. Their flavour has never been matched by anything the nurseryman has been able to put on our tables.

As my sister and I grew older the family's journeys went farther afield. Often we stayed on farms, where we joined the children of the house in their pursuits. One particular farmer cut his corn with a scythe, and it was the task of us youngsters to tie it into stooks. I am sure I could still do it today, only, alas, there is no call for it. The liquid discharged from the cowhouse ran in channels at the bottom of the stalls to the yard outside, where it was collected in a deep pit. Here it remained until the spring, imparting its flavour to the atmosphere of the farm. Special tanker carts, horse-drawn, sprayed the precious liquid manure onto the grazing land belonging to the farm, and it sufficed to provide an excellent hay crop for the winter.

Hay was made twice a year, once in May and once in August. With this job our puny efforts were again welcome, as the cut grass, lying in swathes, had to be turned manually with a rake every two or three days, depending on the weather, to dry it out thoroughly. The greatest excitement came when it was judged dry enough to be carted home to the barn. The extremely arduous work of loading was not for us, but once the cartload was as high as a house and the centre beam, a smooth tree trunk, had been put across its middle to hold it down securely, we were hoisted aloft and taken by the overworked horse at a very slow pace along the rutted tracks through the fields and meadows so familiar at ground level but so different from such a height.

But perhaps the greatest pleasure for me was to join in the herding of the cattle. It meant lazy hours doing little except looking at the sky, watching the clouds riding across it and dreamily eating the hazelnuts and blackberries which grew in profusion at the edge of the pasture. In August these were supplemented by vast acres of bilberries, which coloured one's mouth and tongue a lovely bright purple. One could sit down among the bushes and in a very short time fill a litre tin mug with the large juicy sweet berries.

Townspeople used to journey into nearby woods and, with special metal combs, comb the berries from the bushes, either for sale to a greengrocer or to dry them in the sun spread out on large white sheets of paper for the winter. Soaked in vermouth with a dollop of whipped cream, these made the most delicious dessert imaginable.

From mid-August onwards until the first frosts in October, the mushrooming fever befell the whole population of Austria. Every conceivable kind of edible fungus, and there are many of these besides the well-known nursery-grown champignon, was hunted down, gathered and, if possible, dried. Certain highly prized and rare members of the family were carefully sliced, then threaded piece by piece onto fine cotton yarn to make a long necklace and finally hung up in the sun to dry. Our hall window, facing south, served this purpose admirably and was quite a sight,

49

for any visitor encountering it for the first time, with several rows of these strings of mushrooms across the open space on top, with Mother's tradescantias contentedly growing underneath.

Subconsciously and gradually we learned to appreciate what nature had to offer and, at the same time, came to realise the necessity of caring for the plants and animals which provided us with our food, to say nothing of the beautiful surroundings.

Journeys beyond the frontiers of Austria fell into the category of great adventures. Not that it was very difficult or took very long when travelling either north or south to reach a frontier. A look at the map quickly establishes the closeness of Hungary, Yugoslavia and Czechoslovakia. It took three hours by train to reach Budapest, and until the end of the First World War a tram link connected Vienna with Bratislava. Nevertheless, the holidays spent 'abroad' put one in a special compartment with one's schoolfellows.

One such holiday took us just beyond the Czech frontier to a place called, in German, Frayn-an-der-Theya. It still bore that name at that time, for it was a completely German-speaking area which, lying at the southern extremity of Bohemia, had been included in the newly created successor state. It was a small town on a small river destined to become the site of a large reservoir. Every day, with the exception of Sunday, at certain fixed times in the hills adjacent to the river bed dynamite was set off in loud explosions. One could practically set one's watch by them. We occupied a couple of rooms over a grocer's shop which, thanks to the kindness of the elderly couple who owned it, became a wonderful place to explore and stay in. The sugar came in large cone-shaped loaves which had to be broken up and weighed out in half and whole kilograms. It was bliss to be allowed to unfold the strong blue paper bags exclusively used for this purpose, weigh them and fold the tops over in the prescribed manner. It was riveting to observe the procession of customers passing through the shop and to listen to their conversation. It was also instructive to become acquainted at such an early age with the force of intolerance.

The shop owners, having been Austrians for generations in the past and for the best part of their lives, only spoke German, their mother tongue, like that of the rest of the local population. But the workmen brought in to build the dam and reservoir were native Czechs, and whenever one of them entered the shop our landlords hid themselves in their backroom. Either one or the other of their sons who had, naturally, been to school after the war and there been taught entirely in Czech, or a specially employed assistant were called to attend to the customer, for the use of German instead of Czech would have led to unpleasantness, if nothing worse. Even my father, who had learned to speak Czech as a boy on his grandfather's Bohemian estate, had the advantage over these poor people, who found themselves willy-nilly strangers in their own country.

Coffee was a very expensive import both in Austria and Czechoslovakia, beyond the pockets of most people, and in order to provide a cheaper substitute barley was used. In the spacious passage of the ancient substantially built house leading from the front door and wide enough to permit the easy progress of two horses harnessed side by side to the yard at the back, a coffee roaster was placed once a week. In its perforated slowly rotating metal drum barley was roasted until it looked like the real thing. The smell was quite revolting, and it took many hours for it to become bearable. It filled the whole house in spite of the draught through the open doors only to recur the following week. I am sure I would recognise it at once after all this time, should I be unlucky enough to encounter it again!

The river, as yet quite unspoilt, was a happy hunting ground for human water rats. It also harboured the animal kind, which proved completely harmless. The weather being very hot, it attracted the few summer guests like a magnet. The steps leading from the changing hut to the water, slow-moving and crystal-clear, were hewn out of the living rock which, in turn, was studded with a multitude of garnets, the local semi-precious stone of Bohemia. They were round, bluish, some quite large and of no specific interest to anybody. What did capture our interest was a large raft to paddle down river, and a couple of single-seater canoes which we quickly learnt to handle.

Another abiding memory of those weeks was the wild-growing cucumbers. The town of Znaim, within easy reach of Frayn, was acknowledged to be the cucumber capital of Central Europe, and one could easily see why this should be so. Every compost heap, every wayside rubbish dump was covered in ridge cucumber plants flowering and fruiting to their heart's content. To me as a budding gardener it gave quite the wrong impression that cucumbers are so prolific that the hardest task connected with their cultivation is the picking of them.

A year or two later, at the beginning of the 1930s we travelled right across Bohemia into the Sudetenland to the foothills of the Giant Mountains. At that time the forests there were completely untouched by human endeavours at exploitation, and represented a link with the past going back to the Ice Age. Father took us for long walks along little-used paths leading through tall straight firs of a great age which were so massive that the strongest wind hardly stirred the lower branches. Occasionally, one would happen on a large circular pond called a *Meerauge*, the German for 'eye of the sea', for this was a part of German-speaking Silesia – filled with the clearest water of a beautiful pale green and of an unfathomable depth. It was like being in church. But it was a church with goodies in it. Mushrooms, strawberries, blueberries, bilberries and blackberries studded the forest floor in profusion, well-watered as it was by the frequent cold rains.

The following year brought a complete change from the cold north to the warm and romantic south, and the excitement of a first glimpse of that blue sea, the Mediterranean. We joined a party travelling via Milan and Genoa to the South of France, to Juan-les-Pins to be precise. It was in Genoa that I tasted my first summer orange, as until then oranges had been a winter fruit much connected with snow and ice, a scented reminder of the places where the sun always shone. Juan-les-Pins is well situated for visiting the rest of the Riviera towns. Cap Matin was still an unspoilt spit of land, Roquebrune a small village boasting a few large and beautiful villas, Cannes exclusive and expensive, and Nice quite a large town with its famous Promenade des Anglais. Here we joined the locals in their celebration of 14 July, Bastille Day, by dancing in the street until late into the night.

Monte Carlo's Casino, of which we had heard of course, would not permit my sister and myself to penetrate beyond its entrance hall, neither of us having reached the magic age of majority, 21. This was rigorously checked from visitors' passports which had to be produced before admission was granted. However, the famous gardens facing the Casino's front, with their sinister reputation of being the place favoured by gamblers for committing suicide after losing their all at the gaming tables, held a great fascination for us, for the combination of violent death and the sweet-smelling semi-tropical vegetation, including purple bougainvillea and red hibiscus, seemed quite incongruous.

In 1935 Venice was our holiday destination. No more romantic place existed for the Viennese: was it not where the better-off went for their honeymoon? The journey was long, the train took eight hours to reach it, and the third-class seats were still just hard polished wood. It was with heightened anticipation that we looked out of the windows when crossing the causeway from Mestre on the mainland to the railway station on the island of San Marco. We had heard and read about there being no roads, only canals in this ancient town, but the reality surpassed all imagination.

Travelling along the Canale Grande in a *vaporetto*, the waterbus connecting the various islands of the once so powerful republic, alongside the beautiful if often badly neglected buildings, passing under the Rialto bridge with its shops lining both sides of it, the eyes had difficulty in taking it all in. Our Swiss-owned hotel was right in the centre of this extraordinary city. There, another surprise was in store for us. We had to sleep under mosquito nets, with the chemicals which after the war proved such an effective weapon against the scourge of these malaria-carrying insects lying still in the future. Every night, when going to bed, it was like slipping under a canopy suspended from a lovely white crown over one's head, where the ends of the netting material had been gathered together in that fashion to make its suspension from a hook in the ceiling possible. The dreaded malaria did not find a victim amongst us, but our sense of smell was assaulted by the obnoxious stench from the stagnant canal water when it rained, which it frequently did!

The *vaporetto* became our friend. In it we went across the lagoon to the Lido, an island rightly famous for its stretches of very fine, clean white sand, ideal for the not too expert swimmer, with its long walk down the gently sloping edge of the beach into the shallow waves before one reached deep water. Tide there was practically none, the

Adriatic being in effect a large oblong saltwater lake with its southern end attached to the Mediterranean.

Here it was that a young lawyer from Breslau took a fancy to me, who was quite unaware of what was in his mind since, at the age of 15, my interests did not include affairs of the heart. In any case we girls were always in the company of either our parents or several other young people. I only learnt of his infatuation when he started to write to me once we were both back in our respective homes, but I never saw any of his letters. My mother took it upon herself to open them and to put him off, telling me only the absolute minimum she thought necessary. It surprised me but made no other impression. School was far more important.

1936 saw the first of my journeys alone. In order to improve my command of English before taking the leaving exam in it a year later, I was going to spend the two months of the summer holidays in England. My mother had an old uncle living in London, to which city he had come as a 17-year-old seeking his fortune and perhaps also to escape his position as the only boy in a family of five girls, well before the end of the century. To him she wrote with the request to find suitable accommodation for a carefully brought-up 16-year-old. Uncle Harry, who had turned 70 by then and was on his second, English, wife, must have looked for places advertising for students of English over the summer months. I cannot imagine how else he came upon Dr Evans-Cross and his little empire in Southbourne.

Dr Evans-Cross – I believe his doctorate to have been a theological one – ran a private hotel for retired impecunious gentlefolk. Into this very quiet, sedate, gentle and well-ordered community he injected, for the sake of making money, a number of young Continentals who were anathema to their fellow residents. There were seven of us in 1936, five French boys, one French-Swiss boy and myself. Since all the rooms in the main building were occupied by the 'permanents' we were farmed out along the road in various private houses, but taking all our meals together in the communal dining room of the hotel proper. There we were placed at different tables, no doubt the intention being that we should politely converse with our English companions instead of which, we carried on a loud conversation in French right across the room. My French improved phenomenally! After lunch we gathered on the lawn in front of the building, only to be shushed by the irate takers of a postprandial nap. It was an odd and not very satisfactory situation which only helped to reinforce my belief that I had come to a very peculiar country.

To reach it had been a long and exhausting journey. Under the sponsorship of the National Union of Students of Great Britain a train consisting of six third-class carriages, with every seat taken, had left Vienna at 1 p.m. On it went through the whole length of Austria over the Arlbergpass to draw into Zurich station at 7 p.m. Then it turned north and travelled all night along the fabled river Rhine with its many castles lit by a full moon, across yet another frontier to its terminus at Ostend. Here we embarked on the Dover ferry for the three-and-a-half-hour-long uneventful crossing. In Dover we made a wonderful discovery: third-class railway carriages with upholstered seats! We had to be reassured that we had been correctly placed and had not strayed into second class by mistake.

The journey from Dover to London brought more new impressions. Rows upon rows of interconnected small houses with a forest of chimneys festooning their roofs, all alike, wending their way across the countryside. How could people tell which one they lived in? Back home people also lived in houses, but only if they were well off and wanted a great deal of space and to be away from the centre of Vienna. The normal way to live was in a flat which, as I discovered quite soon, was often much more spacious than an English house. At home people who owned houses had large plots, had each house individually designed by an architect, employed servants and inhabited the upper reaches of society.

My uncle's terraced house in Ealing distinguished itself from its neighbours only by the large pile of books stacked on the front room floor otherwise bare of furniture. During my week's stay with him I used to walk up the short front garden paths and peer into the front room of houses, to my eyes indistinguishable from each other, until I had found the books. Why did I not look for the house number? Well, here was another peculiarity. The houses bore no numbers but had each a name, though for some reason I never got to know my uncle's. Perhaps it had none! Here, too, I came across Camp coffee essence for the first and, as far as I am concerned, for the last time in my life. After Viennese coffee made from unadulterated beans, it was quite awful.

The young soon make friends, and it did not take long before we Austrians from various parts of our country found each other in Bournemouth by wearing our national costume. We spent happy hours driving a hired motor boat on the river Avon, scraping together the necessary pence for petrol, swimming in the chilly and often very rough sea, not at all like the warm blue Adriatic or the Mediterranean, and frequented Woolworths. Woolworths was Aladdin's cave for us. Everything on sale cost either 3d or 6d except for playing cards, which bore an extra 3d in tax. I have the pack of cards still bought out of the scanty allowance my father could afford to make me, for playing cards were extremely heavily taxed back home and worth being taken good care of. There were Japanese-made powder compacts, Japanese teacups of the thinnest porcelain, glassware, vases:

one could practically furnish one's household with all the small items needed to make a home. At the greengrocers there were large bananas at seven for 6d, an absolute luxury for us normally indulged in only on birthdays, and grapefruit, which I had never seen before.

Perhaps the most startling manifestation, however, in the manner of living was the way in which Sunday was spent. For us it was the day on which we went to church in the morning, if so inclined, and, being a Catholic country, most people did. Once having done one's duty by God, the rest of the day was given over to enjoyment. In the summer this took the form of excursions into the countryside or to a bathing pool. In the winter we took our toboggans, skis and skates, went to the pictures, the theatre and the opera, and held afternoon parties with coffee and cream cakes.

What a difference to the English Sunday! The retired Church of Scotland clergyman at Dr Evans-Cross's tried to prevent me from wearing shorts and, what to me was utterly incomprehensible, forbade me to knit. He did not succeed in stopping me from doing either, but that was small consolation for the tediousness of the day. I bought the *Sunday Express* and spent the day and a lot of the rest of the week working my way through it, sport and all, although completely ignorant of cricket, horse racing and rugby union football, the latter being reported from faraway places like Australia and New Zealand, painfully trying to understand. The culture clash was such that even we teenagers were only too aware of it and greeted each other with the question: 'What makes Dr Evans cross?'

The answer, not expressed but fully understood, being our boisterous and, with hindsight, often very rude behaviour.

I cannot remember now how it came about, but I did meet and become friends with some of the locals. One, a girl three years my junior, by the name of Zoë Mortimer, was a cousin of Anthony Eden's on her father's side. For reasons I never found out, even though Zoë and my sister and I remained friends for well over 20 years, her family had fallen on hard times. Her mother, who was her husband's junior by many years, helped to eke out the family budget by baking and selling raised pork pies, a delicacy quite unknown in Austria. They rented a hut on Bournemouth beach, and it was there that I was initiated into the mysteries of beach cricket and the everlasting game of trying to hit a copper penny lying on the sand with a tennis ball from at least ten feet away. We played quoits, which proved a useful skill when I crossed the Atlantic on the *Queen Mary* many years later. Nothing one learns in life is ever wasted.

Another two people, this time husband and wife, I shall always recall with admiration. They must have been in their mid-thirties and lived in a very pretty house. Not only did they frequently invite us sometimes homesick and often lost-feeling foreigners to tea but, something inconceivable today, they left the front door key under the mat to allow us entry into their home at any time, even when they were out. I am certain we never made use of their generosity, probably out of shyness and respect for their privacy, but it was comforting to know that there was a refuge at hand if needed. The love I had felt for the English language from the very beginning was now being greatly reinforced by the kindness shown by complete strangers. Even the astonishing English weather could not spoil the affection I felt.

On the way home life taught me a prime lesson: do not rely on others in important matters unless it is absolutely unavoidable. At London's Victoria station about 600 students assembled for the long journey home. While the hand baggage could be taken into the train compartments, the big suitcases and trunks had to be stowed in a special luggage van. On arrival in Dover there was nobody to unload it except us travellers. I hung around the opening through which young men were handing down case after case, heaving them onto trollies and wheeling them onto the ferry. When the last trunk had thus been shifted I glanced into the dark interior of the van, saw only emptiness and happily, it was a fine warm day, embarked on the ship which was to take us to Ostend.

Halfway across the Channel my name rang out over the tannoy, requesting my attendance at the purser's office. There I was shown a telegram just received from Dover to the effect that my suitcase had been found in the luggage van, the only one to have been left behind. The outcome was not only salutary but also painful, at least for my pocket. From Vienna orders had to be given to a forwarding agent for the case's collection and expedition. The weather in Vienna was exceptionally hot that September, I only had the one thin dress in which I had travelled and had to wear it continuously for the three weeks it took for my case finally to arrive. And to drive in the lesson that taking care of one's possessions was an absolute necessity, the cost, and it was considerable, was deducted in instalments from my meagre pocket money over several months. I have never again anywhere left behind anything more important than a face flannel.

6

Growing up

The major concern of grown-ups since the beginning of time has been the forming of the raw material presented to them on becoming parents. It is amazing how pliable the human child is in spite of heredity, and how the seeds implanted at an early age take root and shape the emerging adult through all the later adventures which present themselves in the as yet unknown future.

My parents were no different from the rest of their generation in trying to instil the niceties of civilised behaviour into their daughters. Mother, whose background, as already mentioned, was entirely Viennese, on marriage spoke the strong local vernacular of her childhood. Father, whose greatest literary success up to that time had been the creation of the schoolboy 'Poldi Huber' with his satirical comments on various aspects of the Austrian scene, spoke the German of the upper, educated classes. The result of this interesting circumstance was rather curious. Not for us the speech of our native town – we had to have a German nanny!

Mother's aunt in Berlin was consulted, and Fräulein Käthe became a member of our household. My memories of her are vague. She slept in our room and was a disciplinarian, which did not prevent her from starting to lead a somewhat unconventional love life in her spare time. After her dismissal all experiments in foreign help were abandoned, but by then what had been intended had been achieved. We two Viennese girls could speak 'good' German, and the dreaded dialect had been kept at bay: until we started school, that is, when we quickly learned to understand, if not speak it from the socially mixed bunch of our fellows.

Fräulein Käthe was followed by Fräulein Mizzi, who was non-resident but came every weekday after lunch to take us for walks in the park of Schönbrunn Palace. There, by the sweeping staircase leading from the state apartments, to the 'parterre', the beautifully laid-out baroque gardens, we joined other children in the traditional games and songs –

> 'Little Mary sat on a stone,
> quite alone,
> when along came a handsome prince
> and wooed her.'

– the wooing being sealed with a kiss on the cheek.

We sang with gusto, making a large circle holding hands. Little Mary sat or rather squatted in its centre and waited to be wooed. None of us really understood what it all meant, but how we enjoyed it.

Then there were the skipping games. One could skip by oneself as fast as one was able, but it was much more exciting for two friends to hold the ends of a long, steadily rotating rope with oneself, often simultaneously with one or two others, skipping in and out without getting one's feet entangled and so bringing everything to a halt. The number of skips was counted out loud, and there was keen competition to come top.

Another way of enlivening the forays into the fresh air was bowling a hoop along as we walked. This was quite a feat on the cobblestones of the pavement and the gravel paths in the park. It demanded considerable skill to keep the hoop running straight and taught a good lesson in endeavour and perseverance.

In the summer there was an ingenious and much loved cross between a toy and a game called diabolo. It consisted of a metre length of strong but thin string attached to two 30-centimetre long sticks. The diabolo – the devil – was made from rubber in the shape of two inverted cones about 8 centimetres across their open ends, with their tips connected to each other with a metal ring, giving it a narrow waist. The game consisted in making the diabolo run on this waist along the string, throwing it up into the air and catching it either straightforwardly or after twisting the string while the top was airborne. The variations were numerous and the challenge to improve one's performance was ever-present.

However, it was not only the young who used the park for their entertainment. Along the immaculately kept paths lined with low, carefully pruned beech hedges, wooden benches were placed at frequent intervals. In the clement seasons these were populated by all kinds of people, none more extraordinary than groups of men, mostly elderly, presumably retired or unemployed. They did not sit down, as one might have expected, but stood in front and behind a bench in a rough circle. On closer inspection it became obvious that they were playing the national card game of Austria, Tarok. It was only when I was living away from my homeland that I learned of the connection ascribed to the tarot cards with the supernatural and their power of seeing into the future. In Austria everybody played Tarok, this very ancient game, with its two different sets of cards all intermingled, making it an excellent mental exercise for the players.

When young university students my father, his brother and two friends had played it when on their way by train to Heiligenblut, the village at the foot of the Grossglockner,

Austria's highest mountain, from where they were going to climb it. It being summer, they had opened the window of their compartment and suffered the mortal blow of having the Stix, the highest card in the pack, worth 22 points, carried out of it by a sudden gust of wind. This unexpected end to what had been so engrossing a game that even the magnificent landscape rolling past could not divert them from it made an everlasting impression on my father and his companions, as if they had lost a very dear friend.

Tarok was part of the national heritage, and in the park these solemn men, well wrapped up against the cold when the spring day was cool and the autumn day cold, only carried on a tradition. No doubt it helped them to forget the hardships of the depressed and sad Thirties, the lack of employment, the cramped and badly heated flats, the uncertain political future.

'*Schönbrunn*' means the beautiful spring and takes its name from a small spring housed in a tiny baroque building in the shape of a sugarloaf. Not many Viennese know of its existence, but Father, who had grown up in the park and had walked every inch of it many times, led us children, as a special treat, to this little temple dedicated to pure water where, for the equivalent of a penny, we could buy a glass of it and convince ourselves of its excellence. There was something mysterious and enchanting about this hidden spring tended by a woman whose job it was to lock and unlock the door and look after the needs of the few callers. It felt as if a fairy story ought to be attached to it somewhere, particularly as the Viennese weave stories around many of their buildings and the great river Danube, although it hardly touches the town. So it was that we learned the story of the knight gracing the top of the townhall, the Rathausmann, courting the lady of the river, the Donauweibchen.

Another of the fascinating features of this great park is

its Zoo. Although we did not visit it all that often, it being expensive to do so, we were well aware of its existence. Just before 3 in the afternoon, with the wind in the right direction, we could hear the lions roaring as they were waiting to be fed. Once we enriched the Zoo's collection in an unexpected manner. On holiday on the Yugoslav coast we had acquired a couple of tortoises which, in those days untrammelled by import restrictions, were easily taken back to Vienna and installed in my sister's and my room. Feeding them was no problem, we could get plenty of lettuce leaves and tomatoes for them, but they made their presence felt in a way nobody had foreseen.

Before the advent of central heating, rooms were heated by means of tall tiled stoves standing in a corner but well away from the wall, with a small open dark and warm enclosure behind them. For reasons of comfort our tortoises hid themselves there during the day, only to emerge at night and walk about with their clawed feet on the polished parquet floor. The noise, until we realised what caused it, was eerie to say the least. It made sleep impossible, so with a heavy heart we had to part with our pets. The Zoo agreed to accept them and, in return for the gift, allowed us a free visit. We did go back to see them again later, but there was no mutual recognition. I have never again owned a tortoise.

Other pets, which lived with us for some years, were tiny green and yellow European tree frogs kept in a large glass jar. They had greenery at the bottom of their container, watered every day to keep it moist, with a small wooden ladder reaching almost to the top of it. When they climbed the ladder it was supposed to indicate that fine weather was to come, and when they sat on the floor looking sad it was supposed to forecast rain. The open end of the jar was covered with a piece of strong muslin into which had been cut small air holes. Feeding these animals was a little more complicated than feeding the tortoises. We bought meal worms from the pet shop, but their main dietary requirement was live flies.

Again Schönbrunn park came to the rescue. Armed with a jam jar with a tight-fitting lid, I made forays along the stone balustrades lining the castle's outside staircases and some of the broader avenues. On them, in sunny weather, flies congregated to wash and preen themselves. With a quick movement of one's cupped hand from behind the back of the fly one could catch it undamaged if one were lucky, and from there transfer it to the jar with lightning speed. It was good practice for the co-ordination of the mind and the hand, if not exactly exhilarating. Somehow we did not greatly mourn the death of our three frogs when, one cold winter's night, they had been allowed to stand in an unheated passage.

Another feature of the park which I came to love, admire and still visit as often as possible is the Botanical Garden. It covers a section near the western entrance gate and includes a large palm house amongst its attractions. Compared to more famous and larger botanical gardens it is insignificant, but its very intimacy is appealing. Each tree and each shrub, each flowering plant and each evergreen is carefully labelled, inviting close inspection and contemplation. The gardeners were only too happy to answer questions, however naive and inexperienced. It is here that a meteorite had found a home, duly labelled as coming from another world. My passion for growing things certainly was fuelled by walking amongst the exquisitely tended flora. The flowering of the Victoria lily in its special greenhouse, an event to be anticipated only every ten years, was not to be missed, a true testimony to the skill gardening represents.

Every autumn an appeal went out from the Zoo for horse-chestnuts to feed members of the deer family. Out came empty sacks to be taken to the park and filled with the shiny hard fruits from the huge trees lining the service road leading past the service quarters to the palace, giving one the warm feeling of doing good. I suppose it did save the Zoo a little money, but its main purpose must have been to make children aware of the needs of animals and the interaction between them and their natural habitats.

This manifested itself also in another, quite different way. Feeding birds and squirrels must have been one of the prime hobbies of the Viennese, perhaps because most lived in flats, perhaps because of an inborn love of living creatures. Whenever one walked in the park one would come across at least one figure covered more or less completely by birds eating breadcrumbs or seed from that person's hands, mouth, hat, from anything capable of holding food. There were all kinds of birds, sparrows of course, blue tits, great tits, coal tits, jackdaws, thrushes and blackbirds, greenfinches, all the birds one would expect – with one notable exception, the robin. This is an extremely shy bird in contrast to its brothers living in the British Isles, and is rarely glimpsed among the trees.

The squirrels, just as tame, would come and eat out of their aficionados' hands after being called to do so. They were and still are the red, often almost black European squirrels, much smaller and daintier than their grey North American cousins, and did not seem to cause any damage to the trees in which they lived. In the depth of winter, when the snow lay on the ground for many weeks and the paths were covered in black ice of which the large notices at the beginning of each gave grave warning, the food provided by these nature lovers was probably the only possibility of survival for many of the park's inhabitants.

It was the Palace of Schönbrunn itself which put the seal on my newly reached adult status when, at the age of 17 and a bit, I was invited to join the 'young ladies and gentlemen's committee' on the occasion of a big ball in the state rooms of this beautiful building. The Emperor Charles VI had the original plans for his 'Versailles', being a contemporary of Louis XIV of France and engaged in a keen rivalry with him as to the importance of their respective countries, drawn up by Fischer von Erlach, the greatest of the architects of the Austrian Baroque. If they had been executed in their entirety the resulting building might very well have rivalled its incomparable French example. But the site, though so beguiling to the eye, was ill chosen, given to flooding and subsidence, and the expense was vastly greater than the Imperial Exchequer could bear. It was left to the Empress Maria Theresia, Charles's daughter and, as his only child, his heiress, to complete a much less ambitious but still impressively beautiful country house, which in the 18th century was set in the countryside, well away from the town.

The Empress loved her castle and made it her main residence as, much later, did the Emperor Franz Josef, whose use of the vast Imperial Palace in the centre of the town was almost exclusively limited to administrative and State occasions. Fortunate man the Emperor! when one compares the restrictions put nowadays upon persons in the public eye to his mode of living, which was only circumscribed by the rigid Spanish court ceremonial to which he clung until the day he died. My father often saw him being driven past his home in an open carriage bound for the office, with the passers-by doffing their hats to their sovereign.

It was here, in the magnificent white-and-gold ballroom, that the aforesaid committee of young men and women was to open the ball in the traditional fashion, with myself included. The general dancing could not begin until we young ones, ceremoniously in pairs and holding hands, had walked onto the dance floor to the strains of Chopin's 'Polonaise'.

For weeks before the great event we had been drilled by a dancing instructor on how to walk gracefully and in step with the music. We assembled well away from the gaze of the other ball guests. Once we had all taken up our allotted places the orchestra struck up Johann Strauss's 'Vienna Blood' waltz, and we performed the specially choreographed 'figures' we had learned with such dedication. Our fond parents, lining the walls in their capacity as chaperons, must have been feeling quite nostalgic at the sight of the young men's dinner jackets and colourful uniforms, for quite a few were cadets at the army's academy for officers, and the girls' ball gowns were being worn for the first time. Little had changed in this respect since the end of the Empire. All girls had to be chaperoned by an older person, usually a parent, who took no part in the dancing but kept an eagle eye on their charges. We did not feel in the least restricted, only loved and cared for.

The next day came the scanning of the social column in the newspapers. How great was my disappointment when, with the description of my dress, not my but my mother's name appeared as having been present at one of the great social functions of the season. That was the disadvantage of having a young and beautiful mother who easily outshone her somewhat awkward daughter.

However, there was one consolation. It was I, after all, who had received the *Damenspende*, the present given to every participating lady, my first tiny bottle of scent ensconced in its lovely little box lined with dark blue velvet. Of course it was never opened, for young girls did not use perfume, and it has remained a treasured possession to this day, though a little diminished in volume through the passing of time, just like its owner.

Schönbrunn and all that it encompassed was an indelible part of our existence. It was beautiful at any time of the year, it implanted in one a feeling for tradition, for the past, for space and orderliness combined with a respect for nature. No wonder the Viennese loved it and respected the notices stuck on every bit of grass exhorting them not to step on it. Possibly the implied threat of the feared two-shilling spot fine helped to enforce the injunction.

In the spirit of the baroque, the art style most closely identified with things Austrian, the deciduous trees lining the main walks of the parks are cut back so as to form a living straight wall. The pruning involved to keep them in line was an activity of great interest to us. It had to be done from a mobile structure two storeys high and running on large wheels, on which stood the gardeners at several levels clipping away with their handshears. It was a never-ending labour. Every so often a niche would be cut into the side of the wall to allow room for a Greek or Roman statue, faithfully copied from the originals kept in museums. The human figure in its natural state, sometimes coyly covered with a figleaf in a delicate place, soon became familiar to us, as did the gods, myths and civilisations they represented. After such an introduction at a very early age to the ancient classical world, the study of the many Latin texts which it later fell to my lot to do was made much easier with one's imagination already stimulated in advance.

7

The Seasonal Round

With Roman Catholicism the religion of 95 per cent of the population, its church festivals punctuated the year. To this were added much older ones which had been fitted smoothly into the religious calendar.

The first of the latter occurred at the very end of the old and the beginning of the new year. 31 December, called *Sylvester* was a night of revelry. Its name, taken from the Roman satyr Sylvanus, god of the woods, points to its pagan, bacchanalian origins. By the time I was old enough to be allowed to stay up and see the New Year in, it had become a rather tame affair compared to Father's young days, and so had Vienna, the hydrocephalitic head of a small, impoverished state hardly able to sustain its diminished population. But *Sylvester* had to be celebrated. The Society event was the *Opernball*. It took place in the opera house's auditorium, from which the seats had been removed to make a large dance floor. We only knew it from newspaper reports. Our celebrations consisted of going to a party at some friend's house where all kinds of attempts were made to divine the future. This took hours and created considerable excitement.

The most highly valued of these divinations was the 'pouring of the lead'. Mother's button box was raided days before for any soft lead buttons which constituted the raw material for this ancient ceremony. Lead buttons came in

71

all sizes and were used in dressmaking, where they were covered with material matching the garment before being sewn to it. They were also sewn into the front lining of lightweight jackets and coats to keep them hanging nice and straight. The lead amalgam had a low melting point, ideal for the *Bleigiessen*. We anxiously watched until a button had turned into a silvery liquid at the bottom of an old spoon over a lighted candle. Then, quickly, this liquid was poured into a bowl of cold water standing next to the candle where, with a hiss, it at once solidified.

Eagerly the now reconstituted metal was fished out and the guessing game began. What image did it convey? How were the coming 12 months going to turn out? Would the longed-for examination success, boyfriend, bicycle, holiday materialise? It was amazing what wisdom and knowledge a lead button from a button box had in it!

Another, more circumscribed way of looking into the future consisted in managing to peel a large apple round and round its circumference without breaking the skin. This, curled as it was, would then be thrown over one's right shoulder onto the floor. The resulting letter of the alphabet, real or imaginary, foretold the initial with which one's new boyfriend's name would definitely start. It was good fun, soon forgotten in the welter of activities of real life.

1 January was a public holiday, and it was very necessary that it should be. For who could have done a day's work after the liquid farewell to the Old and the exuberant welcome to the New Year.

No sooner had the after effects of *Sylvester* worn off but *Fasching* (carnival) was upon us. The Roman Saturnalia had doubtlessly been brought by the Roman soldiery to Vindobona, the fort built as the easternmost outpost of the Empire, where the Danube forces its way through the last foothills of the Alps to make an almost right-angled turn from flowing east to flowing south. After the advent of

Christianity they had continued to flourish while all else Roman was swept away by the tide of restless tribes from the north and east known to history as the *Völkerwanderung* (the migration of the tribes).

Since Christmas for Roman Catholics is an entirely spiritual and religious festival, room had to be found for the pagan one which had become embedded in the lives of the population, and where better than in the following cold dark winter months badly in need of being enlivened. 6 January, the day of the Magi or the 'Three Holy Kings' was the starting date. The day itself was yet another public holiday when a delightful old custom was and, I believe, still is being practised. In the countryside three young boys, dressed up as the Three Holy Kings, one with a blackened face, went from door to door blessing the building and its inhabitants. As a visible proof of their visit they would, with white chalk, write 'K + M + B' (Kaspar, Melchior and Balthasar) on the top of the dwelling's wooden front door, where the letters remained until the following January. In return the 'Kings' received small presents, apples, sweets, a handful of nuts. Whenever today I see these initials on the back of an Austrian inn door, I feel the strong pull of past generations.

Fasching was a marvellous time, even in the lean and hungry days of the Thirties, whose colour seemed to be preponderantly grey. The dray horses, and there were many engaged in the drudgery of heaving heavily laden carts and wagons over the still cobbled surfaces of the streets, were decorated with gaily coloured paper streamers by their proud owners, who themselves sported large rosettes to match in their buttonholes. Every night there were dances and hops, often masked affairs, in pubs, public halls and private houses. There was always live music, for neither radio nor gramophone could make themselves heard over the babble of voices. It was quite common to see men and women having an early breakfast of frankfurters or goulash soup at a roadside stall, dressed in their evening finery. It also was not unusual in the last two years at school to have some of my male fellow pupils sit in class wearing their dinner jackets, having had no time to go home and get changed before the start of lessons at 8 a.m. Nobody remarked on it, possibly because the younger masters themselves had managed a quick wash and change only by the skin of their teeth.

In our last year at school we had a good excuse for appearing in class wan and worn on a particular morning in early January. It was traditional for the top form, all aged between 17 and 19 by now, to throw a ball at that time of the year before the really hard work of preparing for the leaving examinations got under way. We did it in style. As is the case with the inexperienced and young, it never occurred to us that we might be courting financial disaster by being too ambitious and aiming too high. Blithely we hired the ballroom at the Hübner Hotel in Hietzing, one of Vienna's leading hotels at that time, hired the second most popular dance band, led by Franz Totzauer, had beautifully designed and expensive tickets printed, and engaged a dancing master to drill the young ladies and gentlemen of the management committee in a new interpretation of the almost compulsory 'Vienna Blood' by Johann Strauss with which to open the night's proceedings. The expenses incurred were enormous, to say the least.

Now began the task of selling sufficient tickets. Anybody on two moving legs with whom we had the slightest contact was cajoled, persuaded, yes, pressganged into buying one. School work was put aside, nothing else mattered. Slowly we sold over 500 tickets, a record for that event in the school's annals. The dancing master, whom I had first encountered during my own dancing school days, came, with the headmaster's permission, to school and taught us, to the seductive tones of a wind-up gramophone, the intricate steps of the waltz figures on the hard, sticky boards of the art room.

Naturally, it was to be a very formal affair, with long dresses and dinner jackets *de rigueur*. Being tall, I had been paired off with the tallest boy in the class, Edmund, always called Mundy, Arnold. I had never paid much attention to him, nor he to me. However, he knew how a gentleman should behave. On 'the evening' he called for me looking very smart and grown-up in his brand-new dinner jacket and black tie, and presented me with a large bunch of deep purple, deliciously scented Parma violets as a corsage for my dress. This was a cast-off from my mother's elegant cousin Fritzi, consisting of full-length coffee-coloured lace over a silk slip of the same colour with puff sleeves and a discreet V-neck. It had been altered to fit me by our little dressmaker, and made me feel something very special. Mundy had gone to the expense of hiring a taxi, in which we went off in very high spirits, this time with the blessing of the adults but without their company.

It was a magical evening. Most of our masters, those distant, much-respected and usually feared arbiters of our fate as scholars, were present and unbent sufficiently to allow themselves to buy coloured balloons in aid of our form fund. But the fraternisation did not go so far as actually dancing with any of the girls! The ball opened exactly as planned, with the 'young people's' committee performing its much rehearsed figure waltz. We danced the quickstep, the English waltz, the tango, innumerable Viennese waltzes and the quadrille, which had made a comeback from the happier pre-war days. In the early hours of the morning my shoes were scuffed, my toes hurt, but what did it matter, I had had a marvellous time and we had made a profit!!

The intensity of the festivities connected with *Fasching*

increased as Ash Wednesday and with it the end of all gaiety and the start of Lent approached. The pinnacle of abandonment was reached on the Tuesday preceding it, with the *Gschnasfest* organised by the Society of Viennese artists at their appropriately named *Künstlerhaus* (artists' house). Since *Kunst* in German encompasses all of the creative arts, be they painting, sculpting, writing of every variety except journalism, music both composing and performing, etc., *Künstler* is the designation given to any practitioner of the above, which included Father. No doubt, that was the reason why Dorrit and I were invited one year to a *Kindergschnasfest* in the week before Lent. Being still in single figures the joyful anticipation was particularly great, for it was going to be fancy dress.

Mother, resourceful as ever, decided we should go as two roses. Tight-fitting bodices with round necklines and small shoulder straps were made from a cheap shiny green cloth to which were attached hooped skirts. These consisted basically of very stiff organdy on to which had been sewn with much effort large pink rose petals cut from crêpe paper. They overlapped each other, creating the impression of a rose just unfolding. It was a little difficult to sit down in them, but they looked wonderful, at least to our unsophisticated eyes.

On arrival at the beautiful building right in the heart of the city we were each given a large gingerbread heart of a brown colour, attached to which was a long red ribbon to be looped round the neck with the to us puzzling inscription written in white icing sugar under a stuck-on paper picture of a mountain scene: '*Auf der Alm da gibt's ka Sünd*' (there is no sin on an alpine meadow). Very curious indeed for us youngsters, whose comprehension of sinfulness was extremely limited and only to be understood many years later, when one had learned about the way cattle were cared for in the mountains. Driven in May from their stables in the valley to which they had been confined during the long hard snowy winter onto the lush meadows high above their byres, a single cowherd, either male or female, had the responsibility of looking after them. This meant many lonely days and nights but also complete freedom from the conventions and wagging tongues of the villagers. Who was to know who visited whom and what they got up to? After all, yodelling, the way of communicating from mountain to mountain, did give nothing away.

The provisions by the artistic community for entertaining their young guests had been imaginatively made, as was to be expected. There were rocking horses, games of all kinds, a dolls' theatre worked by invisible hands and, not to be overlooked, frankfurters and cakes to eat and lemonade to drink. But what was most intriguing was what had been done to the walls. These carried a large painted frieze of carousing men and women as nature had made them, and each of the many humans had been carefully dressed in pink crêpe paper to hide their nakedness from our childish eyes. The labour involved must have been prodigious and oddly senseless. Did not every public park in Vienna display its quota of classical statues, which were naked and even in reproduction in possession of normal human accoutrements, just as they had been when gracing the cities of ancient Greece and Rome.

In *Fasching* anything went as far as the really rather moral and straight-laced citizens of those days would indulge in. It was quite usual to wander from ball to ball and dance to dance in the course of a night. The resulting hangover from tiredness and weeks of indulgence in a variety of alcoholic beverages, known as a *Kater* (tomcat), conjuring up the image of a fierce black tom sitting on one's shoulder hissing into one's ear, exhorted one to feel with the arrival of Ash Wednesday a natural, indeed, welcome emotion turning the day, a public holiday of course, into a

77

quiet scene of retrospection and vows to be good from now on. Since however the way to hell is paved with good intentions once the worst of the excesses had worn off, Lent was not bad either.

It is true one abstained from eating meat on Fridays, if one was not doing so already as a good Catholic, but fish was permitted. This would be either hake or cod imported frozen by the German Northsea Fisheries and sold in their chain of shops, or dear freshwater fish from Austria's own rivers and lakes. The latter were mostly trout and carp, occasionally pike, and all very expensive. At home we often had home-made soup – all Austrian main meals start with soup – followed by a homemade strudel filled with sweetened ground poppy seed, ground walnuts, apples or curds. The word went amongst housewives thinking of engaging a *Mädchen für alles* (a maid for everything) that one should first test the applicant's skill at making a drawn strudel before even thinking of offering her the job. It certainly is a most skilful task to pull the dough by hand to such thinness that the skin of the cook can be seen through it.

Winter always brought snow and ice in variable quantities. The permanent notices at the beginning of the paths in every park bearing the message 'Beware Black Ice' suddenly assumed an importance quite forgotten in the summer months. The worst winter in living memory and certainly in mine was that of 1929. It was then and still is the law that a houseowner is responsible for keeping the pavement in front of his property free of obstructions and in a fit state for pedestrian traffic. In that year so much snow had fallen early on that the caretakers of the apartment houses whose job it was to carry out this particular duty had built by the sides of the carriage way a snow wall approximately two metres high, with occasional gateways to make it possible to cross to the other side. It was like walking along a sunken road in the realm of the snow queen. The Danube, a very fast-flowing river at Vienna, whose current is so strong that the then existing ferry across it had to run along an overhead cable to prevent it from being swept downstream, froze over completely and built up large blocks of ice along the main river bridge, the Reichsbrücke. Father took us to see it, but would not allow us to walk over it to the other bank as so many people were doing. Coal was in very short supply; it had to be collected from the coal merchant since it could not be delivered in the normal way, and we wore our winter coats indoors. My sister who, in spite of her more felicitous start in life, did not seem as tough as I was, acquired frozen thighs on our walks to and from school through the thick snow covering the paths in the park of Schönbrunn. The intense cold coloured them a nice blue, and they were to trouble her for many years to come. Chilblains on one's hands and feet were commonplace and hardly worth mentioning. The mountainous feather beds with which we covered ourselves at night really came into their own, all the more so since mother, a fresh-air fiend, insisted on opening our bedroom window – even with the temperature at 10 Centigrade below zero.

Of course, not all winters were like that. With the turn of the year and the sun starting to gain in strength there were often perfect, calm, sunny days which, though cold, tempted the flat dwellers not only to take a walk in one of the many town parks, but also to find a sheltered corner or bench for an hour's enjoyment of the free warmth.

Just as winter followed very quickly after the scented days of summer, so spring came in without much ado. Its herald was the warm wind, the *Föhn* from across the Alps all the way from Italy. Although the Alpine regions like the Tyrol felt its full force, it extended its sway as far as Vienna. To me it was the Pied Piper's seductive melody. I had to walk in its face for hours on end and greatly upset Mother, who worried about my disappearance. She, in common with many others, complained about the headache this exotic visitor gave her, and her only word of approval was reserved for its magic power in melting the snow and ice almost overnight. Out came the spring suits and hats, the buds swelled on the bushes long before the trees showed any signs of life – and Easter had come.

Its imminent arrival had been indicated a couple of weeks earlier in the windows of every kind of shop. Tiny bunches of pussy willow decorated the exhibits, tiny fluffy yellow chicks seemed to be hopping all over everything, and the confectioners really went to town. The Easter hare – not bunny – made in chocolate in every conceivable size, always sat up on its haunches with its long ears firmly erect. The larger ones had chocolate baskets on their backs filled with small multicoloured chocolate eggs. Then there were Easter eggs, Easter eggs, Easter eggs, large and small, plain or milk chocolate ones, the more expensive ones filled with sweets. All these one bought if one had the money, but at home we followed the old tradition of making our own. With onion juice we drew faces on the shells of raw eggs, leaving no visible trace of our artistry. Then we boiled them quite hard, and when cold painted the shells again with coloured faces. From white carton we made stiff collars with turned-down lapels to stand the eggs on until we had quite a little army. When we came to eat them and had peeled off the shell, the drawing previously done with onion juice appeared in black on the set egg white.

Easter, however, was not only a time for rejoicing at the arrival of spring but also a great and holy Christian festival. We Lutherans have only two days in the year on which attendance in church is a must: 31 October in commemoration of that day in 1517 when Martin Luther affixed his 91 theses to the doors of the cathedral in Wittenberg, laying the foundations of that part of the Christian fellowship bearing his name, and Good Friday, when Jesus Christ died on the cross in order that mankind should live.

On one such Good Friday Mother had taken us to our quite distant parish church to what was always a lengthy service commensurate with the occasion. Being a good housewife, she had prepared lunch beforehand to be ready as soon as we got home. When the tram eventually put us down at the stop a few yards from the street door of our apartment house, we were astonished to see five fire engines parked outside it. On entering the house, the assembled crowd of fellow tenants soon enlightened us as to what had happened. The saucepan in which Mother had left the haricot bean soup to simmer over a low flame on the gas cooker had boiled dry. The kitchen window being open, the smoke generated by the broiling beans had escaped into the courtyard and risen from the second floor into the blue sky. Somebody crossing the courtyard, sufficiently alarmed by the obvious fire, had called the fire brigade. The firemen had run up their ladder to the open window and, on discovering an impeccably clean floor, had first put down some newspaper before making their way to the cooker to turn off the gas under the offending saucepan. For some time afterwards Mother lived in fear of having to pay for the fire brigade's turn-out for what might be considered to have been a careless action by her. But, no doubt once the reason for its commission, the attendance at a religious service, was taken into consideration, clemency was allowed to gain the upper hand, and Mother could breathe more easily once again, her housekeeping money intact.

The religious significance of Easter was emphasised by the falling silent of the church bells. Instead of announcing the customary services like the raising of the monstrance in face of the kneeling congregation during Mass, silence reigned from the evening of Maundy Thursday to the morning of Easter Sunday. We children were told that the bells had flown to Rome to be blessed by the Pope. I tried to visualise the long long line of bells of all sizes and weight winging their way across the Alps to the Eternal City. It was sheer awe-inspiring magic that each one should be back in its own church or chapel to ring out the joyful message of the Risen Christ on Easter Sunday.

The week leading up to Easter Sunday is called *Karwoche*, the week of the Passion of Christ, but here, too, the more ancient beliefs and rituals have found a place. Maundy Thursday is known as *Gründonnerstag* (Green Thursday). It is the day on which the traditional fare for the main meal is fried eggs with spinach. The symbolism of the egg, just as that of the fluffy yellow chick, is not difficult to fathom, but what about the spinach? With the severe winters, with the great outdoors frozen and covered in snow for many months, fresh vegetables were just not available. One lived on cabbage of the large white variety, and roots like carrots and parsnips which could be stored like potatoes for long periods. What a joy it was to be able to pick the first green crop to grow in abundance, ushering in the return of life to the denuded land, although it was spinach and not to everybody's taste. But it was a firm promise of the good things to come before long.

Another custom going back to before the coming of Christianity was the taking to church of bunches of pussy-willow by Catholics on Easter Sunday to be blessed and then hung up in their homes until the following year, as a token of God's protecting hand. Surely a corollary of the 'Three Wise Men' on 6 January and a proof of the strength of the human need for protection by Higher Powers.

Easter was followed more or less quickly by 1 May, Labour Day, a public holiday of course. We children sang lustily: 'Hurrah for the first of May, then we have three days off from school', which, of course, was quite untrue but rhymes nicely in German. On the contrary, in the second half of the Thirties this was the day on which Vienna's large public sports stadium in the Prater was taken over by the schools for interschool athletics competitions. Being tall and thin with long legs, I was a competent runner and one year made the school team. It was a never-to-be-forgotten experience. The weather was so cold that it snowed on us who, lightly clad in shorts and T-shirts, were standing about in the open, awaiting our turn for what seemed hours until our brief moment of glory came. Lunch, consisting of a knackwurst and a roll, enlivened the proceedings, in particular our hands, which unfroze a little holding the hot sausage. I never again took part in a sports meeting on the First of May!

May itself has its vagaries. Right in the middle of the month come four days when winter usually makes a last stand before beating retreat. These are known as 'The Three Icemen and the wicked Sophie'. The story goes that the 'wicked Sophie' (Sophia) refers to the Emperor Franz Josef's mother, who made herself highly unpopular through her interference in his marriage to her niece Elisabeth of Wittelsbach, Princess of Bavaria. She had even gone so far as to remove the couple's first-born child, a daughter, from the care of her mother whom she, probably correctly, considered too young, too inexperienced in the ways of the Imperial Court, and a little unstable, thus making her unfit to be in charge of the upbringing of an Austrian princess. The consequences of this action were tragic for many people and, possibly, responsible for the turn history took later on. All that is left of what was once of great import is the folk memory of a no-longer-understood chain of events.

May was for us non-Catholics the most attractive month of the school year. It absolutely abounded with Catholic church festivals and going to confession and communion, which all involved a day off from school, so that the standard six-day week was reduced to one of five. After the cold spell summer started, the open-air swimming baths opened for business, and the long holidays beckoned. Whitsun brought another break in the routine, to be followed by Corpus Christi Day and on 29 June by the feast of St Peter and St Paul.

Of all these Corpus Christi was the most exciting and impressive. Several days before the actual day lorryloads of young birch trees were delivered to the blocks of flats along our part of the street, to be planted in between the cobblestones along the roadway in the spaces left by the mature lime trees which scented the air so beautifully when in bloom later on in July. What a busy hammering there was, since it fell to the lot of the resident caretaker of each house to space his share of the young greenery evenly along the façade of 'his' property. The effect was quite extraordinary. The woods had come to town.

Come the great day, always, it seems to me, hot and sunny, when quite a different sort of work began at 4 a.m. We were woken by the unloading of piles of timber and boards at the wide front door of the impressive old house opposite, owned and occupied in its entirety by a wealthy merchant. It was enthralling to sit on the windowsill high above and watch the skill with which the apparently unrelated bits and pieces were turned into an open-air altar with vases of fresh roses, a statue of the Virgin Mary, and Christ on his cross as its centrepiece. All was finished by 8 a.m. At the Catholic parish church the faithful gathered to follow their priest in procession round the circumference of the parish. A short religious service was held at each of the pre-ordained altars and, eventually, the morning ended with Mass at the church.

The whole event was, for me, spellbinding and frightening at the same time. The procession was spearheaded by the adult congregation, followed by a large group of young children walking two by two and dressed in white, each

84

carrying a white lily or a small basket filled with rose petals to be strewn along the way for the feet of the priest to walk on. He moved at a measured pace under a brocaded canopy whose supporting poles were carried at each of the four corners by strong young men. At the rear marched a detachment of soldiers. Having arrived at the altar opposite our house the participants placed themselves in a semicircle and the service began, watched by a large crowd in the street with heads appearing from every window.

As soon as the bell for the blessing sounded I rushed off to the room behind the kitchen, furthest away from the front, where I sat in fear and trembling, with fingers stuffed in both ears, for the service ended with the soldiers firing a round of blanks into the air, the sound of which caused me almost unbearable pain. However, this did not prevent my sister and myself, although of the Protestant persuasion, from taking part in one of these processions, dressed in the regulation white and equipped with the much envied flower baskets. Without our parents' knowledge, our nanny, Fräulein Mizzi, a staunch Catholic, wanted to see her charges included in the high spot of the year for small children, and simply infiltrated us into the procession of the neighbouring parish, well away from prying eyes. It is one of my most cherished memories without having had the slightest influence on my religious beliefs.

June, occasionally, brought unexpected surprises. In 1929, I believe, the *Zeppelin*, Count Zeppelin's original airship, built in Ludwigshafen on Lake Constance, visited Vienna. We were taken to the strategic vantage point of the Gloriette, the pavilion gracing the hill facing the park front of Schloss Schönbrunn, having been apprised of the flight path beforehand. It was an impressive sight to see the long cigar shape coming straight at us in a blue sky at a very low height, scattering small bunches of flowers to the onlookers below. We did not manage to retrieve one but it did not matter, we had been allowed to see one of the marvels of technological progress.

School broke up in June, not to reassemble again until the middle of September. Provided the end-of-year report had been satisfactory and the promotion to the next form assured, two glorious months of comparative freedom stretched ahead of one. Vienna, hot and tourist-ridden in the summer, knew us not for all that time. In common with at least half the population, we fled the town. Notices appeared on closely shuttered lock-up shops saying: 'On holiday for the month of July' or 'the month of August' or even for both of these. The opera house shut its doors and moved to Salzburg for the festival.

And yet, those who stayed because they had to were not entirely deprived of the joys of summer. The many open-air swimming baths and, in particular, those along the Alte Donau (Old Danube) offered a refuge from the heat and an opportunity to relax, provided the gnats and midges were not too bad that year. In the evening there were the 'Heurigen' inns in Grinzing and Sievering on the lower slopes of the Alpine foothills, only a tram ride away, with their gardens shaded by huge horse chestnuts, limes and beeches, dispensers of new wine – the 'Heurige' – of unsuspected potency and sourness, and *Schrammelmusik*.

Josef Schrammel, who gave his name to this type of music, had formed his quartet at the end of the 19th century for the purpose of playing Viennese popular songs and tunes in the establishments lining the narrow alleys of the small villages on the edge of town, whose main streets lead up to the vineyards covering the southfacing slopes of Vienna's local mountains on its north-western aspect.

As a change from the sentimental native product, frequently a Hungarian gipsy band would take the floor and, going from table to table, serenade the ladies while keeping a watchful eye on the banknote proferred by the men in the

86

party, fashioning their musical offering according to its value. The flower seller would call several times a night with bunches of roses and carnations, the newspaper boy would hawk the latest edition of the evening paper and, once midnight had come and gone, the first edition of the morning one.

And yet it was a cheap way of spending some hours away from the treadmill of a humdrum job and poor housing, as the only expense needed to be the wine. Food was brought in by the customer. Out came greaseproof packets of ham, salami and any of the other 50 different varieties of cold sausage available, also a large pickled cucumber or two, several freshly baked and very crisp rolls and, possibly, some butter, provided it had not melted in the heat. With all of Society, high and low alike, acting in the same fashion, all social distinctions were in abeyance. They could not even be distinguished by the clothes worn as they could be at most other times, the national dress of dirndl and lederhosen being universal. It was only in the use of language and the strength of the Viennese dialect that existing differences could not be smoothed over. The graduation of accent and the vocabulary employed put one in one's slot.

At the weekend, which usually meant Sunday, since on Saturday only the afternoon was free, the town emptied into the surrounding countryside at all times of the year. No other capital city in Europe, we used to say, has a countryside like Vienna. There were and still are the Vienna woods with their farms and fields, their pine forests harbouring ancient villages with ancient inns whose walls, often one metre thick, keep them warm in winter and cool in the dog days of summer.

Father, who was a great walker like very many of his fellow Austrians, with the help of a map worked out excursions of not less than 25 kilometres a day which we, children of seven and eight, were expected to accomplish. Having been taught to swim and thus been taken care of in case of a river ducking, he did not see any reason why such a feat should not be within our competence. Off we went with our small rucksacks on our backs to be initiated into the joys of walking through a lovely landscape. There was a feeling of awe when following Schubert's peregrinations or walking in Beethoven's footsteps through the Hinterbrühl. I wonder whether the former would have appreciated hearing his 'Trout' sung, not very well, by a family marching along a well-used riverside path. It would have been amazing if we had not slept well after so much exertion.

Autumn comes quickly in Central Europe. By the end of September cold winds started to blow, October's bright but chilly days caused the Danube, normally a grey colour no different from any other large river, to take on a bluish appearance, and November brought the first snow with its welcome intimations of the approaching Christmas festivities. It was a kind of game to look out of the classroom windows to spot the first snowflakes with their promise of such joys of winter as to supersede the fight against the cold. Four Sundays before Christmas Eve, the *Heilige Abend* (Holy Evening) on which centred all our hopes and desires, the advent wreath, made from pine branches and decorated with four thick red wax candles, was fastened to the centre light of our schoolroom. One, then two, then three and finally all four were ceremoniously lit not, of course, on Sunday as they really should have been, but on the Monday following, heightening everybody's excited anticipation.

But before arriving at the commemoration of the birth of Christ, a strange and somewhat pagan festival, much enjoyed by all who were not at the receiving end of its excesses, took place. 5 December was dedicated to the Devil and 6 December to St Nicholas, the children's bishop. They went by the Austrian names of Krampus and Nicolo and while 6 December was a public holiday and thus meant to be 'holy', the previous day bore quite a different face. Weeks before, shop windows started to be decorated with the colour red. Every conceivable kind of material could be used as long as it was red, while tiny plush red devils were liberally dispersed over the wares exhibited. As soon as it got dark and the younger children were safely at home, there would be a ring at the front door bell. The much desired yet feared callers were the good bishop himself, with his staff and mitre and his sack of presents, accompanied by the devil, a most fearsome figure dressed in a black fur coat down to his ankles. Over his face he wore a terrifying devil's mask with a long portruding red tongue and sharply pointed goat's horns on his head. In his hands he held a clanking chain and a large birch made from swishy twigs. The worst feature, though, of this get-up was the huge basket on his back of the type used by mountain farmers to carry a load of freshly cut fodder from the high meadows down to their stabled cattle. And it was into this basket that all wicked and naughty children were going to be put to be carried to hell unless they passed 'the' test. This, undertaken with considerable dread, consisted of answering questions like:

'Have you been a good child throughout the year?'

'Did you do as you were told by your parents?'

'Can you say a prayer?'

My sister and I stood transfixed in front of the hot tiled stove which was heating our room, and stammered out some answers. Obviously we passed, for we were given our presents and not taken away to roast in hell.

The spell, however, was broken for ever when, on one occasion, our nanny delivered herself of the following: 'Mr Krampus, please don't stand too near the stove or you'll catch fire.'

How could the Devil, the Lord of the Flames, possibly

catch fire? Gone was the illusion, gone another childish belief. But our maid still locked herself in the lavatory on that evening in deadly fear of the man behind the mask. In our case this was an unnecessary precaution, both actors in the little drama being merely fellow tenants well-known to us all, who had been supplied with our presents by our parents. But there was a rough element abroad who liked to dress up as devils and lurk in the large doorways of the block of flats, so common in Vienna, from which to attack any unaccompanied young girl with the birch they all carried. Few young women gave them the chance to do so by walking on their own.

On that evening 'Krampus dances' took place all over town, the girls wearing red dresses and the young men sporting one of those little red devils in their buttonholes. Before going to bed we children would hang a stocking from our bed ends. Miraculously in the morning they had been filled with the traditional gifts from the good Nicolo: a handful of peanuts in their shells, a wreath of dried figs, an orange and a tangerine and a couple of apples. To us it was a feast indeed to be savoured during the quietness of St Nicholas' Day.

If the weather followed the normal pattern, the temperature continued to drop as the days shortened and with it our anticipatory expectations rose. Everything around us added to the rising feeling of excitement. The shop windows filled with desirable things to be scrutinised at length on our afternoon walks, the chestnut vendors appeared at numerous street corners with their large round stoves heated with charcoal, selling not only the sweet chewy nuts but also wonderfully crisp large baked potatoes, whose skins had taken on an almost black brittle consistency. When one had chosen the best and largest, the vendor would split it open lengthwise with a sharp knife and sprinkle its fluffy yellow-ish interior liberally with salt. A penny bought this highly desirable object, which served two purposes at once, for before it was eaten it deliciously warmed one's cupped hands, stiff with the cold in spite of home-knitted woollen mittens.

The days, as is their nature when one is very young, passed only very slowly. Every spare moment was devoted to crocheting a complicated table mat for Mother, who pretended not to notice the half-hidden bag containing yarn, pattern and crochet hook. Since children in general had very little money, being entirely dependent on their parents in this matter, nobody ever bought a ready-made present of any value. One made one's own. And I somehow think that the recipient set much greater store on a gift of true labour and love though, possibly, of little use to him, than on a present casually bought because it was the done thing.

The shops stayed open all day Saturday, and on the Sunday before Christmas, called the Golden Sunday, they opened on that day for the only time in the year. By then the Christmas markets had sprung up in their traditional places. They consisted of a number of stalls lit in the evening by kerosene lamps which made a slight hissing sound, and sold a variety of goods: decorations for the Christmas tree, cheap trinkets, nothing expensive. For me they represented something extra special. The cheerful lights brightening the poorly lit streets, for poverty reached into the heart of the city administration, the bright colours of the merchandise, the sparkle of the glittering chains hung round the stalls, and the chatter of the people carefully considering how to spend their few spare shillings to the best advantage conveyed something quite out of the ordinary to me. Not knowing any better, they portrayed a world of riches with a promise of what the future might bring.

The last day of school before the Christmas holidays finally arrived. Once we had thought of celebrating early and surprising our much-admired form master with a little party. A very daring undertaking indeed. And it all ended quite otherwise than had been planned. Since Christmas trees always had sparklers hanging among the wax candles which, once lit, marvellously enhanced the effect of the rest of the decorations, we spent some of our precious pocket money on four of them, hung them along the top of the blackboard in our classroom and lit them just before Dr Nack entered. The effect was stunning. The sparklers duly sparkled but, at the same time, burned lovely little holes into the blackboard where they touched it with their backs. It was a much chastened set of pupils who, instead of 'Merry Christmas', accepted a stern rebuke and showed its gratitude for not having to pay for the damage.

At last the year had turned and the great festival was upon us. We fervently believed that the celebration of the birth of Christ on 25 December was preceded on the evening of 24 December, 'The Holy Evening', by a visit from the babe himself, bearing gifts which he carefully deposited under each Christmas tree in the land. The tree itself, a fine well-grown fir if one's parents could afford one or a spruce if they could not, had somehow been smuggled into the home and decorated as lavishly as possible. As small children still believing in the fairytale side of Christmas, any sight of it before the appointed hour was made impossible. The *Herrenzimmer*, a combination of father's study and general reception room, very large like all rooms in pre-First World War houses, was kept firmly locked and out of bounds.

On the afternoon of 24 December a stillness descended on the town. We children sat in our room, waiting for the slowly falling darkness which would bring the longed for tinkling of a small bell. With that the double doors to the study opened, revealing the festive tree lit up with small red candles and splendidly hissing sparklers. The green of its boughs was almost hidden by glittering garlands, an assortment of special Christmas biscuits, each baked with a small hole to allow for it to be hung from the tree by a gold or silver thread, as were chocolates wrapped in pieces of fringed coloured tissue paper. There were toffee apples, gold- and silver-painted walnuts, and at the very top a large shimmering star. Having been placed on our grand piano, its tip reached the high ceiling.

We children stood awestruck hand in hand, taking it all in while surreptiously trying to locate 'our' share of the presents lying in small heaps round its foot. But before being allowed to go near them Christmas hymns had to be sung to Father's piano accompaniment. The moving Austrian '*Stille Nacht, Heilige Nacht*' (Silent night, holy night) was followed by '*O, du fröhliche, o, du selige, gnadenbringende Weihnachtszeit*' (Oh, you joyful, oh you blessed, merciful Christmas time) with its final cadence imitating a joyful peal of bells. Then, at last, the electric light was switched on and the presents came into their own.

The meal on that evening was, in contrast to all other days, the main one, consisting either of baked carp or roast goose, or even Wienerschnitzel (escalope Viennoise). Afterwards the grown-ups went to midnight Mass or, we Protestants, to midnight service, for if Christmas was anything at all it was a great religious festival. This feeling of a very special, holy event carried over to Christmas Day, when the all-pervading quietness impressed itself even on us otherwise lively youngsters. We walked in the park, met our friends there, talked about our presents and, after a time, went home to play with them in a subdued fashion. If snow had fallen as it should do in late December, one's footsteps were muffled, adding to the impression of being in communion with a higher world.

26 December brought a return to work for all who had to earn their living, except the teaching profession, who started back on 2 January. Only in Vienna, where St Stephen is the

93

patron saint to whom the city's old cathedral is dedicated, was some concession made to the memory of the first Christian martyr. But for us, whose horizon was almost completely filled with school, the holidays continued. The tree, having served its purpose of combining Christian beliefs with the much older ones in the spirits inhabiting the animals and plants among which man lives, was now ready to be relieved of its unnatural burden. Every day each child could take a sweet, a nut or an apple off its branches until it stood denuded of anything edible by the morning of 6 January, the feast of Epiphany. Every evening the candles were lit for a few minutes until they, too, had been consumed by that date. Then it was quick work to strip the tree of its remaining decorations and turn it into fuel for our stoves.

The atmosphere of that time and the manner of celebrating the birth of Christ are so deeply embedded in my being that any other approach is entirely without any emotional content for me. Certain ingrained attitudes acquired in childhood cannot be eradicated, however hard reason tries to effect a change.

8

Politics

It seems somehow odd when reviewing one's childhood and early years to devote a chapter to politics. What, after all, does a young person know about the grown-up world's favourite game except to suffer from the consequences of human ambition, rapaciousness and the mistaken belief of being able to create for the ages to come a system of government built on the shifting sands of time. Children throughout history have been the victims of changing fashions in everything concerning them from their food, their clothes, their education to their place and treatment within the family. It is proof of the strong inborn will to live that they, like many other living things on this earth, always survived in sufficient numbers to carry on the species.

The vagaries of political life in the Austria between the two world wars of the last century certainly tested to the utmost nature's ingenuity in this field. The year of my birth was also the year of the peace treaty of St Germain, in which the dismemberment of the ancient empire in the heart of Europe found its official endorsement. Away went the monarchy, away went the agricultural supplies of meat, grain and sugar located in the successor states with their newfound independence from the centre, even if many of the problems of mixed populations, arbitrarily drawn frontiers and sheer lack of viable size bore in them the seeds of as yet unresolved quarrels and bloodshed. All that mattered at the time was to leave the German-speaking crown lands to their fate which was, indeed, dire.

The Austria of 52½ million people comprising 14 different nationalities within its borders was suddenly reduced to 7 million. Its capital, appropriate in size for a large empire, housed two million, while the remainder lived in small towns or villages in the beautiful but little fruitful countryside. The protracted war with its ever-increasing shortage of food supplies had left no reserves with which to combat the appalling results of St Germain. Despair and hunger filled the city streets, exacerbated to almost breaking point by the raging inflation which ruined the already beleaguered middle class and made the ground fertile for the political upheavals which were shortly to follow. Having been forbidden by the victorious and vindictive allies to attach itself to Germany in the hope of, at least, being able to feed its population, the struggle for survival split the country into two almost evenly balanced but diametrically opposed political camps. On the right were the Christian Socialists, who had the support of the Roman Catholic church and hence were known as 'the Blacks', while the Social Democrats, for obvious reasons, bore the soubriquet 'the Reds'. With the church's influence strongest in the countryside, where the priest still represented earthly order and tradition and the certainty of redemption from all sins leading to the eternal life, the support for 'the Blacks' continued unwaveringly until the date of the Anschluss in 1938. 'The Reds' had their strongholds in the industrialised towns, with Vienna as the spearhead. The see-saw battle for political power rent the population.

Having conquered the devil of inflation in 1924 the country slowly came to terms with its changed external position, but the difficulties were enormous. After living in a supra-national state covering a vast territory, the new frontiers seemed to be running through one's backyard. Suddenly familiar places changed their names to something unrecognisable. Agram, the capital of Croatia, became Zagreb after 600 years, Laibach, the capital of Slovenia, Lublijana, and dear old Pressburg, where the Empress Maria Theresia had made her bid for the loyal support of the Hungarian nobles with her young son by her side, and which was connected to Vienna by a superior kind of tram taking two hours for the journey, turned into Bratislava, inaccessible to Hungarians and Austrians alike in its new role as the capital of Slovakia. Families were divided, cut off from their areas of origin, if they happened to be a branch who had settled many years before in the territory of what was now called Austria.

Worse was to come. Hardly had the country achieved some sort of stability, when in 1929 the Wall Street Crash and the collapse of the dollar with all its consequences wrought havoc with the fragile economy. The largest Austrian bank, the Creditanstalt, failed, partly due to the fraudulent machinations of its managing director, and a wave of business failures swept away most of the precarious prosperity built up with so much effort. The catastrophic aftermath became soon evident. Unemployment in town rose and rose and continued to do so. The impoverished state could not afford for long to support financially those who needed its support most and had to leave many to the mercy of charity, and in the last resort begging. Busking became a way of life at a time when most people would have been ashamed of having to resort to it. Our courtyard almost every day was visited by one of these desperate people, some of whom were excellent musicians, obviously properly trained professionals. They played or sang or did both until a window opened and a coin wrapped in newspaper would be thrown down to them. When they considered to have received as much as they could expect, they would move on. How they survived in bad weather or during severe winters I just don't know.

The impact of these conditions on the political scene was dramatic. Instead of adhering to the democratic process, demanding submission to the ballot box with due regard by the majority to the wishes and needs of the minority, each of the two main parties believed itself not only to be the only one capable of solving the severe problems facing the country, but attempted to impose its sole rule by often violent means. The rise of National Socialism in Germany through the Twenties was greatly assisted by the dire state of the economy in that country and was observed by its neighbours with growing interest and horror. The visible improvement there in the economic situation once the National Socialists had come to power found an enthusiastic echo among the young unemployed and the more gullible members of the community in Austria.

This witches' brew exploded in 1934. February brought street battles to Vienna between the Reds and the Blacks, and in July home-grown National Socialists murdered the Catholic Federal Chancellor in the most heinous manner. Only Mussolini's intervention prevented the immediate occupation of the country by Germany, giving it another four years to live. Ironically, this short period witnessed a revival of industry, a fall in unemployment, a growth of confidence and a belief in the viable future of the post-war Austria.

The effect of such unquiet times on my early youth was profound. Father who, with the greatest difficulty, had weathered the collapse of his humoristic weekly paper, who had seen his investments in Austrian war loan reduced to worthless pieces of paper and, having had his inheritance stolen from him and the other members of his family in large part by the government of the new state of Czechoslovakia and the remainder by inflation, tried to secure his family's future by taking out life insurance with the already mentioned Creditanstalt. The premiums were high but the sum to be received by his heirs was to be paid in gold dollars, the gold standard still providing the sheet anchor of all western currencies. One of my most painful memories is watching my parents not only receive the news of the bank's collapse but their dawning realisation that the severe sacrifices necessary to find the money for the payment of the premiums had been utterly wasted. The insurance document was redrafted to a pay-out in Austrian schillings instead of the contracted gold dollars and, in the end, was practically worthless after the German occupation in 1938. This was my first lesson in the futility of trying to make long-term plans with any certain prospect of them coming to fruition.

The political instability of the Thirties spilled over into the schools. There were clandestine and not so clandestine members of an embryonic Hitler Youth. They wore white shirts, leather shorts like practically all youths of every and no political persuasion, and long white knitted knee-stockings. In the buttonholes of their loden jackets they sported a cornflower of a bright blue in place of the proscribed swastika. No power could forbid a get-up so near to the common everyday wear of the rural Austrian, and yet it was at once recognisable for what it stood. That the National Socialist party was officially banned did not matter. This group had its counterpart, even if not numerous, in the Communists. They seemed to be flush with money, but never told us others where it came from and what it was for. On the whole we did not take them seriously.

The bombing campaign which hit Vienna in 1933 soon after Hitler's accession to power and was perpetrated by the National Socialists, intruded right into our classroom. One morning, in the middle of a lesson, we heard a loud bang without, of course, knowing what had caused it. Only later did we learn that a Jewish jeweller by the name of Futterweit a few streets away had been blown up with his shop. He thus became the first innocent victim of the great European tragedy of the last century.

Politics and one's party allegiance coloured everything and continued to do so right up to the Anschluss. It affected one's chances of public employment. Father, who was self-employed, did not join anything but took a keen interest all the same, just as he liked to be present at quite dangerous events. In 1927, in consequence of the finding not guilty of a man on the charge of a notorious murder considered by popular opinion, influenced by a press campaign, to be guilty, a riot erupted in the Ringstrasse, culminating in the setting on fire of the large Ministry of Justice building. Mother, with my sister and myself looking on, helplessly stood in the middle of our kitchen crying her eyes out over the loss of her husband, who had gone to witness the uproar and whom she never expected to see again!

In February 1934 the Social Democrats, possibly orches-trated by the Communists, removed the arsenal of weaponry carefully collected and hidden over a period of time, and indulged themselves in a spot of civil war. This was facilitated by the huge blocks of workers' flats which had been built by the municipality in the 1920s to alleviate Vienna's chronic housing shortage. They were very much ahead of their time in design and comfort, and aroused the admiration of other European countries. Edward VIII, when Prince of Wales, was greatly impressed by them on one of his visits to Vienna, bringing news of them back to England. The largest of these blocks, situated in Heiligen-stadt, a district known to all lovers of Beethoven, and as extensive as a village, was named 'Karl Marx' and its inhabitants, tenants of the City of Vienna, lived up to that name. The insurrection started there and quickly spread to our district. Although our end of a very long street was quite middle-class, most of Meidling was lower and working-class.

When the shooting started we had to confine ourselves to the passage running through the centre of our flat, well away from the windows and the stray bullets which, ricocheting, were causing casualties among the curious peering out of their front-room windows. The small Austrian army, 30,000 in all allowed under the peace treaty, was called out and machine guns appeared in the middle of the roadway where vehicular traffic normally reigned. One could go to bed though for, come the evening, hostilities were suspended and, I expect, the hostile factions in true Austrian fashion met in the various pubs for a refreshing drink. This rather frightening state of affairs lasted a few days, then it was all over with the defeat of the insurgents, and we went back to school.

The Austrian head of government in 1934 bore the title of Federal Chancellor. He was a man of hardly 5 feet in height, from the Christian Socialist party by the name of Dr Engelbert Dollfuss. By origin he was not Viennese but came from the countryside and was a man steeped in the Catholic tradition and faith. His party had organised itself in opposition to the National Socialists on rather similar lines by effecting a uniform based on a different variant of the native national costume, of which the most striking feature was a large dark capercaillie feather with its tip curling backwards in the soft grey cap. It added several inches to Dr Dollfuss's stature.

The unsettled disquiet left by the February attempt at removing the government by force seemed to stir the National Socialists into action. Was this not an unexpected opportunity to complete what had been prevented by the victorious powers in 1920 and unite Austria with its northern neighbour? A process begun by Frederick II of Prussia, known as the Great for the many bloody but on the whole successful wars he fought during his reign, including his unprovoked attack on Maria Theresia's Silesia, and continued over more than two centuries in a number of wars, would at last be satisfactorily completed. What was simpler than to mobilise the fanatical National Socialist supporters inside Austria and supply them with the necessaries to mount a violent takeover bid for the Austrian government?

On 25 July of that terrible year a lorryload of men dressed in ordinary army uniforms was permitted to enter the courtyard of the Chancellery building in the very centre of Vienna, being taken by the guards on duty to be their replacement. Once inside the gates, firearms were produced and a posse rushed up the stairs and stormed into the Chancellor's study, where he was working at his desk. Exactly what happened then is not clear, except that he was shot at point-blank range. The bullet tore away half of his jaw but did not kill him. The alarm having been raised by that time, the revolutionaries were imprisoned within the building while lengthy negotiations got under way. Dr Dollfuss, in the meantime, was bleeding profusely and, after several hours, knew that his end was near. But no amount of pleading could sway the assassins to allow a priest to be called to give the last unction and absolution to the dying, deeply religious man. He who had only wanted the best for the country he loved so profoundly was not permitted the consolation of his religion in his greatest hour of need. This single fact shocked people more than anything had done in the recent difficult past, and raised Dr Dollfuss to the status of a martyr. Stamps were issued immediately, after the quelling of the rebellion, in his memory and on the evening of every following 25 July, that is until the German occupation, two lighted candles were placed in almost all the windows of Vienna. The coup itself collapsed, for Mussolini was not ready yet to make common cause with the Germans. His moving of several battalions of his best troops to the Brenner Pass made Germany withdraw hers from the frontier at Passau.

Soon after there came an official directive requesting the removal of all combustible material from attics as a safeguard against attacks from the air. Considering that the attics of our houses contained vast quantities of well-seasoned and dry wood used in their construction, it was a curious and, very likely, futile move of psychological rather than of practical value.

In the aftermath of the revolutionary year of 1934 the political divisions grew and touched us young even more. Our teachers started to sport lapel badges bearing the *Krukenkreuz*, symbol of the right-wing Catholic party, the *Vaterländische Front* (front of the fatherland), and Father took us to watch, from a safe distance, a rally for members of the *Heimwehr* (Home Guard) in Schönbrunn. The whole of the parterre in front of the palace was packed with a solid mass of men dressed in field-grey uniforms not dissimilar to those worn by the army. They must have numbered 100,000 at a conservative estimate, and had come to listen to their leader, Prince Starhemberg, addressing them on the future of their country.

The Starhembergs were one of the oldest and most exalted aristocratic families left from the departed empire, whose ancestor, Count Rüdiger, had been one of the heroes in the defence of Vienna from the Turks in the summer of 1683. Now his scion tried to follow his example by stiffening the resolve of those who felt themselves threatened by the overpowering might across the border. His patriotism, of course, was all in vain. That he should be arrested after the Anschluss and taken to a concentration camp was only in the order of things, but that his 78-year-old mother should be made to scrub the paving stones in the road on her hands and knees was a cruel and typical example of the new barbarism sweeping across the heart of Europe.

But politics had also their less fervent sides. The most memorable event for me was organised by the *Vaterländische Front* and bore the title '*Ball in der Burg*' (Ball in the Imperial Palace), a huge formal ball in the reception rooms of the 'new' wing of the Hofburg in the centre of Vienna. Again I found myself a member of the young people's committee which was to open the ball formally. I was partnered by a young man whom I had not met before the rehearsals for our entry into the grand ballroom, and whom I have entirely forgotten. The matter foremost in my mind was my right leg, encased from hip to toe in plaster of Paris after my skiing accident at Christmas 1937. How did one walk downstairs in a normal fashion, and how did one dance a Viennese waltz with a stiff and very heavy leg? Practice makes perfect, the old adage says, and practise I did. A skilful swing from the hip, and I moved forward. What did it matter if the rehearsals were not exactly as they should have been, I was going to be out of plaster at least a good two weeks before the great day and would, I was quite sure, be as mobile as before.

The five weeks were up, I was going to have the plaster removed, the weight of which had been such a tiresome burden. Out came the doctor's special scissors, and it only took a minute to cut through the stiff material covering my leg. But alas, what a dreadful picture presented itself. There was nothing left of my leg except the bones covered with peculiar-looking skin, all the muscles having withered away. In the middle, where the knee should have been visible with its round cap and smooth sinews, was a swelling the size of a small football. As for standing on this odd limb, let alone walking with it, it just could not be done. The discarded cast had to be bandaged back on to allow me to return home unaided. Then began the slow and very painful rehabilitation process, eventually stretching over years.

However, this obstacle was not going to keep me from

the ball. The date was 12 February 1938, and the air was full of foreboding of what the near future might bring. The Austrian Chancellor, Dr Kurt von Schuschnigg, had flown to Berchtesgaden on that day, having been summoned by Hitler, but we were not going to have our fun dimmed by anything. Mother had gone to considerable expense to see me well turned out, to help minimise my disability. The specially made evening dress was simple, but the material quite lovely. It was French brocade with strawberries in their natural colour on a silver background. Wearing it made me feel ready to face the ball.

Having entered in the company of Mother through the huge front gates and walked up the wide and, fortunately, shallow stairs to the first floor, a surprise awaited us. On the landing outside the state rooms was a table, presided over by a pleasant woman, on which lay rows upon rows of ladies' fountain pens, small enough to be carried in the tiniest of handbags yet with a full-size gold nib and housed in a smart leather case. These were the 'Ladies' Gifts'. Embossed with the 'Crooked Cross' it represents for me the last present I would ever receive in the country of my birth before the new order took over. It is still among my treasured possessions.

After the young ladies and gentlemen who were to open the ball had assembled in an anteroom, we participants lined up two by two and waited for the strains of the traditional 'Polonaise' by Chopin to signal our entry into the great hall. With my stiff leg hidden under the long skirt of my dress I managed to keep in step with my fellows as we descended the curved marble staircase onto the dance floor and encircled it. Then 'Vienna Blood' struck up and we decorously went through the well-drilled motions of the figure waltz, minutely scrutinised by the assembled parents and other frequenters of the ball seated round the sides of the room. The music stopped, we stopped and general dancing could begin. Time seemed to be going backwards in these glorious surroundings, we were once again in the prosperous days before the war, with the Emperor due to pay us a visit at any moment. However, the rude awakening was not far away, for even during the course of the evening rumours about what was happening at Berchtesgaden began to pass from mouth to mouth, only to find confirmation barely a month later, with the complete snuffing out of Austrian independence for the first time in its long history.

Before the curtain finally fell a semblance of normality was maintained. The beginning of March brought lovely spring weather, and with it a certain restlessness among the young. By that time I was a student at the Vienna Academy of Commerce and Trade on a one-year course for holders of the Matura certificate who wanted to enter business with a relevant qualification. Father, who was anxious to equip his daughters as well as possible for life, thought a practical training useful, whatever further academic studies were to be embarked on later. We were classed on a par with other students in higher education, had a student's pass and privileges, few though these were, and thoroughly enjoyed ourselves. The Academy was well placed for Vienna's best artificial skating rink, outdoor of course, and the two Universities. Just at that time the Ministry of Education had decided to increase the study period for aspiring doctors of medicine by a couple of years to seven, making it by far the longest of any of the faculties.

The weather, as I said, being perfect, unrest being in the air, the budding doctors decided to go on strike. They left their lecture rooms and poured out onto the Ringstrasse on to which their buildings give, and shouting '*Studenten heraus!*' (Students out!) marched down to the Technical University opposite the Academy. On their passing our Alma Mater, we with one voice took up the cry, left our lecturers standing and joined in. Eventually several thousand boys and girls walked down the 'Ring', happy and full of the joys of spring, quite forgetting the actual cause of their playing truant. After about an hour we all went back to our classes, wondering what kind of retribution would befall us. But the German army was massing on the border, Hitler was having his last persuasive contact with Mussolini, and the disobedience of students became a non-event. Whether the medical students had to undertake the lengthened course or not, I do not know.

9

Home Life

Like almost everybody in Vienna, we lived in a rented flat
with a landlord who did not live in the same house and
whom we never saw. The previous owners of the property,
who had occupied the flat next to ours, had sold up just
before inflation started to romp away, and were left with
bags full of worthless paper money. The building stood
under '*Mieterschutz*', which meant that it was rent-con-
trolled and only the share of the cost of the upkeep could
be increased without official sanction. Such flats were much
sought after and changed hands only on payment of a great
deal of key money, a completely illegal transaction. Our
family had lived in the same flat for a considerable time,
with my parents taking it over from Father's mother, who
went to live in a smaller one almost across the road from us
next door to her married daughter, Father's sister and my
godmother.

The house itself dated from the second half of the nineteenth century and was extremely well built. It was actually
two houses, standing on a corner and covering two sides of
a right angle. Each side had its separate entrance and was
in a different road, but we shared all public facilities. The
ground floor, as was quite common, was taken up by small
shops selling the necessities of life. There was the greengrocer, Herr Illichmann, just by the side of the house door,
and next to him the tobacconist. The sale of all tobacco

products being a state monopoly, their sale was restricted to state-run shops whose managers were invalided-out war veterans.

Next to the tobacconist's, who also stocked newspapers, picture postcards and postage stamps, was the dairy. There one bought not only milk in its various guises but also fresh rolls and bread. On the other side of the house entrance the hairdresser had a shop extended over two floors, who had a saddler abutting him. He in turn was adjoined by a shop of wonderful smells and an eternal twilight. Here a spinster of indeterminate age presided over such things as household soap, soft soap and packets of fine sand, both used in the washing and scouring of dishes, pots and pans, and general domestic cleaning. In one corner stood an enormous metal tank containing paraffin, which was dispensed from a waist-high tap. This was much in demand, partly still for lamps, which were used in preference to electricity since the running costs were very much less, and partly for paraffin stoves to heat those rooms without a coal stove. The smell from all these diverse articles was singular indeed.

The large corner shop was occupied by a branch of one of the chain bakeries in existence at that early date. There an incredible choice of breads awaited the customer. Anything from almost black to purest white, delicate small square loaves used for delicate open sandwiches to be served at afternoon coffee parties, rye bread of various strengths, country bread in huge round loaves meant to last a family for a week perhaps, rolls of a bewildering variety and with a particular name for each. Not for nothing is Austria known as the country with the best bread in the world. This establishment also sold some cakes and pastries, but the discerning Viennese patronised a patisserie for that.

All these shops opened early, the food shops at 6 a.m., the others no later than 8 a.m., and we were used to being woken up by the sound of their metal shutters being pushed

109

up. The less welcome noise came during the night from the cigarette vending machine outside the tobacconist's. The owning of a car being still in the luxury class, the ubiquitous vehicle used by young men was the motorbike. The more noise it made the more impressed, at least that is what was believed, would the young girls be who were given a lift on the passenger seat behind the rider, known as a *Pupperlhutschen* (doll's swing). It appeared that motorcyclists regularly ran out of cigarettes in the middle of the night, necessitating driving up to the vending machine down below our bedroom window and coming to a screeching halt. The machine clonked nicely whenever the metal arm holding a packet of cigarettes was pulled and pushed back.

There were altogether 26 flats of varying size in the two houses, but we only knew the tenants in 'our' house. They were mainly residents of very long standing, and I cannot remember anybody new moving in or out in the years I lived there. The ancillary accommodation was standard and carefully planned. With each flat came a roomy private cellar with is own lockable door, for the storage of coal and anything else one might wish to keep there. For many years we had a good stock of wine in one corner of it. Ours being an abstemious family, it was something of a white elephant acquired by Father in rather a curious way. As may be recalled, for several years during and after the war he had published a humoristic weekly paper entirely written by him and illustrated by a clever artist skilled in drawings verging on cartoons. It bore the title *Poldi Huber* and had quite a number of businesses advertising in it. One of these had got into financial difficulties. Father, being anything but businesslike when it came to money, agreed to have the debt settled in wine. So we had a 'cellar' never to be tasted, never to be drunk. Did it perish when the house got bombed during the war? Did the alcohol fan the flames, and did the rats which inhabited the nether regions get tipsy on it? Wouldn't it be interesting to know!

The top floor of the building, the attic, was one huge and very airy room with big windows. Along one side of it each flat had its own lock-up the size of a small room, where one kept suitcases and all the odds and ends of no further use but yet too good to be thrown away. The rest of the roof space was festooned with rows and rows of washing lines. It was here where, adhering to a strict rota, each tenant would for two days in the month, dry the heavy laundry after it had been laundered in the 'wash kitchen' in the cellar.

The big wash only took place once a month. It was quite an event for us children. Large bars of yellow laundry soap appeared on the kitchen table on the day before the arrival of the two washerwomen. These were built on an impressive scale which, poor things, they had to be – it was extremely hard physical labour they were called on to perform. The quantity of dirty linen of a family of four plus their domestic help over a period of a month was considerable. All of it had to be carted down three floors to the laundry room which soon resembled something out of Dante's *Inferno*. Duckboards covered the stone floor to prevent one's feet from getting too wet, with the steam from the wash boiler clothing everything in a thick fog. The water in the boiler had to be heated with coal carried in by the bucketful from the neighbouring cellar. The laundering itself was carried out in large rectangular wooden troughs with the help of a metal washboard. It was quite a treat to be allowed to descend into this strange world, bearing the news of the midday meal awaiting the two women in the kitchen.

After the final rinse the wet pieces, heavy with water before the invention of the spin dryer, had to be carried five floors up to the attic for drying, which they usually did well enough. They had to be taken down, however, even if, by chance due to bad weather, they were still damp at the end of the allotted couple of days, to make room for the next tenant on the rota to take his turn.

Now the job of ironing could begin. This was fascinating, on account of the progression of different types of irons used over the relatively short period of my early youth. The first consisted of a small steel shell into whose open back slotted a solid block of cast iron shaped to fit snugly, pointed at the front with a broad back at the rear. This block had a small hole at its back end to make it possible to handle it by means of a long iron rod with a hood that fitted into it exactly. The so-called *Stagel* was put in the fire of the coal-burning kitchen range until it became red-hot, then was quickly withdrawn and inserted into its outer case ready for use. As soon as it had cooled, it was replaced by another one, which had been heating up in the meantime.

This rather dangerous tool was soon replaced by a gas iron. It, too, had an open end of an otherwise conventional-looking metal case with which it was put on a gas burner of the cooker, with the flame reaching up into its inside until it was hot enough to be used. Again a useful tool, but laborious to use, with the long intervals necessitated by having to re-heat it. It was superseded by an iron I loved. This was quite large, probably twice the size of a modern electric iron, with a live charcoal fire burning in its inside. Once lit it would give out just the right heat for many hours, as long as it was vigorously swung from side to side about every half-hour or so, in order to get air to the glowing coals through the row of holes along its lower sides. It was a privilege to be detailed to this task. It involved leaving the flat for the landing outside, taking up a position next to the open window and letting fly, to be rewarded by the bright glow of the newly kindled fuel. The electric iron, which finally won the day, was, by contrast, dull, uninteresting and, of course, uncontrollable as yet as to the amount of heat it gave out. Since I never ironed anything, this was not a problem to worry me.

After the ironing came the time-consuming job of mending, as things had to last and could not be discarded carelessly when in need of repair. Here, the professional home dressmaker and mender came into her own. In our case it was the poor relation of one of Father's cousins-by-marriage, who would normally come for a whole day to put the laundry into good order again with the aid of our treadle sewing machine. Often she would stay for a second day when she was sewing dresses for us girls, though never for Mother. Her meals were part of her remuneration. In this manner she earned a precarious living, having been early widowed, moving from house to house, never quite knowing what feats of ingenuity she would be expected to perform.

As for the rest of the domestic tasks, these were many and varied. The ceilings were high and the rooms very large. The doors, apart from those leading into the service rooms, were all double, with wide thresholds dividing one room from another. They were made of solid polished wood, panelled and with beautiful brass handles. These had to be cleaned once a week to keep them shining. The floors, lovely inlaid parquet, were overlaid with carpets and Persian rugs. Every Friday, turning-out day, they had to be removed by the gentle, mentally retarded but physically very strong young son of the caretaker of the house next door, to be carried into the courtyard to the wall of the neighbouring house. Here, about 6 feet off the ground a horizontal very stout wooden pole had been fixed, over which the carpets were hung and then thoroughly beaten with a carpet beater made from thick, swishy cane. No girl's doll's house was without its miniature brother. In the winter, with snow on the ground, the carpets would be put upside down on the clean white surface and given a good beating. This treatment was supposed to make the colours come up like new, as did cleaning them with sauerkraut spread over them, to be swept up after a few minutes when it was believed to have done its work.

While the carpets were having their outing, the floors got their polishing. Mother, who was of medium height and plumpish, always wanted to be tall and sylphlike. To the many attempts at dieting, as for instance eating nothing but boiled spinach for a week, she added the physical exercise of floor polishing. For that purpose she used a square, shoe-sized flat brush with a strap across it into which she slipped her right foot, while she put her left one on a large soft polishing cloth. Backwards and forwards she went over the floors in a shuffling dance until her breath gave out. It is doubtful whether her figure improved, but our floors were immaculate. This was not entirely due to her efforts, though, with domestic help being part of our lives.

The wide thresholds between the rooms were put to good use. Mother's sewing machine had its place on one of them, where it benefited from the excellent light it received from both sides. The gap between our and our parents' bedroom was utilised in a different way. The wood of the door frame being so solid and the width of the door so considerable, two stout hooks could be screwed into the lintel from which either two gymnastic rings or a swing could be suspended. No need to go to the public playground, no need to take heed of the weather, we could do our exercises at home to our heart's content, – once we had agreed on whose turn it was. The swing was what I liked best. It gave one the feeling of flying, higher and higher, so high that my sister's multitude of dolls arranged on top of our two massive wardrobes on the opposite side of the room seemed to be within touching distance. No wonder we never felt bored.

10

Social Education

The young are just like plants. Each is endowed with an innate set of talents and characteristics which can be fostered or neglected, trimmed or encouraged to wither or to grow and develop following its natural inclinations. The results vary widely according to the attention bestowed on the infant, whether of the botanic or human species.

Being a member of the latter and belonging to a nation with an old and tried tradition passed on from one generation to the next, I early on became an object for social training. The first conscious lesson concerned behaviour towards and relationship with one's elders. Little girls always curtsied to their parents' male or female friends and acquaintances, and politely shook hands. Handshaking altogether was the proper way of greeting and leaving any sort of company. The curtsey was accompanied by the Viennese version of '*Küss die Hand*' (kiss your hand), which sounded like 'xehand' and could only be understood by the initiated. Hand-kissing, sometimes executed in its totality, sometimes just falling short of the act of kissing the female hand, was the normal polite way of greeting from a gentleman to a lady. Boys bowed and, of course, shook hands.

Deportment was next on Mother's list of turning us into young ladies. Aged five and six, my sister and I joined a dancing class of about a dozen boys and girls of a similar age, with the intention of making us stand and move more gracefully. It seemed to consist mainly of jumping around in a circle to the beat of a tambourine played by the young woman in charge. Whether this was eventually followed by anything more ambitious and advanced, I do not recall. Both of us being quite unfitted to make lightfooted ballet dancers, Mother gave up the attempt after a year.

Womanly skills could not be neglected either. Foremost amongst these was needlework, which I loved. Having learned to crochet at the age of six, my instructress being the daughter of the greengrocer from the shop next to our house door, I soon started to do embroidery as well as branching out into knitting. My first major excursion into needlecraft was the manufacture and embroidery of a hand-kerchief sachet in the second year of primary school, which I use to the present day. The finest and most complicated stitches gave me the greatest pleasure, and the hemstitching of handkerchiefs, considered a valuable accomplishment in a woman, was an enjoyable pastime. Only the voluminous white bloomers, which had to be sewn by hand under the eagle eye of our needlework mistress later on in grammar school, while an example of fine sewing, proved to be utterly useless.

We all knitted, Mother being the most even and yet the most reluctant knitter. My sister and I both mastered the craft, and it fell to me to knit the heavy woollen socks worn inside our ski boots. Turning the heel became child's play, like everything in which one is skilled. My addiction to the needles even brought me a quite unexpected gain. Mother's uncle, the same one who had found Dr Evans-Cross in Bournemouth for my sojourn in England, had married as his first wife an Englishwoman and produced a daughter Margaret, always known as Peggy. This Peggy became a ballet dancer who, by what quirk of fate I do not know, was *prima ballerina* at the Rio de Janeiro opera house. There she met and married a man by the name of ap-Thomas, a real Welshman who was manager of Barclays Bank, I believe, for the whole of South America. In other words, she had fallen on her feet.

None of us had ever met Peggy, but news of her trickled through from other family members who had. Great was our excitement tinged with curiosity when Mother received a letter from her, naturally written in English to be translated by me, announcing her arrival in Vienna, where she would be staying in one of the city hotels. She turned out to be small, pretty, delicate and the most dedicated shopper any of us had ever encountered. Her husband's pocket must have been bottomless, for she bought and bought, mostly knick-knacks and other items classified by Mother as rubbish. She also bought several suitcases to transport her purchases. As it was summer and I had been given the task of showing her the town, we also went swimming to cool off. As it happened, in the previous winter, I had knitted myself a bathing costume from the newly imported waterproof wool from England. All bathing costumes were made from wool, but to hand-knit them was a novel and much admired innovation. It was dark red in colour, and to complete its chic appearance I had embroidered a large white fouled anchor in the corner just below the left shoulder strap. It had been worn on a number of occasions, and I was very proud of my handiwork.

No sooner had Peggy set eyes on it but she had to have it. She did not care that it was secondhand, that she was smaller than I was, that I did not really want to part with it. Mother pressurised, while Peggy offered a considerable sum of money in compensation. This was the end of me and my bathing suit. To Rio de Janeiro it was carried off in triumph. Whether this was the last straw for Mr ap-Thomas is debatable, but the marriage broke up soon after Peggy's return, when she moved to New York. I did not knit another bathing suit, embarking on a much bigger project instead by knitting a whole costume consisting of skirt and long-sleeved jacket, which was put together and lined expertly by our dressmaker. It was in navy blue bouclé wool and did good service for a number of years.

Approaching the age of 14, ballroom dancing had to be added to a young girl's other accomplishments. Ladies and gentlemen had to be able to dance anything from a Viennese waltz, a quadrille and a polka to the quickstep, the tango and what was called the English waltz. This was a slow and watered-down version of the real thing. The rumba and later the carioca also had to be mastered. In order to acquire the necessary skills one joined a dancing school, of which the best and most popular bore the name of its proprietor Ellmayer. My sister, eventually, was allowed to attend one of his classes, but for me fate, in the shape of Father, had something else in store.

On one of the lecture tours he had undertaken in the early Twenties all over Germany, filling hall after hall with audiences eager to hear him read from his own works, he had got to know many people in the performing and related arts. One of these was the *prima ballerina* at the Munich opera house, who was a native of Vienna, to which she retired at the end of her active career. In order, no doubt, to help her defray her living expenses, she ran a very select dancing class for about 20 young people of both sexes in her spacious flat. It was thought old-fashioned, well outside the mainstream of modernity. But Father, always ready to assist a friend whom he considered to be in need of such help, decided that for me it was to be dancing at Madame Lind-Winkler's.

Madame impressed herself deeply on all of us. She resembled a minute china doll in a beautifully furnished doll's house who could well have stepped straight from the ballet *Coppelia*. Measuring about 4 feet 6 inches in her tiny shoes, she always wore a black tulle dress modelled on a dancer's

118

The author's parents on their wedding day 30th January, 1918.

The Weil sisters Susi and Dorrit aged 4 and 3.

Dressed for the Schubert centenary with the newly acquired curls.

At the primary school with the headmaster and class teacher Miss Klara Werner.

View of the garden front of Schönbrunn Palace across the Parterre with Vienna in the distance.

Summer 1936 on Bournemouth Promenade. The Austrian visitors with the author far left.

The French/Swiss contingent at Dr. Cross's establishment with the author in the centre.

Summer 1937 on the promenade in Abbazia (now Opatija). From the left: the author's father, herself, her mother with her Croatian friend, Letty, the author's English friend on a visit from home.

Christmas 1937: soaking up the sun while skiing.

The Schlesinger castle, Donje Miholjac.

Anna Schlesinger in her protective outfit.

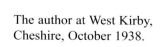

The author at West Kirby, Cheshire, October 1938.

Christmas 1938, West Kirby. The author and her sister.

March 1944. Engaged to be married.

Wedding at St. Martin in the Fields, London, 18th November, 1944.

Back in civilian life.

tu-tu but of a knee-covering length. Years of strenuous physical activity had left her almost lame, moving only with the greatest difficulty by holding on to whatever came to hand. However, her personality was all the stronger, and none of us would have dared to take advantage of her infirmity. She was ministered to by an absolutely devoted maid, who anticipated her mistress's wishes almost before they were expressed.

The actual teaching was done by twin brothers. But as is so often the case with identical twins, the first-born had the stronger, more reliable character and the much more mature looks. The younger by something like half an hour was quite a lad who lived for the day. We sometimes wondered whether he ever wore, or perhaps, possessed another suit apart from his dinner jacket, for some of the girls were occasionally called upon to rub the stains on his stiff shirt front with a piece of white chalk to make them less obvious to the casual observer. What fun it was to be in the presence of this vibrant man, absolutely bubbling over with his enjoyment of life, and what a dreadful day it was when his heartbroken brother had to tell us of his death in a motorcycle accident on the notorious Neunkirchner Allee, which leads in a perfectly straight line from Vienna south to Wiener Neustadt, tree-lined on both sides, an open invitation to excessive speed and the cause of many fatalities.

Life, of course, went on, and so did our classes, but somehow their lightheartedness had been greatly diminished.

Part of the training to make us fit members of Viennese Society was learning to entertain in one's home. Madame took these classes herself.

Lesson No. 1: 'How to walk along a busy pavement without bumping into anybody.'

What an open invitation to have a bit of fun! Lined up in

119

two rows, boys facing girls, we set off towards each other at the word of command. And, naturally, bumped as much as we could! This particular exercise was promptly abandoned.
Lesson No. 2: 'How to receive visitors.'

Again we rôle-played, this time either as visitors calling on a friend at home or the maid – girls only! – whose job it was to open the door, usher them in, help remove their overcoats and show them into the drawing room. This went better, though few of us later on in life had the opportunity or the means of employing resident help.
Lesson No. 3: 'How to serve at table.'

This was our favourite piece of training, since it involved sitting at a beautifully laid table with a real cold spread on the plates in front of us to be eaten at the lesson's conclusion. We learned from which side to serve and from which side to remove the dirty plates, how to handle the assortment of cutlery, and which kind of wine to drink from which kind of glass. If ever 'manners maketh man' this was it.

April heralded the end of the year's endeavours with a dance held at an elegant hotel in town. With it came my first long dress. It was made of white organdie over a lovely salmon pink satin slip. Its lines were classically simple as befitted a very young girl, with its short sleeves in the form of large double ruffs as the only decoration. Suddenly the ugly duckling began to feel like a swan. My dance card – yes, we did have dance cards in those far-off and yet so near days – filled up quickly with partners who wished to try their newly acquired skills against my new satin shoes, and for the first time I became aware that being female was really rather nice. Oddly enough, none of my companions from my dancing class ever became a close friend. For that one had to have more in common than moving together in step with the music.

11

Cultural Indoctrination

The State, too, took a hand in instilling culture in the young. The two classical institutions in Vienna, the opera house and the Burgtheater (the theatre of the palace) had been under imperial patronage since their inception, with their upkeep assured by the Imperial Privy Purse. The demise of the monarchy, however, did not also mean their demise. The extreme poverty of the young republic did not prevent it from taking over the responsibility for these two pillars of Austrian cultural life, they simply changed their status from 'Imperial' to 'State'. (A parallel event occurred after the end of the Second World War, when poor occupied Austria rebuilt its burned-out Viennese opera house and reopened it in 1947, long before the restoration and rebuilding of the many destroyed blocks of flats, with the full support of all its citizens.) The permanent body of performers at both continued their work as established civil servants, with their entitlements as such and a pension at the end of their active career. This included the world-famous orchestra, the Vienna Philharmonic, whose First Violin was given a professorship and treated with the greatest respect and deference. It was, therefore, quite easy for the Ministry of Education to put on at either of these two institutions special performances for schools. These consisted of classical plays of every genre, and operas with the kind of first-class casts provided for normal audiences. They were always

121

scheduled for 3 o'clock on Sunday afternoon and carefully spaced over the acadamic year. Season tickets for them were on sale at school, the prices being graded according to the type of seat, but always at only a small fraction of the cost.

In this way we were introduced to many of the plays of German and Austrian literature, some of which we had studied with divided parts in our German lessons. It soon became clear that Goethe, the great Johann Wolfgang von Goethe, was no dramatist, with the exception of some of his early plays like *Egmont, Goetz von Berlechingen* – the source of the most famous rude quotation in the German language – and *Faust, Part I, Part II* being practically unperformable. How bored I was sitting through the interminable three hours of his *Torquato Tasso*, a play about the limits imposed on human ambition, with its five characters standing about on stage spouting long speeches. How much better it read on the printed page, when the philosophy and the arguments expressed could be mulled over and assessed.

On the other hand, how stimulating it was to see Friedrich von Schiller's *Don Carlos*, on which Verdi based his opera, or the sweet and sour comedies and farces by the two great Viennese dialect playwrights Raimund and Nestroy come to life. What, for me, was always fascinating about Schiller was his incredible skill of enthusing an audience to the cause of freedom, the pleas for which run like a thread through all his work for the stage, and in doing so regularly falsifying history. His 'sire, grant us freedom of thought!' addressed by the Marquis Posa to King Philip II of Spain in *Don Carlos*, more than once roused a prolonged cheer from the spectators during times of political stress. And yet, anybody trying to learn his historical facts from this greatest of all German dramatists would soon discover his mistake. This is all the more surprising, since he was

122

Professor of History at Jena University and must have been well aware that, for instance, Elizabeth Tudor and Mary Stuart never met face to face. This notwithstanding, he made their personal encounter the pivotal scene of the play in the third act of his *Maria Stuart*. It made one wonder how far creative dramatic necessity should and could override fact.

The introduction to the world of opera was skilfully done. It began with *Hänsel and Gretl* by Humperdinck, went on to *The Merry Wives of Windsor* by Nicolai, and from there plunged us into the large pool of Italian and German Grand Opera. Verdi's *Aida* performed on the opera house's vast stage, Puccini's *La Bohème* and Wagner's *Die Meistersinger von Nüremberg* remain vividly etched in my memory.

During the last two years at school we were also given the opportunity of buying tickets, very cheaply, for the 'Week of Music' at the Musikvereinssaal (the Great Hall of the Friends of Music Building) put on during April. There the programme was varied but, again, carefully chosen to foster in us an appreciation of the musical heritage and understanding of it, a heritage of which the Austrians are justly proud. In what other country would the opera house in the very centre of its capital city display a black flag covering the whole front of the building on the death of its ballet mistress, and put up enormous posters all over town welcoming a particular guest singer when seat prices would be raised threefold and tickets become almost impossible to obtain.

Of course we went to the theatre more often than on the half-dozen occasions provided by the subscription, especially when a famous actor or actress was to be seen. Shakespeare has been very lucky in his German translators – Schlegel and Tieck – who produced work of such quality in the middle of the nineteenth century that from that time onwards he has taken his place, an honorary one, among the classical writers of the German language. Werner Kraus in *Othello* was considered the height of great acting, which Father took me to the Burgtheater to see him perform. The impact of evil for evil's sake on the lives of innocent, highminded, yet naïve people was unforgettable.

The cinema, too, was part of one's education. The very early films were Walt Disney's 'Mickey Mouse' and 'Felix the Cat', in black and white and silent, with suitable musical accompaniment supplied by a female pianist on a slightly out-of-tune piano. These were followed by Charlie Chaplin in various predicaments, but alas, he never made me laugh or smile, nor chuckle. In the Thirties came the great epics of the German and American film industries with actors like Emil Jannings in Heinrich Mann's – Thomas's brother – '*Der Weg allen Fleisches*' (The way of all flesh, *The Blue Angel*). Father paid only for one cinema visit per month, for it was not thought that films provided more than ephemeral entertainment.

A great favourite with us were the marionette plays put on in the delightful little court theatre in a wing of the Palace of Schönbrunn. Here I saw the only performance ever of Lessing's scenes – seven, if my memory does not deceive me – from his version of the Faust legend. On other occasions there were short playlets based on folklore from the Austrian countryside, like the one of the three wishes granted by a good fairy to a simple peasant woman who cannot control her tongue and, in consequence, has to use the last of the three to restore the damage done by her careless chatter with the first two.

The history of Austria's past was of great concern to the generation who had experienced the collapse of their world as a consequence of the fundamental changes brought about by the lost war and lost men, followed a few years later by the terrible effects of the Wall Street Crash in 1929, just as it seemed that some sort of social stability had been achieved. What was there left to make the coming generation have confidence and hope in the future, when unemployment was rising like a tidal wave. When the prospects are black and seemingly hopeless, a look back at happier times has an invigorating effect. Not unnaturally it fell to the schools to play a major part in bringing this about. Great emphasis was laid on writers, artists and composers of Austrian provenance, including those from the old empire since, over the centuries, a great cultural amalgamation had taken place. Franz Kafka, for instance, never wrote a word in Czech but only used German for his creative output. Although Prague was the town of his birth, where he lived and worked as a bank clerk, German was his mother tongue, as it was of most of the Jews inhabiting Bohemia. And it was his friend Max Brod, who lived in Vienna, whom he nominated his literary executor. Even this most haunted of writers would, I expect, be amused to find himself included in the parthenon of Czech Great Men.

In addition to determining the syllabus to be taught, the Ministry of Education introduced a day in each semester – the school year being segmented into two halves – when the whole school, form by form, had to go on an 'excursion'. Some unfortunate master or, in the very few girls' secondary schools, mistress, was given the task of taking their 30 charges to some place of educational interest. Usually a day at the beginning of October and again in early May were designated, and the pupils, given their marching orders – in the literal sense – a week or so beforehand. In this way we were introduced to the two fabulous collections housed in the oldest part of the Imperial Palace in the heart of Vienna, one being dedicated to the accommodation of secular and the other to that of ecclesiastical treasures. The centrepiece of the former, without a doubt, was and is the Imperial Crown reputedly first worn by Charlemagne at his coronation in Rome on Christmas Day 800. Its metal, I believe, is iron, and the stones with which it is set are of little intrinsic value were they ever to be removed from their setting and offered for sale. But its history is such that one can stand only in awe before it.

Another never-to-be-forgotten outing occurred in my second year at grammar school. The man who taught us mathematics was, unusually for a logically trained mind, of a dreamy disposition. Perhaps he found solving abstruse problems in his head more enjoyable than the care of what, after all, were still young children. Much to his dismay no doubt, and to a certain extent ours, he was deputed to take us by train to Klosterneuburg, situated north of Vienna where the Danube makes its right-angled turn from the west to the south. Here the builder emperor Charles VI, in similar fashion to his plans for Schönbrunn, had decided to construct a magnificent imperial tract with nine huge cupolas situated within the old monastery, founded in 1106, as an expression of his powers as a ruler over heaven and earth. Just as with Schönbrunn, however, he overreached himself, and only the central pavilion, bearing an enormous imperial crown, and the cupola at the north-east corner, bearing the Austrian ducal crown, were ever built. But even in its diminished dimensions, this Austrian Escorial is one of the country's prized possessions, with which the young have to become acquainted.

Off we went with our lunch packed into our small rucksacks, having assembled as instructed at the appropriate railway station. The monastery was duly visited, including some of the cellars where the highly regarded wines from its own vineyards were laid down, the overwhelming size of the imperial crown gazed at with astonishment, and soon the time had come for the journey back to town. Having been trained to look after my physical needs at an early age, I thought it advisable to make use of the facilities at the very rear of the restaurant in whose tree-shaded courtyard we had been sitting to eat our lunch. When I reemerged there was nobody to be seen! Our dreamer had simply gone off without counting heads. I had just enough money for the railway ticket to our point of departure, but from there had to walk home, where Mother was having hysterics about her missing daughter who, in turn, was really rather pleased with herself for having for the very first time managed a train journey by herself. Whether anything happened to the erring shepherd I do not know. Parents had great respect for the arbiters of their children's schooling in those far-off days.

On another occasion we were taken to the Wachau, Vienna's orchard, where the apricot blossom in spring resembles a beautiful dark pink snowfall covering many acres. Here, on the right bank of the Danube stands the abbey of Melk, which for me is the most beautiful and certainly the most impressive monastery in the whole of Austria and probably the whole of Central Europe. In the days of primitive or nonexistent roads, when the rivers constituted the main traffic arteries, a monastery like Melk was in a commanding position, being poised right above one of the major ones. A masterpiece of baroque architecture, it astonishes the eye afresh at every visit. The spiral staircase alone which, seen from below, has the appearance of a perfect snail's shell delicately decorated and painted, evokes one's admiration. It became the subject of one of my first photographic efforts.

Whether I should mention this last one among a brief survey of educational outings is debatable, but it was a very happy one, signifying the end of childhood and the entry into adult status. This was the *Maturakneipe*. According to tradition, after the successful conclusion of the leaving exams with their dreaded vivas and before parting from school and our colleagues for the last time, pupils and teachers went on a drinking spree. In our case it was a very

127

tame affair. We sat over glasses of wine in an inn with our form master and several other teachers, and made rather stilted polite conversation. It had been a perfect June day, warm, with not a cloud in the sky, and as evening fell the warmth lingered, caught by the stones of the solid buildings around us. For the first time ever for most of us, it meant staying up all night. The long walk home at sunrise under the large stately old trees lining the pavement made a perfect end to a deeply satisfying chapter in my life.

12

The Daily Round

Daily life followed a strict routine which was rarely broken. Mother, always an early riser, was up at 6 a.m. or very soon after, in order to get us children ready to leave the house by 7.30. This was not difficult in the warm and light months, but hard in winter, when the attractions of the large duvets – featherbeds we called them – were considerably greater than those of the world outside. Breakfast was a scanty affair, a glass of milk or tea – this often being Maté, a type of green tea from South America which Mother bought when overcome by one of her health-conscious moods – a piece of rye bread and butter, and that was it. Father, who always rose at 7.30, no matter how late into the night he had been working, had a cup of chocolate to get him started. As soon as breakfast was over my sister and I left for school with a sandwich for the mid-morning break while Father, like many men, whether self-employed, unemployed or even in paid work, went to the coffee house across the road for a cup of coffee and a roll. This was the fee he had to pay to gain access to the many papers available to its customers. Mother, as was the custom, went food shopping every day, the time of the generally available refrigerator had not arrived yet. Her morning was spent in preparing the midday meal and taking the fashionable walk in the park dressed appropriately.

The whole family assembled again for the midday, the

main, meal of the day, the timing of which had to be adjusted in accordance with the ending of the school day. Father often caused delay and not a little annoyance to Mother by locking himself into his study when, on being called to the table, he happened to be immersed in his work. And yet the soup with which the meal always had to start was required to be hot, even on days when the temperature topped 40°C. There was never any dessert on weekdays, just fresh fruit to round off the meal. Sometimes on Sundays cream slices or similar delicacies were bought in from the small patisserie across the road. Occasionally, on a summer Sunday, when the heat became oppressive and cooking a torment, we would conform to the Austrian custom of going out for the midday meal. Our preferred venue was a nearby old-established family-run restaurant whose main attraction was not its cuisine, which was, at best, of moderate quality, but its large gravel-strewn garden overshadowed by massive horse-chestnuts whose leaves, blossoms and fruit sometimes found their way into the dishes of food on the customers' tables placed underneath them. Nobody minded, nobody complained – the relief of being restfully seated in the cool shade and the food, reasonably priced and quite palatable, were sufficient to satisfy the undemanding clientèle.

After lunch our parents retired to their bedroom for an hour's complete rest, when we girls had to be as silent as two frightened mice. In this our parents were not alone. The working day having started at 8 o'clock in the morning at the latest, but often much earlier, offices and many shops closed for two hours over the midday period to enable their staff to go home, have a meal and a refreshing rest. After all, shops and offices did not close until 6 o'clock at night, the former staying open longer if they were food retailers. This exacting schedule was made bearable by the fact that distances to and from the place of work were usually minimal, and could be walked or covered by public transport in a very short time.

The siesta being completed, life resumed once more. Father went off to attend to business or undertake one of his daily extended walks, which he found essential for his creativity to flourish. Notes were made in shorthand on the backs of old envelopes, of which he seemed to have a plentiful supply, and overshoes were left stuck in the snow without his noticing it or the wet-through shoes, much to Mother's great dismay, for money was tight and unnecessary expenditure an added burden.

Father altogether lived much of his waking hours in a world of his own. On one memorable occasion he was wearing his new bowler hat, bought at great expense from Vienna's leading hatter in the fashionable Kärtnerstrasse. Not being by nature a conceited man, he felt considerable pleasure and pride when he noticed people in the street looking at him intently as he was walking along, with what he took to be looks of admiration for his exceptionally beautiful headgear. It was only when he saw his reflection in a shop window that he realised the true reason for the attention that had been paid to him. He had been parading the white tissue paper wrapped for protection round the hat's crown, an unusual sight in the conformist Vienna of the day.

Mother's afternoons were spent in the way Vienna's matrons liked to spend them. She took the tram into town to one of the many coffee houses, where she met her friends for a good gossip, with the Viennese of both sexes liking nothing better than putting the world to rights on every conceivable subject under the sun, whether they happen to know anything about it or not. Having delivered herself of her views, complained about the small irritations of everyday life and the cost of living, having listened to her friends' similar discourses, she would contentedly return home to supper. This was normally a cold collation, its constituents having been supplied by one of the many delicatessen shops. While our parents might be drinking tea or a glass of beer with the evening meal, we girls always finished with a large mug of cold milk. Bedtime for us youngsters was 8 o'clock right up to the day I left home for good at the age of 18, with Mother following no later than 9. Then Father came into his own, for he loved the calm and quiet of the night hours and would often work in his room until 4 o'clock in the morning, only to rise again at 7.30 as already mentioned.

Each part of the day had its own dress code. There were morning, afternoon and evening clothes. Women had special dresses for each section, and Sunday saw the very best of the finery. Not that these clothes were anything special or out of the ordinary, but fashion decreed certain materials and styles, and the hemlines moved in accordance with the *diktats* of Paris. The colours one could wear were also coded. Autumn and winter meant dark muted colours, brown, black, dark green, navy blue and russet. Spring expressed itself in grey flannel suits, beige and lighter shades of the winter colours. When summer brightness at last broke in white became predominant, always excepting the dirndl. All these fashion rules also applied to one's footwear, coats and gloves as well as hats. The latter two were *de rigueur* when 'going out'. Certain colour combinations were quite unacceptable, the main one being red/green. The Viennese had a doggerel about this one which ran as follows: '*Rot und Grün tragen die Narren in Wien.*' (Red and green fools wear in Vienna.) I believe this to be harking back to the outfits worn by the official court fools, employed for their wit and sharp tongues which they exercised under the guise of tomfoolery.

If one could afford it one owned three different types of overcoat: an in-between-seasons one, a raincoat and a winter coat. The latter had to protect one from the severest cold.

In order to do so, it was interlined with a thick fleecy woollen lining. Well-to-do men had theirs lined with fur, and all women aspired to the ownership of a fur coat, of which the most desirable was made from Persian lamb. Mink was in a class of its own, only to be dreamt about. The coats of both sexes, whether of cloth or fur or a combination of the two, usually had fur collars, often made from astrakhan, which could be turned up to protect the ears from the biting east winds which scourged Vienna from time to time, blowing straight from the frozen wastes of Siberia across the flat plains of Hungary's *puszta*. The material of the cloth coats was the best one could afford, for it had to last a long time. 'Made in England' guaranteed quality. Since such an expense had to be spread over many years, it was common practice when wear and tear was becoming too noticeable, to commission a small tailor, of whom there were many, to turn the coat inside out, resulting in the back of the cloth becoming the front. Cleaned and re-lined, it felt and was, in effect, a new garment.

Hats were obligatory through climatic necessity in winter and fashion in summer. They were never bought ready-made, but individually fashioned by a milliner. One of Mother's cousins owned a 'hat-salon' as they were termed, to which we were regularly taken and from where Mother's creations, supposedly copies of the newest French models brought back by Trude from the twice-yearly Paris fashion shows, emanated.

Gloves for the grown-ups were bought in specialist shops, of which there is one still in existence to this day, but those for the younger generation were, on the whole, homemade, knitted woollen ones in winter, lacy ones crocheted from mercerised cotton yarn at other times. This was not as difficult as it may sound, with excellent paper patterns to be bought when purchasing the yarn.

Shoes presented a bit of a problem. Those manufactured

in Austria were not of a very good quality, though expensive, and I cannot remember ever being bought a pair. Father was friendly with the chairman of the Viennese branch of the Swiss Bally shoe company, which had set up a factory after the war and had the deserved reputation of producing a first-class product. We were given access to the small shop run by the firm for the sale of goods not quite up to standard and classified as seconds, where we could satisfy our requirements for half the normal shop price. Mother, like many middle-class women, had her shoes made to measure by the firm of Kučera, of Czech provenance of course, like nearly all shoemakers and repairers of that day. Great was her joy when she was presented with two cured snake skins by a friend recently returned from Africa; after all it meant a pair of extremely hard-wearing shoes in the height of fashion. Our ski boots, like our skis, were made to measure, the latter from black hickory wood by the carpenter up the road, the former by a specialist manufacturer in Innsbruck to whom we had to send our foot measurements.

Father's suits were made by a tailor who came to our flat for the measuring-up and fitting. Since Father was much in the public eye, his clothes had to be well-cut and their cost borne, come what may. In general I cannot recall an instance of an important item of clothing being bought off the peg, with the wholesale clothing industry still in its infancy, the materials used of poor quality and the fit variable. It was on our visits to Czechoslovakia that we were introduced to the excellent and cheap footwear made by the large Batja factory in Slin. It became a game of somewhat dubious merit to walk through the less than eagle-eyed Austrian customs without having to pay duty on the obviously new shoes gracing one's feet.

13

The Coffee House

The first siege of Vienna by the Turks in 1629, while unsuccessful in its aim of taking this bastion of Christianity, left its mark in quite an unexpected but most welcome manner. The Turks having been routed after months of beleaguering the town, fled in such disarray that their tented camp with all its supplies fell into the hands of the victorious townspeople complete and untouched. The Viennese, past masters of making the best of any situation in which they might find themselves, were greatly intrigued with their booty. '*A la Turque*' became the fashion, even though the Turkish advance had only temporarily been halted until its final destruction after the second siege of Vienna in 1683. A new drink, 'coffee' by name, made its appearance. Sacks of dark-brown roasted beans had been found amongst the other foodstuffs left behind, but nobody knew what they were for. When an Austrian who had acted as a spy and was acquainted with the Turkish way of life came forward to claim his reward he was given the sacks of beans as part of it, having professed to know their purpose. Soon afterwards he opened the first coffee house in Vienna, from where this institution spread right across Europe.

Over the centuries the coffee house came to take on a major rôle in the daily life of the country, fulfilling many of the functions of a club and some of the home. The entrance fee was as little as the price of a cup of coffee. This could be any of the half-dozen varieties on offer, each with its own designation, each served in its own special kind of cup. It came on a small, shiny, solid metal tray, always accompanied by a glass of cold, freshly drawn tap water, the pride and joy of the Viennese, which was automatically exchanged every half hour or so for a fresh supply.

This one cup of coffee bought access to a wide range of services. All inland newspapers, together with the major German language ones from beyond the frontier, were fixed to wooden frames with stout handles and hung from hooks along one wall. If they were of the popular kind, more than one copy would be available. It was a common sight to observe a solitary figure comfortably ensconced on a banquette studying a newspaper while the chair next to the reader would be piled high with others still to be read. Quietly one or the other of the coffee house's clients would approach the hoarder and ask politely whether he could possibly part with something from his store.

In addition to the daily and weekly papers there were large piles of magazines in thick brown covers to protect them from the wear and tear of the handling to which they were exposed. Their titles were emblazoned on the front. They were supplied by a circulating library, always up-to-date, with a ready readership. I never knew of anybody who bought a copy for his private consumption.

If one felt the need to write a letter, the ever-obliging waiter, who knew all his regulars and remembered every order without having to make a note of it, would, without charge but expecting a generous tip, bring notepaper, envelopes, pen and ink, often accepting the finished article for posting afterwards.

Habitués who liked to be more active could engage in a game of billiards on the full-sized table in a corner of the establishment. Anybody could walk in off the street to make use of the public telephone booths at the rear of the premises. Telephone directories were available, as was a thick volume named after its original compiler *Lehmann*. It listed the names and addresses of all persons resident in Vienna, and was updated every year.

Another of the coffee house's functions was to act as a contact place where clients could be phoned, messages were taken if they happened not to be present, or information passed on to the caller on their behalf. Home from home indeed. Closing hour was determined by the departure of the last of the paying guests.

Various clubs based themselves in certain coffee houses, like the one run by my aunt and her daughter. Being keen and very good bridge players and in need of earning a living after my uncle's death, they opened a bridge club in one such coffee house. The rent they were required to pay was minimal, the establishment making its profits from the orders of the ladies who came to play. They were always ladies who frequented the club, wives of hardworking men with little else to do.

Of course, there was much more on offer than just coffee. Alcoholic drinks of every kind, non-alcoholic drinks of every kind, light warm meals like omelettes, frankfurters, even Wiener schnitzel, ice-cream of several flavours, cakes of a bewildering variety and excellence – no wonder the Viennese were well-upholstered by the time they reached middle-age – the menu was extensive and available all day. There were no fixed times by which certain items stopped being supplied or the kitchen closed.

One rarely entertained at home unless it happened to be a children's party. The coffee house was where one met one's friends. For many years Father belonged to a chess club based in a coffee house, and we knew where he could be found on certain afternoons. It was indeed quite possible to spend the day from early morning until quite late at night in the coffee house, and only go home to sleep. Its influence on Viennese, and in a wider sense, Austrian culture was all-pervading. Each, and in particular, the inner city ones, had its own character stamped on it, mainly by its clientèle, be they writers, artists or revolutionaries. It is debatable whether the last flowering of cultural life from the turn of the century until its snuffing out by the Great War would ever have occurred but for the ease with which like-minded men could meet on neutral ground for the exchange and discussion of their ideas.

14

Sunset

After his return from the visit to Hitler's redoubt at Berchtesgaden in February 1938, the Austrian Chancellor Dr Kurt von Schuschnigg and his cabinet were convinced that the only way to safeguard the continued independence of Austria was to call a referendum, asking the nation to vote for or against the Anschluss, the integration into the German Reich. The date set was Sunday 13 March. The excitement caused by the announcement could be felt wherever one went, and we students on our course, though not of voting age, which was 21, could talk of little else. The consensus was that the 'Nos' would win by a large majority, as the National Socialists, though very vocal, commanded only about 10 per cent of the general vote. The weather was lovely, warm and sunny – later dubbed 'Hitler weather' as it seemed to be like that every time Germany invaded another country – and we could hardly wait for Sunday to come and with it the lifting of the threatening nightmare. But we had not reckoned with Mussolini's *volte face*. Blithely we went on with planning for the future after the referendum, where we would spend the summer holidays, what avenues were going to be open to us after completion of our course.

Suddenly, on Friday 11 March, the Chancellor resigned. His one National Socialist cabinet colleague, Dr Seyss-Inquart, who frequented the same barber's shop as Father

– in those days men had themselves shaved by the expert after buying a season ticket to reduce the cost of such a service – and who had earlier on, under German duress, been appointed Minister of the Interior, took over the government. Austria held its breath. That evening my sister and I had gone to bed as usual, but not to sleep. Soon after dark the first German troops came marching down our street, which connected the main access road from the west of the country with the city's centre. We lay in the dark room, only lit fitfully by the street lights, without saying a word, just listening to the tramp, tramp, tramping, while our parents, also in the dark, went through Father's papers and books with the aid of a torch, invisible from the street below, removing everything which they feared to be on the National Socialists' proscribed booklist. The embers of the large tiled stove in Father's study which, in better times, had made that room so pleasant even in the depth of winter, worked their magic in consuming what had been collected over long years. Books like Erich Maria Remarque's (Krämer spelt backwards) *Im Westen Nichts Neues* ('All quiet on the Western Front'), Haček's *The Good Soldier Schweik*, a send-up of the Austro-Hungarian army and the men who served in it, and Stendahl's *The Red and the Black*, three great anti-war works, topped the list. It was common knowledge that the Gestapo made its home searches and arrests at about 4 o'clock in the morning, so one had to be prepared.

The next morning a blight had fallen on the town. Of course, those who had been subversives now strutted about in all their uniformed finery like the winners of a cock fight, but there were many more who were walking the streets blinded by the tears running down their cheeks, quite oblivious of the public places in which they found themselves.

140

On the morning of Sunday March 13, this ill-fated day, and another glorious foretaste of summer, my cousin Edith and I sat on a bench outside the main entrance to the park of Schönbrunn and watched lorryload after lorryload of men in civilian clothes being transported in open trucks along the great west road into town, where they swelled the crowds in front of the town hall along the Ringstrasse, waiting for the arrival of their hero Adolf Hitler. How many came in that manner and where they came from I suppose we shall never know.

The journalists from abroad who were covering this event reported the unbridled enthusiasm shown by the assembled mass of people, judged to number 100,000, quite convinced that what they saw were genuine Viennese acclaiming the victorious prodigal son. How competent were they to tell the origin and background of those present? Who among them knew German well enough to recognise the difference in the accents and dialect of a Viennese, a Tyrolean, a Bavarian, a Würtemberger, let alone a North German from Berlin or East Prussia? Most of the occupying army was made up of North German conscripts who spoke a dialect almost incomprehensible to the Viennese who, in turn, could only with difficulty be understood by them. What a prime example of the superficiality of journalistic reporting, of the creation of a myth which becomes accepted as fact.

Over the next few weeks we had to become accustomed to hearing of the disappearance of friends, arrested for their political beliefs or race, and the suicide of many who stood in fear of persecution. Amongst these was the 15-year-old son of a great friend of the family, who had joined the Communist party some time earlier, unbeknown to anybody. No doubt, he considered it a great adventure to be 'underground'. His death, unexpected as it was, came as a tremendous shock. Our family doctor, who had treated us over the years and who was thought to be a friend, telephoned to ask when we would be leaving so that he could take over our flat.

The need to emigrate moved more and more into focus. Decisions had to be taken which would split our family forever although, thankfully, this was hidden in the future. But leave we would have to, if we wanted to make sure that Father, who as a writer was suspect, did not end up in Dachau, which was the camp to which people were taken. As I had passed my 18th birthday I had to get a special permit to leave Austria. This involved me in hours of queuing at various public offices for an assortment of certificates proving that I did not owe any income tax, local tax, water tax, I have forgotten what else. Only after collecting this sheaf of papers could an application for a passport be made. Having been issued with one for one year, rather than the five which had been the rule previously, life as I had known until then with its certainties, its safety, its feeling of security and its parental love and protection, ended for me on 16 May 1938, when I left home for ever, only to return as an occasional visitor many years later, feeling a stranger in strangely familiar surroundings.

The odyssey begun on that day, however, is another story.

PART TWO

The Other Story

ANOTHER FOREWORD

It is unusual, to say the least, to write two introductions to one book. However, the cause for doing so is also unusual. My original intention was to bring down the curtain on my memories of early life when it had came down in my country, Austria.

Nothing made me change my mind until the outbreak of the civil war in the Yugoslavia of my childhood, with the town of Osijek making the news for all the wrong reasons. I had known it and the area around it intimately for a span of time. And I subsequently lived a precarious existence in three different countries until the end of the Second World War brought some stability into my life. How I managed to survive the many vicissitudes to be overcome may be of some interest to the benevolent reader.

1

New Beginnings

LEAVE-TAKING

It was a lovely spring, the spring of 1938. On Mother's birthday on 25 April her favourite flower, the lilac, was in full bloom, which had not always been the case so early in the season, and, as usual, we girls presented her with a large bunch of it, bought from our pooled pocket money in a little street market quite close to our flat. But there was no heart for celebrating as we would normally have done. Instead, family conference succeeded family conference as to what to do for the best in an uncertain future. Finally, arrangements for the, as was thought at the time, temporary dispersal of its individual members were agreed on.

For my sister, aged just 17, it was easy. She was still classified as a child, 18 being internationally considered the threshold to adulthood. She would join our dear friends, the Mortimers, in Bournemouth as their guest on a visitor's visa. After she had reached them she would eventually leave to serve as a student teacher in schools as widely separated as Crewkerne in Somerset and East Dereham in Norfolk. Her pay was £5 per term, but at least her living expenses were taken care of until she was able to leave Great Britain for the United States in July 1940, having been furnished with the requisite affidavit by the wonderful couple who had already taken care of our parents in the previous August.

My journey, or perhaps odyssey, was to prove much more complicated and occasionally fraught with danger, as I had already passed into my 19th year.

On one of our holidays along the Croatian coast in the early Thirties Mother had struck up a friendship with an elegant well-to-do Croatian lady who, like so many of the inhabitants of what had been the Austro-Hungarian monarchy, visited Vienna to shop and refresh her culture and, on these occasions, of course visited us. Now this imposing woman, having been widowed several years before, lived with her grown-up son and lawyer brother in a village in north-east Croatia. Hearing of our plight, she at once offered to find me a job with the rich landowners there, for only in this way would I be allowed to enter Yugoslavia, and, in any case, from now on I would have to earn my daily bread. This was not an easy task for an untrained young woman, taken away from her studies and a very sheltered existence, in a foreign country.

It was agreed that I would take charge of the three children of the Schlesinger family during the long school holidays, with particular care of the youngest, a girl, Anna, aged nine. My specific duties were to teach the rudiments of the English language to the eldest child, a boy of 16, who was later on in the summer to travel to England with a school party; to speak French with his 14-year-old brother, and teach and speak it with my little girl. The remuneration was to be my board and lodging plus 400 dinars in cash per month. This roughly worked out as £1.10.0 at the exchange rate of that time!

Being so young and inexperienced, I rather looked forward to this challenging adventure which, after all, would only be of limited duration until Father and Mother had worked out our common future as a family.

148

Having made the decision to accept the Schlesinger offer, the task of obtaining clearance from the new Austro/German authorities to leave the country could begin. Fortunately, I had a valid Austrian passport, which was a start. The process commenced with a visit to the town hall of our district for a certificate proving that I owed no local taxes. Then an application to the office of the Internal Revenue followed, for a certificate that I owed no income tax. My christening certificate had to be amended to show my mother's religion which, as was the custom at the time of my birth, had been omitted. Armed with these documents I joined a long line of people at a special desk in the Interior Ministry to request permission to travel abroad. After an uncomfortably long wait the desired stamp was finally entered in my passport after payment of the required fee, and the curtain could begin to rise on an obvious track fortunately hidden in the unknown future.

With 16 May 1938 the chosen date for my departure, the preparations could get under way. These consisted in packing and leave-taking. The former was easy enough. My wordly possessions were strictly limited and, in any case, all I was allowed to take were my clothes and a few souvenirs, since anything more would have roused the suspicions of the border control officers at the Austro-Yugoslav checkpoint. My visa had been granted for a period of five months only, on the understanding that my return to Austria was intended to be, at the latest, at its expiration. My very small pocket diary carried reminders of such engagements as a young student had, with the occasional comments written in shorthand, which had to be carefully checked. Any page carrying an entry capable of more than the obvious interpretation, or mentioning the name or names of persons who might be compromised by their acquaintance with me, had to be torn out in case the security men accompanying the Austrian customs officers on their tour of inspection at the frontier station decided to make a thorough search. Out went the name of a dear male friend, whose career in the Civil Service might have been grievously damaged. Today, when I look at my poor little mutilated diary it at once brings back the terrible feeling of fear for one's life we lived under.

While the preparations for my departure continued, my parents pursued theirs. Father, whose attachment to Bohemia was inbred and very great, taking only second place to his love for Vienna and Austria, opted for a new life in Prague. 'If I can't live in Vienna I want to live in Prague,' he used to say with a gleam in his eye. His father had come from there as a young man, he himself spoke Czech quite fluently, and the ambience of the town with its buildings, its layout and the manner of living, so redolent of the close ties which had existed between this beautiful town and pre-war Vienna, were all most attractive to him. The century-old connection between Austria and Bohemia was still in evidence everywhere, and the bonds as yet were not entirely broken.

Leave-taking was a painful business for me. Nobody outside the family could be told that it was not just a long vacation I was going to spend with friends in the country next door before returning to my studies in the autumn. So all of it had to be of a casual nature, while inwardly I had to say goodbye. Not only to my familiars but also to the town of my birth. This town, for which I had suffered pangs of homesickness whenever I had been away for more than a month, for Schönbrunn, whose every stone I knew from my daily walks and which had been part of my consciousness ever since childhood, from the theatre and the concert halls, from my books, my desk and my comfortable bed. I was soon to learn to live in the mind, to conjure up scenes and events to such an extent that I could describe them in detail if only anybody had been interested. Only from my parents did I not take internal leave, since, surely, we would soon be together again.

16 May came and brought a fine morning. Accompanied by my parents I set off for the *Südbahnhof*, the railway terminus serving Southern Europe. I wore my hand-knitted navy-blue suit with a navy-blue hat to match. The excitement of the journey ahead, to be undertaken alone to an unknown destination, greatly reduced the pain of leaving my weeping mother and silently grieving father standing on the platform as the train pulled out. After all, we would soon be reunited, and as to my much loved country, Austria, God would take care of it.

2

Donje Miholjac

It is not far from Vienna to the border with Slovenia by train. The route is an historic one, leading across the Semmering, the ridge dividing the Vienna plain from the Styrian hills and mountains. And the Semmering railway was the first mountain railway to be built in Europe, built by Stephenson himself and still doing its duty to the present day. Being so close to the capital it quickly became a welcome retreat from the hustle and bustle of a big town, and started to sport some of the grandest hotels in the land, much frequented in all seasons. Past this lovely countryside the train went, past the pilgrimage churches dotting the hills, past Vienna's 'home' mountain, the Schneeberg with its eternal cap of snow, a provider of clear, fresh water for the Viennese, through Styria's capital Graz with its 'Schlossberg', its castle hill in the very centre of the old town, and before one realised it we had reached the frontier. The customs and passport controls went without a hitch, but two persons from the neighbouring compartment were, protesting loudly, led away by men in uniform not of the accustomed cut. One could have dropped a pin in our little enclosed world. Then this, too, was over and on we went to Zagreb, my destination for changing trains.

I knew Zagreb quite well and had stayed there with my family on a number of occasions on our way to and from Circvenica on the Dalmatian coast, which was a favourite

152

holiday resort for Austrians. Zagreb held no terrors for me, although I could not speak Croatian. After discovering the platform for my train to Donje Miholjac, I crossed over to it and entered on the last part of a long day's journey.

The train was like no other I had ever been on. It is true, Austria, too, had its relics from another age still running on its minor branch lines. There had been the memorable journey into Styria on a skiing holiday one Christmas, when the carriage transporting us had as its only means of heating in sub-zero weather a small domestic paraffin stove placed in the middle of the gangway, from where its weak radiation of warmth battled in vain against the icy air entering freely through the cracked windows. Of course, this was third class. How we passengers escaped either being burned to death, had a sudden jolt knocked over the stove in a carriage liberally furnished with wood including the seats, or suffering severely from frostbite, has puzzled me ever since. The latter was probably prevented by the thick skiing outfits we all wore. And yet the little train I had now boarded must have been a relic from the early days of the railways, and would have graced any museum devoted to the preservation of industrial artifacts. Since it was already summer down here south of the Alps, there was no question of feeling cold. On the contrary, the windows had been removed so that plenty of air could circulate. It could not be called fresh, though. The engine, in the mode of an updated Stephenson's 'Rocket' was wood-burning, belching out vast clouds of dense smoke which wafted into the carriages' interior. It smelt quite pleasant, certainly better than smoke from burning coal, and nobody commented on it.

The wooden benches consisted of uncomfortable narrow slats, but that did not seem to worry the passengers either, whether of the human or animal kind as it was the only reliable means of transport available to the peasantry populating the countryside outside the few towns with their metalled roads. There were baskets with chickens and geese, the occasional ducks and cocks, one or two small pigs, it was a farmyard on wheels, with all the noises and activities connected with it. What the atmosphere must have been like with the windows shut does not bear thinking about.

So we trundled along at a sedate pace, stopping frequently at small village halts until we, at last, reached Donje Miholjac, which was to be my home for the next few months. The train went on its way for another 30 kilometres to the provincial capital Osijek, whence it turned round for the return journey to Zagreb. Mother's friend was waiting for me at the station to take me to her house, where I was to be a guest for my first night in a completely different world from the one in which I had grown up.

The introduction into it was not too abrupt, as it was only later that I came to realise that, apart from the Schlesingers' mansion, my first refuge was the only properly equipped house in the whole village. The next morning I was taken to meet my employers and my young charges. The building, set in a well-kept park, was certainly the most impressive privately owned one I have ever stayed in in all my life. It was extremely solidly build, dating back to well before the First World War, when it served as a hunting lodge to a member of the imperial family. Its style was that of an imposing English country house, with turrets on its four corners jutting out above its three floors. The entrance at the side was guarded by the butler, who had a room on the left just inside the front-door.

Before meeting the family I was led upstairs to two interconnected rooms of a good size on the first floor furnished with a washbasin, but without a bathroom, which had to be shared with the children. They were airy rooms which were being used to store a variety of disparate objects soon to become familiar. They exuded a particular musty scent which I had never encountered before, and which was probably due to their venerable age. The most interesting feature of the rooms, extending to the whole house, was the windows. As on the train, the glass in their frames had been removed for the hot summer weather and been replaced with tight-fitting, very fine-meshed thick wire netting, letting in the air but little else. This was a vital precaution against the vicious mosquitos which took over outside as soon as the light began to fade in the evening. After 8 o'clock any outdoor activity became very hazardous indeed, and keeping these pests out of the house was a concern shared by all its inhabitants.

The day after settling in I was introduced to the family. The parents were an ill-assorted pair. Father Arthur, small, stocky and middle-aged, lived for his large estate, which he managed single-handed. He was up long before any other member of the family, supervising the varied activities of a mixed farm. The actual labour for running it, and it was very labour-intensive, with little in the way of machinery, was supplied by the *Meierhof*, literally 'the dairy', a village close by, owned by him, whose people were entirely dependent on the work available to them in the fields and animal sheds.

I got to know some of them quite well, this being a region of Croatia which had been an integral part of Austria only 19 years before. Even the most simple peasant over the age of 30 spoke German, sometimes quite fluently, as well as Croatian and often also Hungarian. Our coachman, turned chauffeur along the metalled road to Osijek, all of 30 kilometres long, on which he could drive the family car, was trilingual, as was the butler. This did not apply to the two footmen or the parlourmaid, while the cook spoke Hungarian with a smattering of German. However, she had a sufficient knowledge of the local language to boss the kitchenmaid about. Communication did not seem a problem to me. Only when I had to supervise the parlourmaid in the sorting and counting of the dirty linen once a week prior to its laundering did it become necessary to learn to count up to 20 in Croatian. The only items normally exceeding this number were the handkerchiefs, when I started again at one. I can do it still.

There were other permanent residents in that large house apart from the owner's immediate family. The most important of these was without a doubt old Mrs Schlesinger, the master's mother. She was a Viennese, born and bred in that city, who had married a Hungarian. By the time I got to know her she had lived away from her native land for well over 50 years. Yet, steadfastly, she refused to speak anything but German, although she understood both Hungarian and Croatian perfectly well, which was obvious from her participation in any conversation in those languages.

When the company was seated at the enormous oblong dining table, there were never fewer than 12 persons gathered around it. The lively conversation was being conducted in a mixture of the three familiar languages, but it was only grandma I could understand, with her stubborn insistence on German. It was a brain teaser trying to understand and to guess at the subject under discussion.

Dora Schlesinger, father Adolf's beautiful wife, was nominally the *chatelaîne* of the household. Although surrounded by the trappings of great wealth, she was one of the most unhappy creatures I have ever encountered. She was just like a fish out of water. What had induced this entirely urban, elegant, pleasure-loving, beautiful blonde girl from Budapest to marry the humourless farmer from the back of beyond can only be surmised. It must have been the lure of a life of ease and considerable social standing. After all, it was not everybody who entertained the British Ambassador to Yugoslavia, at that time Sir Neville Henderson, I believe,

156

as house guest for a shooting party. When I knew her she was in her forties, although she strictly insisted that her age was kept a secret even from her children, and I had instructions not to answer their questions and there were questions, since children are curious, regarding it. Her days were spent in utter boredom, with her often staying in bed for most of the day until it was time to dress for dinner. Contact between her and myself was extremely limited, confined to absolute necessities.

That she was a woman of character showed itself in a particular way. As a girl she had spent two years at a Bavarian finishing school, which left her with an excellent command of well-spoken, grammatically correct German. Considering Hungarian, the language used by herself, her husband and his bachelor brother who lived with the family, to be of limited use, she had made it an iron rule, certainly never broken in my hearing, to bring up her children speaking only German with her. Any other approach she utterly ignored. The result was as one would expect. All three offspring spoke German well, in addition to Croatian, which they used in school and in the village, and they understood Hungarian without difficulty. Whether they could speak it I never found out. Now they were also learning French, and Dury (George), the eldest, only two years younger than myself, English. He was being sent to England for the months of July and August to perfect his knowledge.

It was wonderful to see how Mrs Schlesinger came to life when she was preparing for her annual week's visit to her sister in Budapest, who, in turn, came back with her for a week's return visit. What a lesson in futility it all was.

The bachelor brother I remember mainly for his prowess at tennis and skill at the bridge table. Having been driven indoors at dusk due to the clouds of midges hovering over the tennis court's surrounding bushes, bridge took over for

157

the rest of the evening, played in the big drawing room. Since my duties did not include bridge and I was normally quite worn out from being on the go all day, my memories are of four people peacefully battling it out.

A fairly frequent visitor to the house, where he was treated with great deference, was the most interesting inhabitant of the village. He was a Russian member of the nobility who had been a General in the Czar's army, who had found refuge in Donje Miholjac after the Revolution. What he lived on was a mystery, for he had no family and was much too old to earn a living. I would not be surprised if the master had not quietly and secretly supported him in his very modest way of life. He was a tall man, thin as a beanpole and rather unsteady on his feet, supporting himself with a walking stick. But his back was ramrod straight, and his white general's uniform, which included a smart cap, though much worn, was always spotlessly clean and well-pressed. How the few hours he was able to spend at the manor house in the company of educated people must have lit up an otherwise mournful existence. I cannot remember ever having spoken to him, being, possibly, invisible to eyes used to higher things. One can only hope that this poor old man was spared the horror of falling into the hands of the Communists led by Tito.

3

A Summer's Tale

My duties were quite extensive and far heavier than I had been led to believe. Apart from being in almost constant attendance on the children, I had certain household tasks to perform. Of these, the one that gave me the greatest pleasure was keeping the flower arrangements, so liberally displayed in the reception rooms, fresh and attractive-looking. They had to look good in a multitude of different containers to meet with the mistress's approval.

Every sunny morning, and in my memory it never rained, I made my way through the park with its large shade-giving trees, a rarity in that part of the world, to the section of the garden given over to the growing of fruit, vegetables and flowers for the house. Here, an old gardener was seemingly permanently employed looking after his green empire. Between us we decided on what should be and could be cut to please the lady of the house, it being one of the few things in which she took any real interest. I was allowed to roam amongst the soft fruit bushes growing in abundance, picking and eating to my heart's content. What a treat for a fruit devotee like me! My particular delight was a strain of raspberries I had never encountered before or have seen anywhere else since. They were large white berries of the most delicious flavour, making a wonderful mid-morning snack.

The supervision of the big wash I liked rather less. It

meant seeing the white sheets, pillowcases and towels laid out to dry on the luscious green grass. The hot sun acted as a natural bleaching agent, and as there was nothing to pollute either the grass or the air, the linen – and it was the real thing and not some cheaper cotton – was a lovely pure white.

My forays into the kitchen when sent there on an errand were a truly great experience, after our small urban domestic arrangements at home. Electrical refrigerators being either unknown or unusable for lack of sufficient electricity to work them, the only source of that energy being a petrol-driven generator just powerful enough to light the house, an oblong icebox had been installed along one wall of the large storeroom adjacent to the kitchen. In the winter, when the nearby river Drava froze solid for several weeks, large blocks of ice were cut from its surface and carted up to the house to fill the icebox with a big enough supply to last through the summer. The other walls of the storeroom bore rank upon rank of shelves on which stood the bottled fruits from the kitchen garden. There were white cherries in their sugar bath, pickled cucumbers, peas in salt water, and much else. Cook fed me on bits of fried chicken, a rare treat for me indeed, and I filled out nicely in consequence.

My position in the house was ambivalent. I was not a servant like the domestics, but neither did I belong to the class of those who lived there by right. This made itself particularly felt at table, where I was the last to be served among that large assembly. It required very fast eating, or I would have gone hungry. The order of service was fixed. Grandmother and the mistress, having been served first, followed by the master, his brother, guests and the children, had practically finished by the time my turn came. Once their plates were empty everybody else's was removed to clear the table for the next course. Fast eating has been a habit of mine ever since.

Once the settling-in process had progressed a little towards familiarity with my situation, the exploration of the world beyond the castle gates could begin. Donje Miholjac, as has been stated already, is situated very close to the river Drava. This river rises in Austria, where it is known as the Drau and is part of the county of Carinthia. Once across the border into the Slav-speaking regions, it changes its name, but for me it was, of course, still a lifeline to home. For a considerable distance it formed the border between Hungary and Yugoslavia. In the hot afternoons, when I was given time off, I would pedal down to its banks for a swim. It was pointed out to all who engaged in this activity that the middle of the river constituted the boundary between the two countries, crossed at the risk of one's life. The two nations being at daggers drawn just then, something which comes natural in the Balkans, the Hungarians had put up watch-towers on their side, manned day and night by a well-armed soldiery with orders to shoot any person attempting to swim across the river. It was a novel experience, and perhaps a good preparation to what lay in store for me hidden in the mists of the future, to have the watchful eye of the army trained on me while taking a few strokes.

The village itself was typical of its kind. Nothing much had changed since the days before the First World War. It consisted of low, single-storey whitewashed houses bordering the broad village street in a long line. This was the only street, there was no other, and there was no depth to the village. From the front door one stepped out onto the unmade-up, potholed pavement. Then came a grass verge edging the deep, dusty, equally unmade-up roadway which, in the wet season, must have been a frightful quagmire. It made the most suitable footing for the horses which provided the means of transport. The geese, being communally driven along the verges every morning and night, kept the grass short. At night, unless there was a moon, all was darkness and utterly quiet. The potholes demanded their victims from those who were intrepid enough to be abroad, whether or not they carried a torch. I cannot remember venturing out often. There was nothing to venture out for, anyway.

For transport the choice was limited. Having never ridden a bicycle, since Vienna with its cobbled pavements and very busy streets was not a cyclist's paradise, we were not encouraged to learn. Now I was introduced to this mode of locomotion. It was not easy to balance in a good two inches of solid dust, which made pedalling very hard labour indeed. It was made even worse by the strong brake built into the pedals, which brought the machine to a sudden fierce halt when, as sometimes happened by mistake, one turned the pedals backwards instead of forwards. This way of braking was in many ways much more efficient than the customary wheel brakes, but the learner had to pay for this efficiency with many a spill.

Having mastered the art at last, it did allow for quick trips to the river and along the narrow paths through the fields mainly growing head-high maize. Riding a horse was standard practice for the children of the family and, of course, I was made to try to master the art of horsemanship. Once was enough, though. It seemed a very long way down to the ground from the back of the patient old mare, and my legs did not take kindly to the effort of controlling the animal.

There was, however, a means of transport which has remained my favourite ever since, although it completely disappeared from my life once I had left Donje Miholjac. That was the pony and trap. What a pleasure it was to sit on the box of that light little carriage moving at a comfortable speed behind a docile little horse. In it we would visit the stables, the *Meierhof* and the surrounding countryside. This was dominated by vast fields of maize grown as cattle food for the winter. We would stop the trap, get off and disappear into the forest of maize stalks towering over us. They provided us with a great delicacy. The unripe white cobs were full of sweet, thirst-quenching juice, as were the delicious melons ripening in the fields in the hot sun. Once a peasant woman working in one sold me a sun-warmed perfect large fruit for one dinar, which was less than a farthing. Nobody, however poor, went hungry in this land of plenty.

The only time when we all suffered from an acute shortage was when the dairy herd contracted foot and mouth disease and had to be put in quarantine. Nobody would have dreamt of slaughtering the animals, they were much too valuable, and there was no benevolent government to compensate the poor afflicted farmer. It took seven weeks before the cattle were declared disease-free and milk and cream once again appeared on the table. A supply of butter was always stored in the icebox, so at least this food item had been safeguarded.

As soon as the outbreak had been confirmed, the cow houses were declared out of bounds to anyone but those who had business there, with bulletins given by word of mouth as to the progress of the disease. While it was recognised that the milk-yield from the affected beasts would be much reduced once they had recovered, this was judged to be much less important than their complete loss.

The world around the small circle of people living at the castle hardly impinged on their daily lives. But even despite this, the events brewing up north of Yugoslavia managed to break through with some violence. My parents, having decided to settle in Prague, had packed up their belongings ready for the move. Even the furniture had been either stored with an aunt or sold. This aunt, my uncle's wife, who was to be widowed when the National Socialists did away with the inmates of institutions, was called Leonie and lived fairly close to us with her daughter, my cousin, Edith. They had a roomy cellar which went with their large flat. There were stored the big wooden crates containing the household goods of a once happy family. One housed the china, some of it inherited from my great-grandmother, as well as Mother's collection of much-prized cut lead crystal dishes and bowls, collected over many years and only used on special occasions. There were also kitchen items of little value in money terms, but bearing witness to the activities of a home. Another crate contained the household linen. There were tea towels from Mother's dowry bearing her hand-embroidered initials, the tablecloths worked by her in the most intricate manner, and the beautiful muslin curtains from Father's study with their inset embroidered lacy picture scenes, the result of many hours spent by Mother bent over her embroidery frame. The furniture aunt Leonie found room for in her commodious flat. Having thus disposed of and drawn a line under 20 years of a settled existence, they flew to Prague in July 1938.

Now began Father's fight to gain a foothold and earn a living in this beautiful yet strange town. As a writer, the word was his tool, and this tool was German. I waited for each letter with much longing, for homesickness coupled to worry about one's loved ones is a terrible affliction. They could also give me news of my sister, who had safely arrived in Bournemouth, where she was received most warmly by our friends, the Mortimers, mother and daughter.

With the advent of August the sky metaphorically darkened dramatically. There was talk of Konrad Henlein and his Sudeten Germans agitating for secession from the Czech republic in order to join the Greater German Reich, there was talk of imminent mobilisation of the Czech army and the outbreak of war between Germany and Czechoslovakia, and there were my parents stuck in Prague and in the greatest danger. How ironic it would have been to have left

Vienna, only to be overtaken a short few weeks later by a similar even if not worse fate. Refugees have few rights. Hiding my distress from my employers, many tears were shed in the solitude of my bedroom. I was certain that I would never see my parents again, that I was left to face the darkness unguided, helpless, friendless. However, God or who or what watches over us did not desert them in their desperate hour of need.

Aunt Leonie was Swiss by birth and, like practially all Swiss, never renounced her nationality. Her sister, Martha, was married to a well-to-do business man and lived with him and their three children in a large village halfway between Zurich and Basle. After learning of my parents' predicament, Uncle Jean, who had never met them, willingly stood surety for them to make it possible for them to enter Switzerland on a visitor's visa. Not only did he deposit the, at that time, vast sum of SF 20,000 as a guarantee that they would not become a burden to the Swiss state, but he and Aunt Martha threw open their home for the period of their stay, undetermined as yet, and met all expenses arising from this generous gesture. So it came about that my parents managed to catch the last plane to leave Prague for Zurich before Chamberlain's flight to meet Hitler at Munich. Even today I cannot adequately describe the relief felt by me at that news. It was as if my parents had come back from the dead.

4

In Alien Fields

Until joining the Schlesinger family I had spent my short life in the way middle-class Austrians did. Townspeople rented flats according to their means, lived in villas if they were very rich, which few were, employed domestic help, which might be a live-in maid if funds ran to it, or a daily cleaning woman if they did not. One's existence was firmly home-based and, on the whole, lived according to fixed rules. One went to bed early most nights in order to be able to rise equally early in the morning. Business, shops and offices, schools and higher Institutes of Education, began at 8 a.m. at the latest, often earlier in the warmer months, and the working day did not finish until the late afternoon or early evening. Vienna was a small enough town to allow the two-hour lunch break for office workers to be just that. It was common practice to walk home for the main meal at midday, then take a short rest afterwards before returning to work. One's entertaining was done in a restaurant or coffee house, hardly ever at home, with the opera houses – there were two to cater for the serious and less serious musical tastes – the concert halls and theatres offering a wide choice of cultural fare at reasonable, often State-subsidised prices. Music was a staple of life.

All this dramatically changed for me once I had become an employee of the Schlesingers. Instead of a restricting flat, I now lived in a castle with more rooms than I ever discovered. Instead of a daily domestic help, there was a hierarchy of staff with, at its head, the middle-aged butler in his smart uniform, who could usually be found in his room by the front door if not engaged in other duties which he was a master at hiding, while his assistants combined the rôle of footmen with that of general factotums permanently busy at a multitude of tasks. There was the parlourmaid in her black dress, white muslin apron and headband who, I suppose, supervised the cleaning of the house. As already mentioned, my contact with her was mainly over the dirty laundry. In the kitchen the ample Hungarian cook ruled over the kitchenmaid, who appeared always up to her elbows in raw vegetables waiting to be prepared. I never discovered the size of the outdoor staff, but it must have been considerable with a tennis hardcourt as well as the park and the kitchen garden to be maintained.

Somehow I had to fit into this quite alien way of living. Of the meals only the main one, again at midday, was taken by the whole family and visitors together. We sat around an enormous oval-shaped table which easily accommodated a dozen persons as its normal complement. It could, of course, seat many more should the necessity arise. The tablecloths of which there were just two, had been made to order of heavy linen damask, one light blue and one pale pink. Since the laundering of such a large heavy piece of cloth proved extremely onerous, a thick sheet of plate glass exactly covering the top of the table was put over it. Not only was this easily washed down, but it also looked very attractive and impressive while reducing the laundering requirement to twice a year. Wiping one's hands on the overhang was not encouraged!

My day was an organised one. I met my young charge at breakfast. From then on I was on duty. She was a pleasant little girl, but rather lively and quite headstrong, who wanted to enjoy her school holidays and did not always appreciate the need for extra lessons. She was meant to have daily French instruction, with as much as possible of our conversation carried on in French. This worked reasonably well. The difficulty arose when it came to piano practice under my supervision. Playing that instrument had been one of my passions. Father, who was a splendid pianist and had studied with one of the leading masters of his time in Vienna, would not allow me to start lessons at an early enough age, as he held the only too well-founded belief that my practising would be disturbing the domestic peace and grate horribly on his musical ear. In consequence I did not start proper studies until I had reached the too advanced age of 15. In spite of hours spent in daily practice, I never progressed beyond the simplest pieces. But still, I knew about scales, Czerny exercises, sight reading and fingering.

My little girl either did not or did not want to know. Unhappy hours were spent with my ears being assaulted by a cacophany of wrong notes until, one day, I lost my temper and slapped her on the offending hand. Large tears silently started to run down her cheeks, cutting me to the quick. Why somebody who obviously had no aptitude for playing an instrument, nor any liking for music, should be made to waste precious time in the pursuit of the unobtainable for the sake of conforming with a preconceived idea of what society considered to be a feminine accomplishment, is beyond my understanding.

Another difficulty, not of our making, was the fact that her mother forbade the slightest injury to be sustained by her daughter. Forbade is the word specially chosen. How she imagined that anybody, let alone a lively nine-year-old leading a very active life out in the open air, could be protected from the smallest physical danger like taking a tumble or grazing a knee unless protected by a glass case was not made clear. The result was that a fall resulting in the tiniest bruise had to be hushed up. An ingenious method of doing that was quickly found. Anne's riding kit, consisting of a long-sleeved jersey, breeches and boots, left little skin exposed to the eye. She spent a lot of time in that outfit, even on very hot days. Fortunately, nobody thought it odd, with riding demanding the correct accoutrement, although it often was not a horse but a bicycle that saw her in the saddle.

Sometimes, when visitors called and even more so when they came to stay, I would be given time off to spend in any way I might wish. No restrictions were imposed – there was no need for that, as there was nowhere I might have gone, and nobody with whom I might have misbehaved. Through my mother's friend I had met her student son, home for the university vacation, and also the only other educated young man, living almost next door to her. The son, a well-brought-up youth, did not impress me. His head somehow seemed to have been made for a much smaller body. The young man, also a student but from a less well-endowed background, was more to my liking and had many uses. When my bicycle had one of its frequent punctures, he would patiently find the hole in a bowl of water and carefully patch the inner tube. When I wanted to go down to the river to swim he would come with me, provided I invited him, to guard me from only God knows what dangers. In fact, he was smitten! I, being a child of my age, had little conception of what it was all about. If I had wanted to, and with a little encouragement he would probably have married me, but that thought never crossed my mind. Our last day together was spent on my stop-over in Zagreb on my way to Switzerland in October 1938, when we went to the cinema to see Walt Disney's runaway success *Snow White and the Seven Dwarfs*.

The village boasted a small draper's shop selling the usual assortment of cheap wares bought by the peasantry. There I purchased a small quantity of white cotton cloth to be made into tiny handkerchiefs with the minutest hemstitching round the edge. I never used them; they were, practically speaking, quite useless and hence have survived among all my other beautifully embroidered handkerchiefs from many countries, much too good ever to be used. Looking at my handiwork now, I can only marvel at the patience and the good eyesight with which I must have been endowed.

One of the highlights of my stay was the invitation to join a party, not including 'my' family of course, who were above such things, for a roast sucking pig picnic. The day chosen for that event was as hot and dry as its predecessors, but pleasant enough when we gathered in the castle forecourt to mount our horse-drawn vehicles at 10 o'clock in the morning. After an hour or so of ambling along we arrived at the edge of a small woodland, where we disembarked. In the shade of a large horse-chestnut tree sat a man on a log in front of a wood fire, over which had been rigged up a substantial turning spit on which a plump sucking pig was slowly being roasted. The process had been started at 5 a.m. and would not be concluded until noon, the hour set for the feast.

After a glass or two of the local white wine, the taking of the group photograph and the exploration of our surroundings, the party livened up and began to gel. Even language did not present a problem. However, I was due for a disappointment when the actual meal began. Chunks of meat dripping fat, crackling and strips of pure fat were passed from hand to hand to be eaten with dry bread. There was nothing else. Anything fat and, in particular, crackling was, at that time, inedible for me. I was physically sick after trying to eat it. All I could do was to nibble politely a little lean meat and make do with a generous helping of bread. And yet, it had been a lovely and memorable day.

Occasionally Mr Schlesinger would invite my charge and myself to accompany him on one of his rounds. In this way

I saw the terrible suffering of the cattle infected with foot and mouth disease, as they stood in their stalls unable to eat and hardly able to stand on their sore hoofs, crying pitifully. Another time, in the evening, we went to call on the people in the *Meierhof*. Partly, I suppose, in order to keep the hungry midges at bay, they had lit a large camp fire round which the young members of the community were seated. To while away the time they were holding large metal griddles over the glowing embers, on which had been placed handfuls of ripe yellow maize. Before our eyes these hard, pea-sized pieces of corn puffed up to at least twice their original size, became crunch and fluffy and very good to eat. It must have been from this part of Europe that immigrants took this simple way of preparing a nutritious staple food to the United States of America, from where it conquered the world under the short and snappy name 'popcorn'. Whenever I come across the word I am back amongst the kindly hard-working people of Donje Miholjac.

Time passes whether we want it to or not, and my visa was shortly due to expire. If no other arrangement could be arrived at before the date set for my departure from Yugoslavia, that is if no other country could be found to give me shelter, I would be forced to return to Vienna alone and with nowhere to go. Aunt and Uncle Troesch in Switzerland again came to the rescue. I received a letter from Uncle Jean, offering hospitality. Armed with this precious document, I travelled again to Zagreb to call at the Swiss consulate there, it being by no means certain the necessary visa would be mine for the asking had I applied by post. With my passport in my handbag I found my way to the building housing this dispenser of happiness. On entering the waiting room, it was difficult to see how many more human beings could have been squeezed into the limited space filled to overflowing with a completely silent crowd.

A seat was found for me, and I began to wait full of apprehension, with my whole future at stake. After a short time the consul himself came out of the door on the left in order to cross the room, glanced at me, sat down by my side, asked me a couple of questions, and the much longed-for visa was mine! Admittedly it was only for four weeks and granted only for me to see my parents, but what matter. Once on Swiss soil it would surely be possible to straighten matters out, of that I had no doubt.

With the precious stamp in my passport I returned to 'my' family with a light heart. The last few days were spent in making my goodbyes to all the people who had accepted me into their midst, little thinking that I would never see any of them again. The winds of war and revolution have swept over that hard-working, industrious and above all peaceful corner of what had once, and that not so long ago, been part of my homeland, Austria. Are they any happier today, I wonder, with bloody ethnic strife poisoning their daily lives? The much-vaunted progress may manifest itself in an easier external life style, but since everything in life has to be paid for somehow, the ease of mind, the feeling of having one's proper place in the order of society, the firm belief in a definite purpose to living and dying are largely gone. Real tolerance, not to be confused with liberal licence, consists in respect for the world in which we live, by which we are surrounded, and of which we are only a tiny part.

My experience of almost feudal life ended with my journey by train to Zurich at the beginning of October 1938, where another chapter in the saga of my wanderings was about to begin.

5

Swiss Interlude

The year 1938 had, by now, already been an extraordinary one for me. It had brought my 18th birthday and with it the wonderful feeling of being at last grown-up. It is a curious thing that, when we are very young, we long to be older, even to the extent of adding years to the few so far accumulated. And yet, having once passed the halfway mark of life we desperately cling to the belief that time can be confounded and we, though if few others, will be able to drink from the cup of eternal youth.

In more general terms the weather, too, had been quite extraordinary. In Vienna, with the threatening, ever-thickening political clouds gathering, in the March of that year summer decided to make an early call. Blue skies and lovely warmth greeted the German troops as they marched into Austria. It is not surprising that the name 'Hitler weather' attached itself to it, particularly after it had happened also at the German occupation of Czechoslovakia. Now the autumn continued to present an unusual weather pattern.

On my arrival in Zurich in early October, summer had decided to linger on. It did this with unaccustomed if very welcome force, pushing the cold winter days, which had to come eventually, further and further into the future. It permitted the indulging in outdoor activities not normally possible. Shortly after my arrival, I was invited to join a party driving to the Halwyler See (lake), where the Troesch

173

family owned a substantial boathouse which served as a base for all kinds of water sports. All records were broken when my cousins and I swam in the warm waters of the lake on 16 October, a date usually marked by chilly winds and warm clothes.

Another aspect making 1938 stand out from the ordinary passing of time was the increasing political unrest spilling across borders and, in this manner, setting in motion a second *Völkerwanderung* (movement of the tribes) not seen since the early centuries of the Christian era, and of which the end is not yet in sight.

Switzerland was not exactly new territory for me. In 1935 my sister and I had been sent by our parents to spend the long summer holidays, as members of a small party of Austrian school-children of both sexes, to a convent school at Thonon-les-Bains on the southern, French, shore of Lake Geneva. As part of our education we frequently took one of the lake steamers across to Lausanne, Geneva and places in between, gorged ourselves on Swiss chocolate, considered to be the best in Europe, travelled on the little rack-railway running up the slope on which Lausanne is built, and marvelled at the way in which the staid and solid Swiss celebrated their National Day on 1 August. In the evening of this public holiday the large ferries set out from the Swiss side of the lake fully laden with merrymakers, while fireworks constantly lit up the night sky. All this was accompanied by typical, cheerful Swiss music wafting across to our side from the Canton of Vaud, and was in celebration of the famous victory won by the three founder Cantons, Uri, Schwyz and Unterwalden, over their deadly enemy, the Austrians, at the battle of Moorgarten in 1315.

Now I was going to live in the heart of German-speaking Switzerland. While the French spoken in Francophone parts was generally held to be the best to be found anywhere, it was quite a different story when it came to German, the native tongue of two-thirds of the inhabitants of the country. For historic and geographical reasons a multiplicity of German dialects have come into existence in every Canton, differing quite considerably from each other, and in common daily use by high and low. Their use is entirely confined to the spoken word, always excepting the highly specialised dialect literature. The written language has always been, and still is standard German in its most precise and accurate grammatical form. I had encountered both types during my studies of literature in the German language, but nothing had prepared me for a situation where I was only able to understand, on average, every third word. It took me a good month to get attuned to it. As to speaking it, that remained beyond my powers.

Wohlen, situated in the Canton of Argau where the Troesch family lived, and to some extent still lives, lies between Zurich and Basle and was then a large village of about 5000 souls. It had a railway station with a good train service to either of these two towns, and made its living mainly from millinery straw. With Milan, the capital of the straw-hat manufacture, just across the Alps, the demand for the raw material was great. Uncle Jean was a factor for it in a big way. He very likely dealt in other things as well, but one did not ask questions as a poor guest of the house.

For me there began yet another mode of life differing from the previous two in several respects. Of course, it was marvellous to be reunited with my parents. We had always been a very close-knit family and had never been separated from each other, unless it was for a specific purpose and always for a relatively short time. But it was not and could not be like home. Here, Father, who had stood firmly on

175

his own feet, keeping himself and his family with the work of his brain and hands, was dependent on the most willingly given charity of another man. Here, Mother, who had managed a household for over 20 years and had led the life of a middle-class Viennese woman, was relegated to doing nothing except making herself as inconspicuous and as little intrusive as possible in the home to two other women. To this had to be added the constant worry of what was to become of the three of us.

Physically, my situation had dramatically changed. After the fairly easy-going conduct of life in Austria and the almost feudal conditions in Croatia, I now found myself in a country as well regulated as the proverbial Swiss clock. The roads which in Austria, once one left the main arteries in the countryside, were still the dusty ones used, for generations, with horse and cart by the peasantry, the roads which in Yugoslavia, apart from the single one connecting Zagreb and Belgrade, were all in that state, here were beautifully metalled, with some of them, especially round Zurich, lit up at night by sodium lamps giving out an orange glow. They were a revelation to me. In the dark there was no need of a torch to avoid tripping over a pothole! There were no potholes!

The spotlessness of every nook and cranny was impressive, the houses in a process of a constant spring clean. The Troesch home, built on the site of an old farmhouse Uncle and Aunt had bought for that purpose, was and remains for me the perfect design for comfortable living. It faced the main road, looking very substantial in its grey stucco coat, with wings extending on either side of the centre steps leading up to the front door. It accommodated Uncle's office on the left of the front hall. This was out of bounds at all times, unless one was specially bidden to enter or, when the need arose, to use the telephone. The latter caused some anxiety. Uncle, this most generous of men, had

176

a fixation about telephone charges and made liberal use of a special clock set in motion as soon as a number had been dialled or one had answered a call.

Further along from the front door was the kitchen, again on the left, a veritable cook's paradise. It was very large and airy and the domain of Annie, the maid. It contained not one but two cookers, one gas and one electric. They shared the functions of what is normally the rôle of one of them only. The top of the gas cooker was used for boiling saucepans, and anything else that required to be heated from below, while the roasting and baking was done in the electric stove. One could only marvel at this provision of cooking facilities, when even a cooker of any sort other than a coal-fired range was quite unknown to us in Vienna. One used a two-ring gas *rechaud* and a free-standing large gas-fired metal tube, the so-called *Rohr* (tube) fulfilling the functions of an oven. To have something which would not be out of place today was breathtaking, and that in duplicate!

Next to the kitchen was a small room where everyday meals were taken. From there a door led into my favourite room at the back of the house overlooking the large garden. It could be called a glassed-in veranda. The huge windows, reaching from the bench round their base right up to the ceiling, held a surprise in store. On fine warm days they could be tilted up so as to make one feel right out in the open. The bench was amply provided with comfortable cushions for sitting, and it was here that breakfast was served.

On the right-hand side of the hall opposite Uncle's office, one entered the extensive drawing room with its beautiful furniture and its *pièce de resistance*, the huge, pale yellow round-bellied tiled stove reaching almost to the high ceiling. It was the only item in this functional house which refused to function. Although central heating was a feature in the building, the size of the drawing room on cold days benefitted from extra heat. However, something was wrong with this lovely stove, and it filled the room with acrid smoke when an attempt was made to burn logs in its interior. As a consequence, the architect, ever resourceful, had it converted to burn Switzerland's abundant white coal, electricity. It was hardly every used, but lent tone to its surroundings.

The first floor, reached by a flight of stairs from the hall, contained five bedrooms and two bathrooms. One of these was *en suite* with the master bedroom and equipped with two washbasins side by side, making for cosy intimacy during the ablutions while preventing any vying for first in line. All other bedrooms had washbasins to prevent arguments about the use of the other bathroom, particularly during the morning rush. The second floor was judged not to be of a par with the rest of the house. It contained several rooms which could be used as bedrooms, and was built mainly of wood, giving it a rustic appearance. Here Annie had her room, and here my parents were lodged. The sanitary fittings were similar to the ones on the floor below.

With my eldest cousin, Trudy, away in Italy, I was given her attractive room. The large garden was Aunt Martha's realm. Every morning, weather permitting, she would don her apron and work in it for at least two hours. The vegetable plot received her particular attention. This, while a surprise to us town dwellers, whose gardening expertise did not extend any further than the windowsill, was ordinary practice in the Federation. Gardening was a compulsory subject in all secondary schools, underpinning the strong ties between town and country. A desert island would not hold much terror for a native-born Swiss when it came to food production.

There were also a number of soft fruit bushes and fruit trees, whose produce was stored in the basement. And what a basement it was. The building, straddling a downward-sloping hill, housed a semi-basement rather than the usual dark and dank affair. The ample space provided, with its garden aspect, was used to the full. On the left side of the house was the driveway down to the garage, completely sound-proofed to prevent any noise from escaping into the upper regions. The passage leading towards the entrance door into the hall was furnished with hooks along its walls from which to suspend any bicycles requiring storage, to prevent the tyres from growing soft from prolonged standing in one spot. One door from the corridor led into the laundry, furnished with a washing machine and strings across the ceiling for drying in wet weather and, of course, the winter months. It was a large, very airy and light room, very different from the one I had known at home. The ironing, too, was taken care of. For large pieces like sheets a properly equipped table served as a surface, while smaller items like shirts, pillowcases and handkerchiefs were finished on an ironing board.

Next to the laundry came storage rooms. One, dedicated to the preservation of apples from the trees in the garden, had rows of slatted shelves running round the walls on which the fruit was individually spaced out and maintained in a controlled temperature. Another, also with shelves round its walls, harboured the bottled garden produce and the various jams and preserves made in long sessions in the kitchen upstairs. And, of course, as one would expect, this being a Swiss household, everywhere was absolutely spotless. I was to become quite well acquainted with this world below stairs.

Uncle Jean was the head of the family, the hub around which life rotated. He was a man of middle height, always immaculately dressed, who lived by the clock. All meals had

179

to be served at the prescribed time. If, for instance, lunch was scheduled for noon, he would take his place at table on the stroke of twelve o'clock and expect the dishes to be put on the table there and then. Having worked his way up to his position of prominence in the small community and in business through extremely hard work, he continued to organise his days on the basis of strict order. This went with a deep sense of civic duty and generosity to his fellow men.

Aunt Martha, the younger sister by two years of my father's brother's wife, was a cheerful, happy woman who brightened, by her mere presence, any company. Long ago, when first married she had to accept that her sister-in-law, Tante Elsie, who had looked after Uncle Jean until he left to set up his own home, and who had never acquired a husband, would be coming too. After some sparring an agreement had been reached. Elsie would look after the housekeeping, while Martha would concern herself with everything else. By the time we came to know them we, perhaps being outsiders, certainly did not feel any friction or tension. Of course, by then the children had grown up and were on the point of striking out for themselves.

The eldest of the three was Trudy, whom I hardly got to know as she was based in Milan, working for a dentist, I believe, and learning Italian, one of the languages of Switzerland. She was extremely good-looking and, being a few years older, quite out of my ken. She came home for Christmas when we met. The second child was Yvonne, 18 months my senior who became a very close friend. The youngest was Walter, of my own age but still at the grammar school in Arau. At Aunt Elsie's insistence, he had to be treated with the greatest consideration. When at home at weekends and during the Christmas holidays, he was allowed to sleep late when strict orders were in force that, on passing the door to his room, neither talking nor walking past in a normal, slightly noisy manner were permitted.

180

Tiptoeing was mandatory. After my recent experiences, this appeared rather odd.

I greatly admired Walter. He was an extremely gifted athlete, an accomplished skier and, in addition was capable of a feat I have never seen repeated by any other person. Not only could he roller skate, but he could tap dance on the whizzing wheels. At his school fête he performed in white tie and tails before a large audience, including his family and us, who were just as impressed as I had been when he had been practising at home. If he had wanted to he could have turned professional, but this would not have accorded with the wishes and aspirations of his father.

Winter comes almost overnight in the mountains. Once the exceptionally warm October weather had given way to November cold, a phenomenon unknown to us continental city dwellers made its presence felt. And that was fog. Thick, white, very clean – how could it have been otherwise – impenetrable fog. Wohlen lies in the valley of a small and insignificant river surrounded by hills which keep the winds, the enemies of fog, well at bay. This makes for calm days in the warmer seasons and for fog in the cold winter months. Of course, it made little difference to my parents, who rarely ventured further than the village centre, and that on foot, but it had its effect on me.

Very much on the quiet, for it would very likely have been against the restrictions imposed at my entering the country, I had obtained a part-time job in Zurich for one day a week, helping a cancer specialist with his secretarial work. It brought in a little pocket money and opened my eyes to a medical speciality not before encountered. Foggy conditions made time-keeping a hazardous undertaking. Having reached my employer's by train, fog or no fog, I seemed to spend my time typing passages taken from a variety of books. These were all liberally illustrated with the most appalling pictures of cancer victims at various stages of the disease. I never discovered what eventually happened to my efforts.

At other times my aunt invited me to accompany her on a shopping trip to Zurich, which always proved quite an event. Since she was a very well-to-do lady, this took us to the leading shops in that beautiful town, amongst which one has left a lasting impression in my memory. Its name was and is 'Seidengrieder', the founder's name being Grieder and silk being an indicator of the quality of the fabrics and clothes offered for sale. We were received with every courtesy and, comfortably seated at the counter, my aunt took her time over making her choice. I have never again been made to feel such an important customer.

Since everybody understood that we, the Weils, were birds of passage in Wohlen on a short break on the journey into the unknown, we had to try and find a country or countries which would offer us a permanent refuge. Hardly a day went by without a confab between the three of us. My parents' case proved to be extremely difficult. Father was by then 58 years of age, relying entirely on his skill with his pen and the German language to earn a living Although a splendid linguist and highly educated, he did not count English amongst his accomplishments. Mother, as was the custom, had no skills, nor had she been trained for any occupation other than that of a wife and mother, competent at running a household in the manner of a Viennese establishment.

Indefatigably Father wrote letter after letter to his contacts in the literary world beyond the orbit of Germany, but just as regularly the rebuffs would arrive. The high hopes with which the daily postal delivery was anticipated were dashed again and yet again. A sense of desperation slowly built up until there was a hint of contemplating suicide as the only remaining way out. Just when things seemed to have reached an almost unbearable low, fate took a hand. The American radical writer Upton Sinclair had entered the best-seller list with his book *The Jungle* exposing the horrors of the cattle trade of the Midwest and the slaughterhouse world of Chicago. I had been reading it, and Father was interested to hear my enthusiastic comments. Was it possible that here was someone who would and could help? A letter was written to the famous author and the wait for a reply began. Eventually it came. In it he explained that he was in no position to help in person, but that he had passed on Father's plea to Mr and Mrs Scheuer of New York. The address followed. And the miracle happened. The Scheuers, millionaires, parents of five sons, took my parents under their wings, keeping in benevolent touch with them for many years. The much longed-for affidavits guaranteeing that my parents would not become a financial burden to the public purse arrived quite soon after contact had been made, followed by tickets for the journey to the aptly named New World. This journey at last took place two weeks before the outbreak of the Second World War on the *Aquitania* out of Liverpool. This enabled my sister, who was well ensconced in her teaching work, and myself, whose life had taken a quite different direction, to spend a last week as a complete family at Herne Hill in South London, as the guests of yet another Swiss family. It was to be another eight years before I saw my parents again.

As it had been impossible to include me, now an adult as far as the authorities were concerned, in my parents' arrangements, something else had to be done to see me on my way. As it was well known that Great Britain was desperately short of domestic labour, enquiries elicited that I would be granted a working permit as a domestic servant but not admitted otherwise to the United Kingdom. A suitable household would be found for me by a refugee agency in London. This sudden pool of willing workers for the unpopular employment as resident maid at a regulated wage seemed to the British government a heaven-sent opportunity to solve an inconvenient problem. Nobody seemed in the least concerned about the suitability of the women and girls thus to be engaged at a distance, who, indeed, were queuing up to accept the conditions of service laid down by government edict. Anything to be safe again. The pay was to be 15/- per week with full board and lodging. The hours of work were not specified, except for a two-hour break every day and a half day on Sunday, the latter by agreement with the employer.

Once my application had been sent off, Aunt Elsie decided to give me some domestic training. She was faced with a blank page, housekeeping not having figured amongst my interests until then. I had observed others carrying out domestic duties, but had never progressed beyond clearing the table. The schooling I was now to receive was hard and thorough. Every Thursday I had to spring-clean my room. This involved polishing all the furniture, well-made solid large wooden furniture, as one would expect in an Alpine country, and giving special attention to the parquet flooring. Even the tiniest spot had to be scrubbed with wire wool before the electric floor polisher could be put to work. Down in the basement I was introduced to the mysteries of wielding an electric iron, the ironing of men's shirts receiving particular attention. So much devotion to the needs of a Swiss home, and so little knowledge, how differently things were done across the Channel. However, at least I had been given a taste of what my life would have to be like in the foreseeable future. Luckily, cooking was not on my tutor's timetable. None of my eventual employers required that skill for, after all, the English cuisine was very different from that of the rest of Europe.

In spite of the compulsory training I was made to undertake and my part-time job in Zurich, there was still plenty of time to engage in other activities. Just after Christmas Yvonne, Walter and myself set out for Engelberg for a few days' skiing. Engelberg itself lies in a deep valley and offers little to the more advanced skier, but a cable-car connection to Grindelwald, well up the mountainside, makes up for this deficiency. It put my recently damaged knee to the test in accordance with the generally held opinion that a return to skiing as soon as possible was absolutely essential if one was not to lose the courage to engage in this dangerous sport once more. Well, I passed the test, and the sun and the snow did the rest to help my leg along.

New Year's Eve brought the introduction to a welcoming custom of the dawning year. On the stroke of midnight we, the young, clambered onto the window seat and jumped 'into the New Year' before settling down to pouring the lead, as we had done at home. February was carnival time. Most Swiss in the German and Italian parts of the country adhere to the Catholic faith and, therefore, follow the same traditions and rituals as in Austria. Carnival stretches from the day after Epiphany, 6 January, to Ash Wednesday. The town of Basle had a reputation for making merry, but the neighbouring Cantons did not lag far behind.

The four days preceding Ash Wednesday turned the population from a staid, upright and rather self-contained society into a bacchanalian one. We outsiders could only goggle with surprise. It was difficult to accept Aunt Elsie, the bedrock of the Troesch household, the stern guardian of our behaviour, whose character was reinforced in its unbendingness by her spinster status, becoming a costumed and masked figure who took herself off to the ball being held in the largest hall in the village. But she was not alone, the maid went too, and so did all the other members of the family, with the exception of Uncle Jean. I suppose he considered himself above making a fool of himself. I, who

185

longed to be part of the general merriment, was not allowed to do so by my mother who, with hindsight, rightly judged it unfitting activity for a poor refugee. She did, however, take me in my everyday clothes to sit in the balcony of the hall, from where one could overlook the festivities in progress down below.

With the advent of Lent, my looming departure in a few weeks time, and the many gaps in my preparation for yet another way of living, an attempt was made to rectify this situation. Walter having obtained a record of the 'Lambeth Walk' and being familiar with the steps, we assiduously practised that dance without having the slightest idea where this much praised thoroughfare might be. What a disappointment it was when, years later, I discovered the truth about it.

Other friends had records of Stanley Holloway. When it became known that I would be working for a family in the Wirral which, although in Cheshire, was exactly opposite to Liverpool, they played over and over again his famous monologues 'Sam, Sam, pick up thy musket' and 'Albert and the Lion'. I could not understand a word, which they found amusing, but which frightened me a little on being told that this, as it turned out quite rightly, was the common way of speaking in that part of England.

My work permit and visa duly arrived, together with the name and address of a family in Greasby, Wirral, Cheshire. We looked it up on the map. It was a tiny dot south of Birkenhead, unknown to any of my friends who knew the country well. The date of my leaving was fixed, it was to be 18 March 1939, and preparations for my departure had to be made. It meant taking leave of my parents yet again, but the most worrying aspect of travelling was how I was to reach my destination. France had closed her borders, not only to potential refugees but also to those who had to cross the country to get to the sea. By now I was travelling on a German passport, my Austrian one having expired.

The morning of the day when I was scheduled to visit the German consulate in Basle to apply for another passport, I overslept for the first time in my life. No doubt, my unconscious tried to prevent me from entering the lion's den, but enter it I had to, only to emerge with my new nationality confirmed for a year, which was all that could be done outside the borders of Germany. While it would see me through the various border controls, it did not make it any easier to overcome the obstacle of the French barrier. There was just one way of doing the almost impossible – I would have to go by air, but this was a very expensive business. Once again friends came to the rescue. The kind couple, owners of the Stanley Holloway records and my hosts on many an evening, took pity on me in my plight. Not only did they pay for my flight ticket, but they also provided me with £5 to tide me over until I had earned my first wages. It was a lot of money in those days. Later on in London I kept myself entirely on £3 a week, paying for room, food, etc., and even managing to save 5/- out of it most of the time.

Flying was not the everyday occurence it has become today. One knew hardly anybody who had flown but, at least, I had had a taste of it, which would make the prospect of the long haul to London less unsettling. On a beautiful Sunday in October 1938 my cousins and I had attended a display by the aero club of Arau, the capital of the Canton in which Wohlen is situated. There were a number of tiny, privately owned machines to be inspected and marvelled at. Some of them offered, for a small fee, to take passengers on a trip over the surrounding countryside. My cousin, kind boy that he was, invited me to join him on what was for both of us a first. The plane we entered was just big enough for three persons, the pilot in front, sitting by himself at the controls, and two passengers behind him, strapped into their seats. Off we went, watching the houses and fields getting smaller and the horizon wider. Suddenly trees appeared over our heads while the plane's wings slid across a deep blue nothingness. The pilot was proudly putting his prized possession through its paces by turning somersaults in order to impress us. We were impressed but not in the least frightened. It was an introduction into a mode of travelling the importance of which none of us dreamt of.

Now I was going to be initiated into the world of commercial flying. It was not possible to fly direct from Zurich to London without changing planes in Paris. A tiny Swissair machine with six single seats on either side of a narrow gangway took us to Le Bourget, then serving as the gateway to Paris. Here I had a couple of hours wait confined to the airport hall, not being permitted to set foot beyond customs control. Fortunately, an old student friend of mine who had Czech nationality, and with it his liberty of movement, was living in Paris. In response to my telephone call, he took the trouble to meet and keep me company until it was time to board the Imperial Airways plane bound for London.

It was considerably larger and more impressive than the little Swiss machine. Night had fallen by the time we approached Croydon, the airport for London, and all that could be seen were a few lights in a sea of nothingness. On passing through immigration control, the difference in my status from my first visit three years earlier became at once obvious. My passport was stamped 'Refugee from Nazi Oppression, admitted on work permit No . . .', and I was told to report to the police on the very next day, to register as an alien. Since my final destination was Victoria Station, I had to take the airport bus for, as it seemed, a never-ending journey through unbroken lines of buildings, to disembark finally disorientated, tired and fearful of what was to come.

Once again my good friends in Wohlen had made provisions for me. Two English ladies whom they knew well had offered to accommodate me for the week it would take to fulfill the formalities connected with my new life before I could take up my post. They met me at the station, only to take me on another interminable journey to Highgate, where they lived in a small house.

The date was 18 March 1939. In Switzerland spring had put in an appearance, people wore their spring clothes, and one could sit in the sun during the day without feeling uncomfortable. Suddenly the brightness had gone out of the day, and it was so cold that the bathroom filled with clouds of steam whenever one took a bath. The rooms felt icy and damp, the trees were bare. Beautiful, sunny, rich, well-ordered, super-clean Switzerland containing my parents, my family-by-marriage, my dear caring friends were all behind me; I was on my own at the great age of just 19 in a country of which I had only a superficial knowledge, whose language I had mastered only imperfectly, and whose customs and manners would take more than the couple of months I had previously spent in it to learn.

Looking back, it must be considered a quirk of fate that Croydon, where I first set foot not as a visitor to England but as a homeless, displaced, persecuted human being, should become my home town, my permanent place of residence, with the now disused airfield a short walk from our house. The Odyssey has come full circle.

PART THREE

England

1

The Domestic Servant

The morning after my arrival in London presented a very different aspect from my first visit to England. Now it was no longer to be a holiday of limited duration in unusual yet congenial circumstances, but a fight for survival. There was no back-up from home to take recourse to should matters get out of hand, there was nobody I could turn to in case of need. There was the post, the frequent letters which travelled between myself and Switzerland, constituting an illusion of tight bonds which, in truth, could and did not exist. As a family, we were torn apart and powerless.

The first thing to be done on that grey, damp and chilly morning, so different from the bright early spring I had left behind, was to join the crowd beleaguering Bloomsbury House in Bloomsbury Square, where an agency set up by the Society of Friends to help 'Refugees from Nazi Oppression' as we were dubbed, had its headquarters. The staff, as far as I am aware, were Quaker volunteers trying to do their best with the never-ending stream of assistance-seekers. These consisted mainly of persons like myself, who had been admitted to the country in an attempt to meet the demands for the kind of labour the native population would not provide in the quantity required.

The working permit, the magic key to residence in the United Kingdom, was stamped in our passports at the immigration control at the place of entry. Now, at Bloomsbury House, instructions were issued on how to reach one's place of employment. Mine as I knew was with a family in the Wirral at a place called Greasby. My prospective employers had paid for my train ticket, the cost of which was to be deducted from my wages over a period of weeks. At the same time I was given my 'grey book'. This was a kind of internal passport complete with photograph, obligatory for every foreigner intending to stay for longer than three months whether as a worker or holidaymaker. It had, as may be guessed, a grey cardboard cover and contained one's personal details. The police could ask for its production at any time, and any change of address was carefully noted in it.

After the week in London, during which neither contact with my, by now, ancient great-uncle nor my sister, living in Crewkerne in Somerset, had borne any kind of fruit, I journeyed up to Liverpool, where I was met by my employer and taken to his house in the heart of the Wirral. There I was received by his wife and two of their four children. It was evening, almost dark, and the little room allocated to me seemed quite inviting, except that there was no key in the lock. I had never slept with an open door in strange surroundings before.

The next morning revealed a, for me, dire situation. The house itself, a small detached structure, stood on a building site, being one of the first to be completed on a new housing estate. The family consisted of husband, wife and four children, all of school age, two of whom were weekly boarders while the other two went to local primary schools. The wife, suffering from some mysterious complaint, probably just overwork, had to be brought breakfast in bed on a tray after the other members of the household had been catered for. She also did the cooking and the laundry, the latter with the aid of a state-of-the-art washing machine. I was expected to carry out every other household task, including the ironing for seven persons. The cleaning had to be very carefully done, Lancashire women, of whom she was one, having the reputation for particular cleanliness, with the kitchen floor washed daily on one's hands and knees after the cooked midday meal. For this I was paid the legal minimum of 15/- a week.

According to the labour regulations in force, I was entitled to two hours off duty each day, which I liked to spend either walking in a little copse near the house, or sitting in the garden reading, if the weather happened to be warm enough. This was greatly, if silently, resented. Then, eventually, there grew the uncanny feeling – and I was quite naive and inexperienced in such matters, as was normal for girls from a good continental home – that the husband had designs on me. It was the way he tried to help me get down from the stepladder whenever I needed to reach the top pantry shelf, the way there seemed to be something strained in the relationship between husband and wife, and the way my door could not be locked. Additionally, and probably quite wrongly, I gained the impression of somebody moving about outside my door late at night. Lastly, and most decisively, I could not cope with the demands made on me.

Before my final day, though, I had taken the bus into Birkenhead to call at the Labour Exchange, where I was found employment with a much smaller family in Wallasey. At least I would have a roof over my head. What I remember most clearly about this trip is walking along Birkenhead Dock Road in the rain with tears streaming down my face for having been condemned, through no fault of my own, to live in such a God-forsaken place. For that is how that town appeared to me, with its dirty brick buildings, its mean houses and the soot descending just like rain from the weeping sky. That Birkenhead also had a superior part I only discovered very much later. Suffice it here to say that my second foray into domestic service was also of short

195

duration. This time, I believe, it was the unexpected cost of maintaining a resident servant which proved unsustainable for my employers. It marked the end of my efforts to earn my living as a skivvy.

With my carefully saved wages plus the £5 from my Swiss friends, I moved to Liverpool into a slum rooming house. Perhaps it was not really in the slums, being quite near the University buildings, but it seemed to be so. The room on offer was of a good size, and the rent was 10/- per week. The first thing to greet me on entering it was a couple of dead mice on the floor by the outflow pipe from the washbasin. On closer inspection I discovered a bed consisting of the lower, sprung part of a box divan without the mattress which should have gone on top of it. As I was in need of shelter and almost penniless, it seemed quite acceptable. I spent the next day washing everything washable, the ornate fireplace minus a fire, the floor, the window, the bits of china, until it felt more like home. Now the problem of how to keep myself alive arose. With minimal cooking skills and little understanding of the strange weights and measures in use in this suddenly so hostile country, confronted by a single gas ring as the only means of boiling a saucepan, the possession of just a few pounds in money and with no prospect of obtaining any support from anybody anywhere, I had reached the end of the road. I lay down on my uncomfortable bed and decided to die.

However, unless you are a member of a certain Polynesian tribe or James IV of Scotland after the battle of Flodden, dying by simply wishing to do so is a near-impossible thing, particularly for a healthy 19-year-old. After a night and a morning, the urgings of nature took over and I got up. The problems confronting me suddenly became less pressing with the arrival of a neighbour. While I had not noticed them, a young couple in a room on the floor below had observed my arrival, discovered a little of my history from the landlady and were concerned about my 'disappearance'. The husband worked at some lowly job bringing in about £3 per week, just enough to keep them afloat but with nothing to spare. And yet they stretched out their hands to me in my need by inviting me to join in their very frugal evening meal and generally taking me under their wing, which included introducing me to some of their acquaintances. Amongst these was a student on a long-forgotten course at Liverpool University. He it was who, in turn, introduced me to the Students' Union.

Young people easily make friends. Among the crowd I got to know another young man, whose home was in West Kirby on the estuary of the River Dee, next door to the very upmarket town of Hoylake with its famous golf links. At his mother's bidding, with whom he had discussed my situation, I was invited to go and stay, as a guest, with his family. I jumped at the offer.

The journey to West Kirby on the Wirral Railway through the Mersey tunnel and then across the peninsula takes less than half an hour. The sight that greeted me on leaving the station was a revelation. What a difference from dusty, builder-ridden Greasby. Here and in neighbouring Hoylake lived the rich Liverpool cotton merchants and shipowners, some of whom I was to meet later on. But for the present I was taken into my friend's home, which turned out to be a narrow Victorian house where his widowed mother earned her living by letting furnished rooms to Liverpudlians spending a week's holiday away from the poor streets of their home town. I was given the little attic room with its sloping rafters and accumulated heat from the infrequent hours of sunshine in that summer of 1939. It suited me very well to be warm, at least at night.

After a few days of settling in, it was suggested that I might like to repay my hostess for her hospitality in giving her a hand with the housework. Within a short time I had to look after seven furnished rooms excluding my own, make the beds, tidy and clean them as well as the one and only bathroom, for which work I received, in addition to my keep, the princely sum of 1/- per day. But I was kindly treated. Apart from the son, of whom I saw little since he worked in a Liverpool office, there was a daughter a little older than myself. Three adults was a great improvement on young children.

From childhood on I had been passionately addicted to swimming, and it was only natural that in my quite ample free time I should seek out West Kirby's swimming baths, carved out from the River Dee and not subject to the considerable tidal fluctuations of the large estuary. The water was very cold, and it required a determined effort to strip off one's warm clothes and take the plunge. There was not much competition, and the few persons who braved it got to know each other within a few days. After dressing, a hot cup of tea slowly dispelled the blue colour from lips, cheeks and hands, and the conversation started to flow. Although completely unaware of the effect I was having, I must have appeared a strange, exotic bird to these folk who, on the whole, had never set foot outside England, and whose knowledge of the Continent did not stretch any further than the bits of French they had learnt at school.

In this way I met and fell in love with a very good-looking man four years older than myself. What we had in common was youth and a great interest in the arts. He was quite a competent artist, and knew a lot about birds and the beauties of the heatherland covering Thursterton Hills. Hilbre Island at low tide was a favourite spot for picnics and sunbathing, always weather permitting. It was an enchanted few weeks. But the stormclouds gathering ever more fiercely over Europe turned one's thoughts first to the possibility, then to the likelihood of war. Both he and my hostess/employer's son were in the Territorial Army. Both were called up to join their respective regiments, the former the Royal Artillery, the latter the Liverpool Scottish. It was the first time I was to see a man in a skirt which, after all, is what a kilt looks like to the untutored eye. My friend, worried about my safety in the case of the outbreak of hostilities, persuaded his aunt to have me live with her as her house guest. She and his mother each had a spacious flat on different floors in a large block along the promenade. Yet another change in my physical circumstances was about to take place. Having moved in, I found myself propelled into a well-established upper-middle-class family. With war having broken out, my friend insisted on us getting engaged with a view of marrying as soon as his military duties would allow. An announcement appeared in the *Daily Telegraph*, I received a beautiful solitaire diamond ring, and another adjustment in conducting myself had to be embarked upon.

2

Engaged to be Married

The immediate effect of the declaration of war on 3 September was to turn me into an enemy alien. The refugee from Naxi oppression, who had been admitted to the United Kingdom as such only six months earlier, was now considered a danger to the State. I was summoned to appear before a vetting tribunal staffed by, what seemed to me, extremely elderly people. Since I was by that time living with a Justice of the Peace, the procedure was gentle and the restrictions imposed those demanded by law. My little old camera, bought by my mother secondhand years before, had to be given up, and any journey of more than five miles from my registered address had to be notified to the police both on departure and return. Our one and only policeman soon got to know me, with Liverpool just outside the five mile radius, as any shopping trip to that town involved going to see him twice on the day in question. His familiarity with my position in the relatively small community was to stand me in very good stead later on.

Having been considered a fit person to be left at liberty, and living in the bosom of the bourgeoisie, I was drawn into conducting my daily life in accordance with their rules. Some weeks earlier I had decided to train as a hospital nurse, this being the only legally permitted alternative to domestic service. Liverpool General Hospital had accepted my application for the three-year course, I had passed the medical and been measured for a uniform. This was before learning that my future husband, and especially his mother, were fervent Christian Scientists who did not believe in illness except as a mental aberration, and considered medicine, hospitals, drugs and anything else to do with 'artificial' healing, completely unacceptable. Out went my wish of making nursing my career, out went my desire to be financially independent, in came gradually the pressure to accept Christian Science for myself. Fate and, perhaps, my cultural background, as well as a nascent scepticism, intervened to blow away a form of belief quite alien to most people.

However, for the present I was entirely dependent on the goodwill of two women, aunt Phyllis and mother Nora, whose only real concern was my fiancé's happiness. My first activity, even before the engagement had been officially announced, was to act as one of the clerks dealing with the evacuees pouring into West Kirby from the Liverpool slums. While that town, with its huge port and industry, was rightly considered a prime target for air attacks, the places lying on the other side of the Wirral were believed to be safe in that respect. Householders willing to take in evacuees had their names put on a list well in advance. Now they gathered in the large church hall to await their guests. There was an excited buzz in the air, for nobody quite knew what to expect.

And they came by the trainload. I am sure none of these well-bred ladies had ever seen anything like it. Dirty, uncared for, often not even housetrained. An abiding memory is that of a stately matron with mop and bucket cleaning up, while we clerks, sitting at a long table on the platform at one end of the hall, waded through the lists. It was a drawn-out and quite traumatic business. The crowd thinned, the newly matched strangers left the premises, leaving a group of mothers with numerous offspring sitting round the walls, with nobody having shown willing to take them into a private home. Finally a solution was found. A big old house which had been standing empty for some time was requisitioned and the families were lodged there. Very quickly the necessary furniture was collected and installed. By the time I left West Kirby they were still there, a very noticeable blot on the immaculate landscape.

Other problems took longer to solve. Among the children was a group, as was soon discovered, who ran a temperature sometimes only in the evening, sometimes, though lower, also in the morning and at night. Then there were others covered in large impetigo sores, a very infectious skin disease prevalent where cleanliness is not. There were yet again some infested with lice, this even occurring among the adults who had evacuated themselves without official authority. One poor man, the worst case I ever came across, was infested with these pests in every bit of dense hair on his body.

With the greatest urgency a children's emergency hospital had to be set up by taking over another large empty house. By this time, together with my fiancé's cousin Joan, I had joined the Red Cross, proudly sporting the white headscarf with its red cross on the front. Together with volunteering matrons who, I am sure, had never held a scrubbing brush in earnest before, we cleaned the designated hospital from top to bottom. Iron bedsteads were procured and filled in no time.

Our greatest worry were the feverish children, whose foster families could and would not allow them to stay on in their homes. The medical officer appointed to this make-shift hospital was an old doctor well into his seventies, who had retired from general practice some years earlier. He had no idea what the cause of the fluctuating temperatures in otherwise apparently healthy children could be. The puzzle was solved towards the end of September on a day when I happened to be on duty. Together with two other nurses I was drinking tea in our common room, when a young man walked in and identified himself as a teacher at the Farzakerley Open Air School close by Aintree Race Course. This was a special school for children suffering from tuberculosis, the scourge of slum-dwellers. The new term having started, he was anxiously trying to locate his charges who had been evacuated from their homes during the school holidays by officials unaware of the illness from which they were suffering. There was the answer, but not one we had wanted to hear. All tubercular children were at once removed and isolated from the general population. We were left with the run-of-the-mill complaints and illnesses.

The treatment of some of them was primitive in the extreme. Impetigo presented the greatest challenge, especially when it affected the head. Every day the thick crust covering the sores had to be torn off with a strong pair of tweezers before a soothing and, possibly, healing ointment could be applied. The pain these poor children were made to suffer does not bear thinking about. Through years of neglect the ulcers had sometimes eaten into the flesh to such an extent that, having at last healed, an ugly scar with a permanent depression marked the spot for life.

The other task greatly disliked by all the nurses was dealing with head lice. It was common practice to shave the victim's head, which made sense and dealt efficiently with most of the infestation. However, and quite rightly, our doctor would not countenance such an act, for it at once stigmatised the person in question. Everybody knew the meaning of a shaved head. Instead, every morning one of us was detailed to go to work with the finest of fine-tooth combs, patiently removing as much as possible of the unwanted ballast while the child amused itself with a picture book. We young girls quickly learned to lose all squeamishness and, at mealtimes, to enjoy our food while discussing activities which, only a short time before, we would have considered utterly disgusting. If proof were needed for the adaptability of the human being this, surely, is a very good example.

My fiancé having been posted to France with the first contingent of troops to be sent to that country, almost daily letters went back and forth. Of course we did not know his exact whereabouts, just the postal address of BEF followed by a number. His were as explicit as the censorship would allow regarding the boredom and deprivations suffered by the men in these months of the 'phoney' war in the coldest winter for many years. Mine tried to paint a picture of a provincial society slowly adapting to a more stringent way of life, which included the first effects of food rationing with the introduction to dried eggs. There was much to fill my time apart from my nursing duties. Not personally involved, I was nevertheless caught up in the loss of the submarine *Thetis* in the Dee estuary, with all the public distress caused by such a disaster – a foretaste of what the war would eventually bring. There were the Red Cross classes in 'First Aid' and 'Home Nursing' with their end-of-course exams and certificates proving one's skill at bandaging and common sense practices. My English colleagues in possession of these precious pieces of paper one after the other left our little hospital to enter the professional world of nursing by being drafted to the large public Clatterbridge Hospital. I, the enemy alien, had to remain behind, not being allowed near the place, for servicemen were amongst the patients whose secrets I might have wormed out of them to pass on to the Germans. In the end our emergency hospital closed, and I was left with looking after evacuee children two afternoons a week under the auspices of the Toc H.

As long as the weather permitted, we would go down to the beach to play rounders. However, this had to stop when the most atrocious winter anybody could remember befell that part of the country. Even the incoming tide turned to

204

ice, and the crested waves frozen at their highest made an unforgettable picture. The public tennis courts were flooded to turn them into an ice rink where, with borrowed skates, I engaged once again in a skill I had acquired back home. At least it warmed the blood, although the surface of the ice was gritty and difficult.

The grooming for my allotted place in this circumscribed, yet physically very comfortable world went on. Mother Nora's sister Kitty was married to aunt Phyllis's brother Rollo, the owner of a works manufacturing extremely expensive furnishing materials. The premises were located in Birkenhead and specialised in the production of very beautiful handblocked linens and cottons, requiring great skill on the part of the operators. The firm had supplied the *Queen Mary* and other large passenger liners, which provided a very good income to support an impressive life style. The family with their children, two boys and a girl, lived in a large house in Caldy, the best part of West Kirby, surrounded by an extensive garden with tennis court and croquet lawn, of which a gardener took good care.

Every Sunday mother Nora, aunt Phyllis and I went to Caldy to take tea. A strict protocol governed almost every move. We had to arrive on the dot of 4 o'clock and leave on the dot of 6. We wore our best afternoon frocks which, in my case, were of a very limited range while Joan, the daughter of the house, displayed a large variety of the most expensive order. Once, when I remarked on how nice she looked, I got a reply to be remembered: 'Oh, it's last year's, I don't normally wear such old stuff.' And there was I, not knowing when or whether I should ever acquire an addition to my Viennese wardrobe.

These weekly visits caused me some unexpected embarrassment. In the servants' quarter a Viennese couple, refugees like myself, had been installed as cook and houseman. They wore uniform and were treated as ordinary servants, except for the rates of pay, amounting to the legal minimum. Naturally, I called on them in the kitchen and found them to be two nice people, just as much strangers and just as unhappy in their enforced occupation as I had been, the only difference being that, having been married for some time, the wife could cook and knew how to run a household.

Their unhappiness became almost unbearable when they came under the suspicion of having stolen a quantity of jewellery. Although nothing was said in so many words, everybody was aware that the family had left the house for a short time, and that the pieces in question had disappeared when they returned. The two hapless, defenceless creatures had been in the house on their own during the family's absence, and since there were no signs of a burglary having taken place, the black cloud of suspicion settled on them. I felt very sorry for them believing them absolutely innocent, which, as it turned out, they were. A couple of weeks later, aunt Kitty was putting on a pair of boots she only wore in very bad weather and stubbed her right toe on something hard. On closer inspection it proved to be the lost jewellery which, she now remembered had been hidden there for safety reasons. While this may have been a satisfactory outcome for her and the family, I doubt her 'servants' ever forgave her for casting them, who had lost so much, in the part of thieving villains.

There were other remnants of the way of life of the favoured well-to-do in the recent past. This was illustrated when aunt Kitty invited me to lunch to meet some of her friends. To be properly dressed out of doors women wore hats to complete their outfit, as car travel was, as yet, not the common mode of locomotion, eventually making the wearing of headgear a hindrance to free movement into and from the conveyance. Great was my astonishment to find not only the guests still wearing their hats to sit down at the table, but aunt Kitty donning one of hers before joining them. I wonder whether my hatlessness became a topic for discussion! A strange custom indeed to which, fortunately, the war soon put an end.

Another, to me, irksome routine was changing for dinner every evening. This I could have understood if aunt Phyllis and I had been living in a house with servants at our beck and call. But as it was, it was mostly just the two of us, with her cooking dinner and me laying the table and washing up afterwards. But changing into a long dress was *de rigueur* and I courted a ticking-off when uttering some remarks as to how ridiculous it all was.

Since I was not going to risk my irreplaceable two evening dresses, I sent off to Dickens & Jones in Regent Street for a long, dark-red corduroy housecoat with long sleeves and a zip all the way down the front at the cost of one guinea (£1/1/0). For that money one could get an excellent pair of walking shoes but, never mind, my hostess approved. So we sat after dinner facing each other on either side of the fireplace, the stern old lady, a spinster and a magistrate, used to command and obedience, and the very young girl, cut off from everything she cared for. How adaptable the human being has to be to survive.

Christmas came, my first English Christmas, with its memories of the past. How was it going to be this time? Uncle Rollo and his family were very friendly with the Liberal Member of Parliament for Birkenhead, Graham-White. So friendly in fact that all eight of us were invited to their Christmas dinner on 25 December. 'My' eldest cousin, Dennis, could not be present, having been granted a commission in the Cheshire Yeomanry. I hardly knew him. Later on that winter he saw service in North Africa, where his tank was blown up, killing the crew. His place round the festive table was taken by Pamela, aunt Phyllis's charming niece, who came to stay with her aunt from time to time, showing me nothing but kindness and understanding. There

207

must have been at least a dozen persons sitting round the long dinner table, all dressed in their best clothes, the men in black tie, the women sporting their impressive jewellery. The meal, served by the English chambermaid, was a revelation to me from beginning to end. Apart from the vegetables and bacon rolls, I had never eaten any of the dishes put before me. I particularly remember Christmas pudding with brandy butter. It was only much later in life that I learnt not only to tolerate, but actively enjoy such heavy fare. After a jolly meal, so utterly different from the reverent way of celebrating the birth of Christ of my recent experience, the entertainment began in earnest. We played musical chairs and Chinese whispers, with it all culminating in certain antics involving rolling about on the floor and turning a series of somersaults. I was appalled, added to which, I was greatly concerned for the possible damage done to one's clothes, which did not seem to worry anybody else. I sat in a corner of the large room in an armchair, listened to the rough voice of Gracie Fields singing Schubert's 'Ave Maria' and felt desolate. I expect the others thought me lost in thought for 'him'. But no, it was my parents, my lost home, my lost culture I was mourning.

Time passed. I made friends among the mostly married young women who had to learn to manage without their new husbands. There was one who, although without having a job which might have tired her out, had decided to spend every Thursday in bed to have 'a good rest'. There was another, who became a very close friend, with whom I started to look at flats to rent after marrying, who had me round to her house almost every day and helped me to adjust to my new style of living. There were the young scions of the old shipping dynasties, like the Bibbys, who lived in grandeur along the road from West Kirby to Hoylake, a kind of millionaires' row, and there was my

208

bridge table once a week. The months passed, the phoney war continued, winter gave way to spring, the ice and snow disappeared. Suddenly, the world seemed to explode into violent activity with the invasion of Belgium and Holland by the German forces in May 1940.

Mother Nora started to worry even more about her only child, whose father had been killed in the First World War without ever seeing his son. Out of the blue I received a summons to appear before a tribunal in Liverpool, to be again judged as to whether I presented a danger to the State if left at liberty, or whether it would be better to have me interned for the duration of the hostilities. I packed my possessions into the one suitcase I owned, and mother Nora and I set off on the appointed day for the Bankruptcy Court building.

This was a different examination facing me from the gentle one in the previous September. Three judges sat on the platform in the courtoom, while I was placed in the dock. It was established that I had arrived in Great Britain as a refugee from Nazi oppression, that my parents had settled in New York, that I was engaged to be married, and that I was living with my future mother-in-law, having moved in with her after Christmas. It was her turn in the witness box now. What I heard stunned me. She refused to speak on my behalf, and on the contrary stated that she could not vouch for me, that, at best, she was prepared to keep me for another four weeks by which time my father, to whom she had written without my knowledge, should have been able to get me admitted into the United States. The internment camp yawned until West Kirby's one and only policeman took the stand. His statement that he had known and observed me for ten months and had found me innocent of any wrong-doing carried much weight, and I was reprieved. Back to West Kirby we went. It was only now that I learnt what had brought on these trials and tribulations after my previously best friend refused to speak or even look at me.

After that terrible winter, spring had come in softly with warm winds and clear skies. The trees put on their green finery, and the rhubarb on mother Nora's allotment was growing apace. In March she had been approached with a request by a family living in 'Millionaires' Row' concerning me. The husband, a Brigadier in the regular army, had departed at the outbreak of war, leaving his wife in charge of their little boy who was recovering from a debilitating illness. Having regained his health, he was due to return to school in the autumn after an absence of a year. Somehow the gap in his education had to be filled to allow him to join his age group, rather than the one a year younger. With my background, I was considered a suitable person to dispense the remedy for closing this gap. The proposition greatly appealed to me, I liked children, liked passing on such knowledge as I possessed and, last but not least, relished the opportunity to earn a little money of my own. Lessons started. On account of the lovely weather they nearly always took place in the solidly built summerhouse, watched over by nanny who brought us the mid-morning drink, milk for the boy and coffee for me. The few weeks my tutoring lasted I only once set foot in the house, and never encountered anybody apart from nanny. The whole episode filled me with a sense of freedom, the walk in the morning under the flowering may trees lining the road was an absolute delight.

In the meantime the war did not go well. Having overrun the Low Countries, the German troops invaded France itself, and the family's concern for my fiancé's safety grew in proportion. It was decided, without my knowledge of course, that, should he survive, he could not possibly contemplate marriage to an enemy alien. Mother Nora knew what to do. She denounced me as a spy, citing my employment in the Brigadier's household, told my best friend that I had spoken about her in a derogatory manner, and that I considered the evacuation of the Allied troops from the beaches of Dunkirk a terrible defeat and setback which would prolong the war for years to come. My fiancé, on succeeding in getting across the Channel, was stationed in a camp in North Wales across the river Dee. In my utter despair and deep unhappiness my one thought was to see him, my last refuge in this shameful affair. But no, mother Nora would not allow it, and went on her own while I, the enemy, was left behind in the flat to look after myself.

Aunt Phyllis came upstairs to see me. If I were to break my engagement and leave, she would subsidise me to the tune of £2/10/0 a week until I departed from the country. I suppose there was a vestige of decency left in these people, who must have realised that, having prevented me from entering a nursing career, there was nothing to support me until the longed-for affidavit arrived from my father. After that meeting I knew the situation to be hopeless; I agreed and again packed my belongings. During the time of the engagement my fiancé had made me some expensive presents, amongst them a couple of beautiful large Peter Scott paintings of wildfowl and a few nice pieces of family jewellery. With these I covered the top of a table, wrote the fateful letter breaking off the engagement and duly handed it to aunt Phyllis, keeping only my engagement ring and a gold artillery brooch which had been a special gift. Then I caught the train for London even before mother Nora had returned.

On receipt of her letter my father had gone into action. Again it was the generous Scheuer family who came to our assistance by providing the necessary guarantees. Until officialdom had done its work and issued my entrance visa to the USA, I had to find accommodation. In happier pre-war times father had known what proved to be the last ambassador from the First Austrian Republic to the court of St James. Sir George Franckenstein, a baron from the days of the old monarchy, had been granted British citizenship and was knighted after the fall of his homeland. All he could come up with was the address of an emergency hostel in Westbourne Terrace, within walking distance of Paddington Station. When I presented myself there I found something akin to the hospital set-up in West Kirby for the evacuees from Liverpool. It was a large end-of-terrance house equipped in the most primitive fashion to offer shelter to as many people as possible. Apart from an overcrowded common room, every other room had been turned into a dormitory lined with rows of iron bedsteads. The sexes were separated at night but mixed freely at all other times. The daily charge was small, nobody had any money. The administration lay in the hands of the Austrian Centre, a refugee organisation set up by emigré Austrian left-wing politicians in agreement with the Home Office, hiding their Communist faces behind the mask of Socialism. It was violently anti-war and in support of the Soviet Union's pact with Germany. Once the fortunes of war had changed after the invasion of Russia in 1941, their wind, too, changed its direction quite dramatically.

I settled in as well as I could, feeling depressed and empty, indeed betrayed after the dreadful days I had just lived through. Another blow was to fall almost immediately with aunt Phyllis's first cheque accompanied by a letter. A careful check had been made of the items I had left behind, but much to their surprise my engagement ring and artillery brooch had not been amongst them. It was hinted that my weekly allowance might be stopped unless they were produced and returned. I packed them up and sent them by registered post direct to my ex-fiancé, whose address I knew, at the same time asking aunt Phyllis to let me know whether or not they had arrived. I never again heard from the man who had professed undying love for me.

212

3

Another Leave-Taking

By the middle of June my sister's affidavit and ship reservation had come through. She left her teaching post in East Dereham and joined me in London, where I had found a furnished room for us at the Portobello Road end of Westbourne Grove. The owners of the little house were an Italian couple who ran a grocer's shop on the ground floor, lived upstairs and let a room to poor people like us. Its furnishings consisted of two single beds on either side of the room between the door and the window. There was a small wardrobe, a washbasin and a gas cooker, two small wooden chairs and a tiny rickety table. For this we had to pay £1 a week, affordable only with the two of us sharing the cost. Our landlords employed an Austrian girl on a normal work permit as a general factotum, a fact which proved very advantageous for us. She would supply us with the occasional broken egg or any other foodstuff in a non-saleable condition. For fruit and vegetables it was only a few yards to Portobello Market, with its stalls devoted to the produce of Mother Earth, but as yet nothing else.

In the coming days we got to know an assortment of people carried along by the maelstrom of war. Among them were French refugees who had managed to escape on one of the dozens of small boats fleeing the German onslaught. Our exchange of experiences with one of them determined a course of action which would have far-reaching consequences for me. Due to the restrictions in available space on the craft, each person was only allowed one piece of luggage. My sister's passage to New York was booked on a vessel setting out from Liverpool in the middle of July. When the departure date finally approached, we decided that she should take all my possessions while this was still possible, leaving me with just enough to fill a medium-sized suitcase. After all, I would be following her in a few weeks, and certainly before the onset of winter. I was left with a couple of warm dresses, two pairs of shoes, a change of underwear and, most fortuitously, my winter coat. The rest was light summer clothes and odds and ends.

On the day of our parting we went by bus to Euston Station in the early evening, where we took leave of each other in the depressing gloom of the compulsory black-out, waving until the train had disappeared into the distance. How could we have known that eight years would pass before I saw her, our parents and my clothes again, for the contingencies of war decreed that, although my affidavit came through exactly four weeks later, no passage for the Atlantic crossing could be found for as unimportant a girl as myself, in spite of Father's most strenuous efforts. The inevitable had to be accepted yet again; a new chapter started.

4

Doing My Bit

On the way back from Euston Station I realised that, for the first time in my young life, I was completely alone and entirely dependent on my efforts. It is true, there was the small weekly allowance arriving regularly from aunt Phyllis as her part of the bargain, but it became clear that this could only be a temporary measure due to cease fairly soon. Aged 20, an enemy alien in a country engaged in a mortal struggle, which might soon be lost for all anybody knew, with the dire consequences such a defeat would bring for me, my hope for the future centred on the firmly held wish of a speedy departure for the bosom of my family. But until that longed-for day, life had to continue.

The first thing to be done was to reduce my expenditure, my sister's contribution having ceased. I went room-hunting. In Northumberland Terrace, a turning off Westbourne Grove, in one of the houses lining this street, I found a basement room for 15/- a week. It had a comfortable bed, an open fireplace, a heavy consumer of expensive coal, and the usual sparse furniture. Its little cross-barred window looked out onto a small garden. The bathroom on the first floor, shared by all the occupants of the house, provided hot water by means of a penny-in-the-slot Ascot heater. It took four of these coins to half-fill the bath. Once a week was my ration, while one penny sufficed for a basin-full in the morning. I became proficient in washing myself from head to toe in this meagre provision, carrying soap, towel, toothbrush, etc. backwards and forwards. The middle-aged couple who owned the house showed me considerable kindness by inviting me to wash my hair in their kitchen, using the hot water from their water heater for free. Occasionally they also offered me high tea, much welcomed by an incompetent and poverty-stricken cook. Only once did I offend against their goodwill, this, as it seems to be my fate, for a reason beyond my control.

The war had hotted up considerably. In August German aircraft bombed the London Docks, visible in Westbourne Grove with the night sky a flaming red in the east. The bombing increased. On 15 September, a lovely, sunny, early autumn day, I happened to be standing at the corner of Bond Street and Piccadilly when my attention was caught by little flies high up in the blue sky engaged in a fascinating dance. Although aware that these were deadly serious dogfights between the two air forces, it was hard to think of the participants as being vulnerable human beings threatened with death at any moment. By that time, aunt Phyllis having stopped my allowance, I had found employment, approved by the Home Office of course, with Maples the furniture firm.

Unbeknown to the general public, Maples owned not only the shop premises facing Tottenham Court Road, but also vast workshops behind these and on the opposite side in Euston Road. Here war work was in full swing, here the gas mask bags, standard issue to the forces, were sewn, here an array of tents for the armed services was manufactured. Being an outcast from the mainstream of war production, I was given the job of checking gas mask bags in the various stages of manufacture, making sure that the seams were straight, the side-pieces with the metal rings holding the shoulder straps did not budge under stress, and cutting off the numerous threads left dangling by the machinists. Anything not completely satisfactory had to be returned to the worker, whose number was attached to the bundle submitted for inspection. Since the only people being on a fixed wage, albeit the extremely low one of £2/15/0 per week, were the checkers, and everybody else was on piece work, any reject meant a loss of earnings for the machinist.

After a few weeks of the impressively named but mind-numbing activity of an inspector, I was allowed to join the superior rank of machinist. Whether this was sanctioned by the Home Office is more than doubtful, for the possibility of sabotaging the manufacture of gas mask bags presented a danger to the war effort. However, like the rest of the country, Maples were short of manpower, I was on the spot, knew how to use a sewing machine and was a willing worker. My promotion led to a seat in front of an industrial, heavy electric sewing machine at the end of a long line of similar ones, with two always facing each other. A wooden trough ran down the middle between them, containing the bundle of cut-out cloth pieces allocated individually to each operator. It was quite common to find rat droppings deposited amongst the canvas on starting work in the morning, but nobody complained, nobody seemed to care.

We worked long hours and as intensively as we were capable of, for our income entirely depended on our output. Piece work, lowly paid, reigned supreme. If there was a canteen I never found it, for even if I had I would not have been able to afford to eat there or to spare the time. My lunch consisted of a couple of thin paste sandwiches, paste being unrationed, and an apple eaten at my machine. Sometimes, when I was unlucky or, perhaps, a little careless, the fast-moving heavy needle stitched not just the cloth but also my index finger, with painful and time-wasting results. A visit to the factory nurse led through a series of extensive rooms, where the incessant work going on was very impressive. The pay packet on Friday, however, was less so after such an episode. Another and far more serious cause for a drop in one's income was a breakdown of the machine. There were a couple of mechanics whose job it was to affect the necessary repairs, but having succeeded in running one of them down in the rabbit warren of the two buildings, it often meant waiting in a queue for more than a day before one could resume earning one's living again. It was a precarious existence. The most anybody in our shop ever managed to take home did not exceed £4 per week.

The hours of work were from 8 a.m. to 6 p.m. daily, with Sunday a welcome break from the drudgery. A good night's rest is what we all longed for, but seldom got, with the bombardment of London in full swing. From September 1940 onwards, bombs rained down night after night. At first I followed the crowd and took refuge in a public air raid shelter, consisting of a cellar in somebody's house, requisitioned by the authorities for that purpose. Into this makeshift shelter, with its single access down a flight of stairs, trooped an assortment of every kind of humanity, carrying chairs of all shapes and sizes. And there we sat in almost complete darkness, listening to the explosions outside. The thickening atmosphere made breathing difficult, at least for me, even though I moved my little collapsible chair as close to the exit and the open air as possible. Sleep was impossible.

After four nights of this, I decided that it would be preferable to die in my bed. I never again spent a night in an air raid shelter. I pulled the blankets over my head, thought longingly of my parents, and put my trust in God. For many a day I returned from work in the dark at the beginning of an air raid and left again in the morning, still in the dark, with the same air raid in progress. The damage caused was evident all around, one no longer stopped to look, survival was the ticket.

In spite of everything, youth will have its day. Some of

the people I had met in the hostel, in refugee restaurants and cafés, had become friends with whom to spend the little leisure at my disposal. One of them was a well-built, tall and very blond young man, in his early twenties, from Berlin who, although presenting the picture the world normally made itself of the perfect German, had two Jewish grandparents and thus had fallen foul of the German race laws. When we met in the late autumn of 1940, he was serving in the British army. The authorities had decided that enemy aliens, including refugees from German-speaking countries, meaning Germany and Austria, had their uses. The Pioneer Corps of the British Army was permanently short of recruits, for not many indigenous men, and later women, fancied the life of ditch digger, kitchen skivvy, servant and similar lowly occupations. My new friend looked very smart in his rough khaki, and made a presentable addition to the small group of young people with whom I mixed. Without any encouragement on my part he developed a passion for me which became troublesome, particularly when he urged me to marry him. Nothing could have been further from my mind. I was still hoping somehow to get to New York, and had no intention of getting involved with a man again.

It is ironic that it was this very young man who nearly got me thrown out by my landlady for improper conduct. I had been to the Austrian Centre club for an hour after work on that evening. 'My' friend offered to walk me home, which I was glad to accept as the air raid sirens had just sounded. On arriving at my front door, and all hell having broken loose, with flying shrapnel being as dangerous as the explosion from an actual bomb, I asked him in to await an abatement in the attack. I settled on the bed on top of the bedspread, while he made himself as comfortable as he could in the only chair in the room. Nobody in the house slept for the duration of the raid, it was too fierce for that.

One bomb exploded so close that the blast from it shattered a pane of glass in my little window. Eventually things quietened down and he was able to leave. The next morning I got a fearful dressing-down for harbouring a man in my room, for creasing the bedspread and for, possibly, indulging in unseemly behaviour. All this for a man I could only endure with difficulty!

5

Learning to Cope

October turned into November. The absence of aunt Phyllis's allowance made itself more and more felt, with my small cash reserve shrinking almost daily. What I earned had to suffice in its entirety for my upkeep, including any expenses incurred travelling to and from work, keeping my teeth in order and buying the occasional pair of lisle stockings with one clothing coupon. I joined the Hospital Saturday Fund by paying a weekly contribution of 3d, which not only assured me of help with any hospitalisation but also contributed to half of any dental bill. The heating of my room became a problem, the open fire difficult to maintain while out most of the day, the coal having been bought in small bags was dear and heavy to carry home, the cleaning of the grate in the morning an added burden.

On approaching my landlady I was offered and accepted a tiny room on the ground floor for 10/- a week, representing a considerable saving in relation to my income. It was at the very end of the hallway, exactly opposite the front door. My only neighbour was the communal lavatory serving the whole house. It took a little time to get used to the nightly interruptions. The room itself probably measured six by seven feet. The rear wall was entirely taken up by the bed. On the window side, facing south, stood a chair flanked by a washbasin. On the side facing the bed and next to the door stood a small hall wardrobe, and opposite the washbasin was the gas fire, with the usual attached gas ring representing the only cooking facility provided. A narrow chest of drawers next to it, and a small hexagonal bamboo table pushed against the wardrobe door completed the furnishings. Whenever this door had to be opened, the table, being very light, had to be put outside the room and into the passage without obstructing the access to the lavatory. However, the accommodation answered my simple needs.

Just once did I fall victim to the appalling lack of space. In order to save money – the penny-in-the slot gas meter had to be fed frequently to keep the warmth flowing – I kept the fire at a very low level, just enough to warm my feet with the chair drawn up to it as close as possible. On a cold November day I was deeply engrossed in a book, when a searing pain in my right big toe jerked me back to reality. Inadvertently I had touched the open flame with the top of my shoe, burning not only a hole in it but also causing a bad burn, which quickly brought out a large blister, on the side of my toe. The blow was a severe one. It was not just the great pain which upset me, it was, in particular, the damage done to my shoe, being my only pair of walking shoes and quite difficult to replace, a repair proving to be impossible. Nature has endowed me with long, very narrow feet, considered to be aristocratic, but has neglected to bestow the requisite financial means on me. It has always been troublesome to find a suitable make which, once found, would normally be three times more expensive than the average article. On this occasion I had to carry on with the damaged shoe covering the hole from the inside with a bit of cardboard brushed over with dark brown shoe polish.

Christmas was in the offing, my first Christmas on my own. For Christmas Eve the mother of my dear friend Marietta had invited me to share their meagre meal, and I gave myself a present since nobody else did. Marks & Spencer's shop at Marble Arch, small though it was, already proved a magnet. I had saved £3 with which to buy a cinnamon-coloured, long-sleeved woollen shirtwaister dress, my pride and joy only to be worn at weekends and on special occasions. It lasted and lasted until holes had been worn at the elbows. It was never forgotten.

The arrival of 1941 brought no change in my living conditions until one morning in April. Instead of being able to ride on the bus to the junction of Tottenham Court Road and Euston Road as usual, we passengers were set down on the Regent's Park side of Euston Road. Firehoses were lining the gutters and snaking across the pavement in the direction I was going. Their target hove into view. It was Maples, whose workshops having been hit by an oil bomb during the night, were still being doused with copious streams of water from several fire engines. The road between the two buildings was filled with hundreds of workers milling aimlessly around and wondering what was going to happen next. Eventually we were called into a large empty store room, told that our employment was terminated, that we would be paid what was owing to us, and that we could move to Nottingham to work for the firm there. By now I had taken root, especially thanks to Marietta and her family, who were showing me much kindness. When I turned 21 on 15 January it was Marietta and our mutual friend Irmy Verity who had invited me to the former's home for a little celebration. We were an unlikely trio, but we stuck together, with only death finally parting us. No, I could not leave London.

6

A Change of Fortune

Since it is trite but true that important events rarely come singly, it was only appropriate that my mode of living should at this point undergo quite an unexpected change for the better. During my abortive engagement in West Kirby I had acquired a godson, the second child of my fiancé's closest friend. The purpose of this godmotherdom was to tie the two families even more closely together. Well, the tie which bound my fiancé to me was snapped, but that between myself and his friend's family still continues. My godson's mother had a maiden aunt living in a small modern flat in Russell Square. Her income, as far as I am aware, was largely derived from a superior rooming house in Notting Hill, which she either owned outright or on which she had a long lease. I was suddenly approached with the proposition to move into one of the furnished rooms and live there rent-free, in return for looking after the building and collecting the tenants' rent. What a gift to fall into my lap!

The building, No. 6 Pembridge Gardens, was one in a terrace of spacious houses put up round the turn of the century for single family use. It still had a certain elegant air. The rooms on the ground and first floors were let to permanent residents of a rather mixed background. There was the elderly spinster living on a miniscule income, yet keeping herself and her little realm 'respectable', there was the retired, widowed lowly clerk who could not understand why I did not go back to Austria – and this in the middle of the war – and there were several service personnel of all ranks stationed in London, to whom the location and the moderate rent were most welcome. They spilt over onto the second floor, where my room was. And what an attractive room it was after my previous experiences! The furniture was of a reasonable quality, the window let in the light, and the heating and cooking facilities, though still primitive, were at least unobtrusive. I collected the rents, handed them over as agreed, and stayed there until the ever-changing demands of my life made the obligations too burdensome.

Being so unexpectedly relieved of factory work, I decided to try and better myself. As luck would have it, the couple in the flat below my friend Marietta's were also refugees from Vienna. The husband had set up a small trading company in an office in Dean Street on the corner with Soho Square. He had managed to obtain a contract with Woolworth, to supply their myriad of stores with comparatively small quantities of knitting wool. Each consignment had to be invoiced individually to each store. There was also trade in other commodities, requiring a voluminous correspondence. When I was asked to join the firm, the staff consisted of a very competent coloured girl, who held my hand whenever I floundered, and a young one fulfilling the rôle of the office boy.

My particular brief was to take dictation in English and German shorthand, to type the letters, specifications, etc., and, my special bugbear, to check the reams of invoices before they were sent out. Having written German shorthand since my schooldays I now adapted it to English, an attempt to acquire Pitman's having ended in abject failure. The summer of 1941, a cool and sunless one, turned into autumn. My boss found his wholesalers gradually unable to accept his orders. Business shrank, and the day came when I lost my job once again.

And once again it all turned into an opportunity to progress. Many young Austrians, myself included, had, understandably, having made contact, kept in touch with each other. Who else was there with whom to talk in one's mother tongue and who understood the situation in which we found ourselves in the middle of a, by all appearances, war that was going badly with the Continent occupied, North Africa almost lost, and the unrelenting battle on the high seas. We depended on our efforts to keep ourselves alive.

Whether it was a spontaneous act by the few Austrians of public repute who had found refuge in England, or whether it was an action instigated by the Home Office, which to me seems the more likely, a formal club was set up, called the Austrian Youth Association, AYA for short. Its organiser and guiding light was Peter von Albert, an Austrian aristocrat in his early thirties, who had left his home unable to bear the occupation by Germany of his beloved country. At least, that is what we were told. He certainly found life as a refugee extremely hard. I got to know him quite well, since he and one other member of the Association lodged in 'my' house under my administration. With his superior connections he somehow persuaded Lord Melchett of ICI fame, the owner of a house in Wilton Place, Knightsbridge, which was standing empty like so many during the aerial bombardment of London, to let us use it as our club house for the duration of the war.

A considerable number of young Austrians between the ages of 15 and 30 had by then joined the AYA, been issued with a membership card, and were now asked to help make 'our' house habitable. We washed and scrubbed the floors, distempered the walls, installed the furniture donated by well-wishers, and put the kitchen in working order. Peter engaged a cook for the evenings and weekends, the times when the members could make most use of the facilities.

The AYA became for many of us the mainstay of our existence. Friendships entered into were made for life, even when in the course of it close contact was restricted to the infrequent letter. There were a couple of weddings to celebrate, and it was thanks to my involvement with it that I met the man I was eventually to marry.

War has an unsettling effect on the social order. That this is so was very evident in the kind of people with whom we youngsters from a variety of backgrounds were brought into contact. Most of them, the majority of us, would normally only have known as the names of persons too far removed from our place in society ever to be approached, let alone to be met on the same level. There was the day when Jan Masaryk, the ill-fated post-war president of Czechoslovakia, stood aside on the stairs in our HQ to let me pass. There was another day when Archduke Robert of Austria, the second son of the last Emperor, attended a private meeting with Peter in his office, the result of which was a concert in aid of Austrian refugees given by the famous pianist Bruno Moisewitch at the Dorchester Hotel. Nobody else expressing any interest, I asked and was given his letter addressed to the Archduke, thanking him profusely for his patronage. It is still in my possession.

The Archduke and myself, when he was leaving and I just arriving, encountered each other on the stairs, where I acknowledged his presence with a nod of the head. This earned me a severe rebuke from Peter, a staunch monarchist, for whom only a full-blown curtsey would have been proper. Well, Peter had been born under the monarchy, while my cradle had stood in the new-born republic. It can be assumed, that the Archduke, a tall, thin, fair-haired young man, minded not at all.

Another concert which came our way was that given by Peter Stadlen, an unprepossessing yet highly gifted pianist. But as far as I am concerned, the outstanding event, for which I shall always be grateful, took place on 20 January 1942. The Dowager Lady Townshend had no doubt felt that the pre-war social graces should not fall victim to the upheaval caused by the war in London, where life, with its constant threat of obliteration from the air, had taken on a heightened urgency. The restraints imposed by a settled existence in a settled place hardly any longer existed. The town was full of service personnel from Europe and overseas who, in a sense, were rootless and often disorientated, though bound by a common purpose.

It was very much in the interest of the host population to offer some sort of entertainment to its guests, especially on Sundays, when the lack of normal weekday activities and the special meaning of the day allowed homesickness and loneliness to put in an unwelcome appearance. Much to her credit, Lady Townshend had founded the 'Officers Sunday Club' sometime in the previous year. It was the name given to a very formal tea dance held every Sunday at 4 p.m. sharp in the big ballroom of the Grosvenor House, Park Lane. As its title implied, it was for officers in uniform, with or without their ladies. Girls from good families supplied the female component. Its modest cost included as near a pre-war afternoon tea as it was possible to provide, with the thinnest of sandwiches, cake and the best quality tea from the hotel's peacetime stock.

In order to give these functions a more interesting and purposeful character, one or the other was occasionally dedicated to an allied country. Thus there was a 'Free Czech' afternoon, a 'Free Polish' afternoon and a 'Free French' afternoon, when the ballroom would be decorated with the appropriate flags, officers from the relevant armed forces specially invited to be present, and attention publicly drawn to their respective countries' contribution to the war effort.

Peter, always one to push the cause of poor occupied

Austria, considered it only right and proper that our native land should be included in the roll-call of countries to be liberated. Archduke Robert, whose connections to the ruling classes were excellent, persuaded the good lady to hold a 'Free Austrian' afternoon, at which he would be the guest of honour. Out went the word to AYA members to present themselves in their national costume, if available, at 3.30 p.m. on that Sunday in January at the side entrance to the Grosvenor House Ballroom. Not every member possessing a national costume, nor being able to come to town, the group eventually numbered about 25. The excitement was enormous. At last we poor downtrodden enemy alien refugees would receive some recognition!

At 2.30 p.m. the pay phone in the hall of the house in Pembridge Gardens rang. It was Lady Townshend's secretary. The afternoon had to be cancelled forthwith, for the Czechs and the Poles were objecting vigorously to Austria's inclusion in the list of oppressed countries, when its people were happily engaged in being oppressors as part of the German Reich. The Archduke had left for Scotland for a spot of hunting, and that was that. To our protests that it would be impossible to contact the participants in our party, who lived all over London and often were not on the telephone, a grudging concession was made. We could still attend as non-paying guests, but would not be given or shown any special treatment.

As can be imagined, those of us in the know, being restricted to the few who could be contacted, dressed ourselves in our costumes with a heavy heart. It was as if a pall of grey fog had descended on us. On arriving at the entrance to the ballroom, those of us who had come together joined a long, slow-moving queue waiting to be admitted. It did not help to lighten the atmosphere when a young woman near us addressed her partner in a loud voice with the words: 'I did not know it was going to be fancy dress today.'

We tried to make ourselves look inconspicuous, which proved rather difficult.

The ballroom is built for maximum display. On entering one is faced with a wide curved staircase leading to the main floor capable of accommodating 1200 persons. In full view of all those already present, one had to walk down the stairs after having been presented by name by the Master of Ceremonies to Lady Townshend standing at the top of them. It was a depressing moment. If we had been able to turn round and go home without causing a scandal, we would have done so. As it was, we were shown to the oblong table reserved for our party, well away from the dance floor, where we sat trying to look small and unobtrusive. How could we even think of joining the dancing when feeling so completely out of place? Of course, it was pleasant to take in the splendours of the room, the beautifully laid round tables set for eight, and to listen to the first-class band. The food, too, made a change from our normal frugal diet.

After sitting for a time round the table in a cowed fashion, Peter told us to take part in the dancing. He thought it bad manners for us to appear glum when we were, after all, present as the guests of Lady Townshend. At the next 'Paul Jones' most of us did as we were bidden. And that is how I met my future husband. At that time he was a Lieutenant in the Royal Navy Volunteer Reserve, stationed at the Admiralty, who in civilian life had been a schoolmaster in the Wirral, teaching Physics, with a First Class degree from Cambridge University. Now he was attached to the Gunnery Division and living in London. Although he looked very smart in his uniform with the wavy gold braid round the sleeves, and proved to be an excellent dancer, the impression he made on me at first sight was minimal. Somehow he managed to face me again in the course of a second 'Paul Jones', then he asked me to dance.

230

Towards the end of the afternoon he invited me out to dinner. Nothing could have been further from my mind than to go out with a complete stranger. I had come with my friends and would leave with them. However, I thought it judicious not to turn him down flat but to make him withdraw his invitation. Knowing how particular English men were about one's physical appearance, I accepted but regretted being unable to change from my national costume into something more conventional. Surely this would do the trick! Not at all. That was just fine, he told me, we would go to Schmidt's, the German restaurant of repute in Soho, where I would look just right.

With apologies to my surprised friends, we set off on our walk there. It was slightly snowing, but we chatted without taking any notice of the weather until we reached our destination. Schmidt's displayed a large notice 'Under British Management' but the food was still German and the waiters still wore long white aprons wrapped around their legs almost to the ground. The evening was not very entertaining, for Tony thought it proper to talk mainly about his Dutch girlfriend back in Holland, whom he had been visiting at the outbreak of the war and had known for a number of years. I was not impressed. He saw me home and promised to keep in touch. Inwardly I gave him two days to do so before I would write him off. Two days passed without any news, and I dismissed him from my mind. Then the telephone call came. He had been away at sea, that was all he could tell me. Much later I learned that he had to be present at the test firing of certain naval guns. And that was the beginning of yet another chapter in my life.

7

Of Wine and Bombs

The loss of my job with the Austrian firm necessitated the search for another one with some speed. I bought the *Daily Telegraph* and studied the 'Appointments Vacant' column. One caught my eye as being, possibly, suitable. It was with a wine and spirit wholesaler by the name of 'Montclare & Co' of 49 Old Bond Street, almost on the corner with Piccadilly. At the interview I discovered the owner, a Mr Fenveszi, to be a middle-aged Hungarian of rather large proportions whose second language was an excellent German, who needed somebody with that language and English to take on the office work single-handedly. A bargain was struck and I joined him in his enterprises in the autumn of 1941 for almost two years, two very happy years, until the day came when I was due to be called up into the armed forces.

No. 49 was solid and old-fashioned, the world of wholesale trading in alcoholic beverages a revelation to me, whose upbringing had not included close acquaintance with the oldest aid to good cheer. Customers, mainly hoteliers of the calibre of the Imperial Hotel, Torquay, called to taste the goods before placing an order. Blind wine tastings were organised for the experts, which fascinated me. The expertise on display was breathtaking. Only a lifetime spent acquiring the knowledge of being able to identify wines by their bouquet and flavour could produce such astonishing results.

The country, having been cut off by the war from its natural sources of supplies, had to be replenished from cellars stocked with years of laid-down reserves. These came up for auction at regular intervals held by the city firm of Restell & Co., at which my boss was a regular attender and buyer. We had no storage facilities of our own and, apart from a sample or two, I never saw his purchases.

Cognac, too, was much in demand. When one buys a bottle it is of a light brown colour with the quality carefully stated on the label. Now I learned about the life cycle of brandy. Like all spirits, casks were held in bond by the Customs and Excise until the requisite duty had been paid. Since supplies of matured cognac from France soon ran out, wholesalers, my boss amongst them, undertook to produce their own unbranded kind. With great regularity I was despatched to the bonded warehouse in the Minories for samples drawn from casks belonging to the firm. To my astonishment on the first occasion I came away with a quarter-pint bottle filled with a greenish-white liquid and another filled with a slightly more yellowish fluid. It was explained to me that the young spirit was colourless for the first three years and only assumed the, to the consumer, familiar golden brown after maturing in old oaken sherry casks. The longer it was allowed to mature, the darker the colour and the finer the quality.

Our one and only store cupboard housed a number of undistinguished small bottles containing samples at various stages of development. They were carefully inspected by my boss, on whose judgement rested the decision how and when to proceed. For brandy, as we know it, is a blend of several cognacs according to well-guarded formulae, and the final product is the result of skilful 'cutting' as it is called in the trade. In this way our firm, on occasion, produced its own blend, but more often sold a cask on to an established blender. I cannot remember ever seeing a full bottle in the office. The samples, being 90% proof, hence almost pure alcohol, were undrinkable. And yet a little sip was an excellent way to cauterise a sore throat. A tiny quantity seemed to kill all pain for a short time, at least.

The most demanding, because the most exacting, task to be performed was keeping records for the Customs and Excise of all spirits physically passing through the office. With whisky in exceedingly short supply, my boss found the gift of a tiny quarter-pint bottle of the much sought-after Scottish gold to be most acceptable to anybody he wished to impress or reward for services rendered. These, almost miniatures, usually came in boxes of one dozen and were stored in the already mentioned cupboard. It was up to me meticulously to write out a Customs and Excise certificate countersigned by the recipient, who was given the top while we kept the bottom copy in the large book provided for the purpose. At any time a Customs officer could and did descend on us to check the cupboard contents, the invoices from the suppliers and the copies of the certificates. Woe to my boss and, afterwards, me if any discrepancy were to be discovered!

An additional duty laid upon all tenants of the building was firewatching. Incendiary bombs would rain down in quantity, especially during night raids, when the offices were unoccupied. Triplex Glass, who had large premises overlooking Picadilly, were the firewatch point. It fell to me to come in on a Sunday morning and keep a look-out for anything falling from a hostile sky. What exactly would have happened in such an event has escaped my memory. This imposition did not last long once the daylight raids had stopped. At night I was on a much more professional firewatching rota. In the summer of 1941 I had been accepted into the service, issued with a membership card, and joined a team based in a large old house near my home.

Here, the extensive front room had been designated a fire watch post.

Once a week I had to do duty for several hours stretching into the early morning, but only after I had received considerable training for the task. This consisted in attending lectures on how to cope with a variety of incendiary devices, how to cope with smoke – this included crawling through a smoke-filled hut wearing one's gas mask – how to handle a stirrup pump and, very importantly, what to leave well alone. Into this category fell an anti-aircraft device. It consisted of half-a-pound of high explosive encased in metal and looking like a hand grenade, around which was fitted a freestanding thin metallic ring attached at one point to a firing pin. The bomb, in turn, was secured to a large spool of piano wire suspended from a large balloon. Once the balloon was released it rose to a height sufficient to exceed that of an oncoming aircraft. On its upward journey the wire unravelled and, being invisible except when seen close to, would touch the aircraft, the ring round the bomb would touch the aeroplane, the firing pin would be activated and the ensuing explosion would destroy the target. This was the theory. As was explained to me after the war by my husband, who had been intimately involved in the project, the practice looked rather different.

I learned about this weapon during one of the lectures, when it was shown to us without any reference as to its origin and function, except for the stern warning neither to touch one of these 'things' were we to happen upon one, nor to try and remove any kind of dangling wire caught in a tree, on a roof or just about anywhere else. The reason for this injunction emerged only much later. It was an anti-aircraft weapon developed by the Department for Naval Weapons Development (DNWD) to deal with air attacks, particularly at night. Whole squadrons of balloons were released into the paths of intruders, whose speedy demise was sanguinely anticipated. Only nobody had taken weather and, in particular, wind conditions into account. Instead of intercepting the enemy coming in from the east, the north-easterly winter winds carried the balloons all over southern England as far as the West Country. The damage done by the bombs, which were so sensitive that the slightest touch on the ring would set them off, was as nothing compared to that caused by the heavy empty spools which, once the wire had unravelled, fell to the ground. Roofs which might never have suffered any other damage were holed, people were injured, and in all likelihood even killed. One of my husband's duties became the gathering and making safe of these deadly gifts from on high, and, since the population at large knew nothing about them, one must marvel at the small number of casualties.

Having completed my training, long hours of tedious duty followed, only occasionally interrupted by involvement with a fire raid. It was fortunate that there seemed to be a fair proportion of duds amongst the incendiaries. Those that did explode were quite sufficient to have to be dealt with. The hours spent on duty were not, however, entirely wasted. Our post boasted a dartboard and a billiards table. The introduction into the highly skilled game of darts gave me a lot of pleasure. Billiards less so. My civil defence duties continued for more than three years until I got married, and I am very proud to have been awarded the Defence Medal in recognition. There cannot be many civilian enemy aliens so distinguished.

8

Reserved Occupation

Soon after meeting the man I was eventually to marry, I was persuaded by him to find safer accommodation than a room at the very top of a tall house. It was lucky that not a stone's throw away at No. 18 Pembridge Square a tiny self-contained furnished bedsitter on the ground floor was to let. The rent was affordable. The door had its own Yale lock, and there was a walk-in cupboard, almost as large as the room itself, for storage purposes. The tall, narrow window overlooked a garden, which made for silent nights only disturbed by the wailing of the air raid sirens and the sound of exploding bombs. An even tinier room had been created by putting up a less than sound-proof partition almost across the centre of what originally must have been a fair-sized one. My intimate neighbour, whom I did not know and never met, and I had our washbasins back to back. In this manner we could follow each other's ablutions morning and night. The ubiquitous gas ring was built into the wall, making stooping unnecessary when handling pots and pans, an activity I engaged in only on rare occasions apart from brewing tea or warming up a tin of soup. Divided by a narrow road from the building, United Dairies had a large depot, from where the clinking and chinking of bottles could be heard in the early morning, acting as a reliable alarm clock.

The move having been accomplished, I had to concentrate on a more worrying matter. Women, having been called up for National Service, had been joining up in ever-increasing numbers, but the hunger of the war for human beings constantly grew. The call-up went according to the year of birth, and by 1942 mine had been reached. With the shortage of labour, the concept of the 'enemy alien' took on an elastic nature. The effect of this was that army service loomed on the horizon for one to whom the wearing of any kind of uniform has always been anathema. Coupled to this was the fact that the tasks to be performed would again be those of a skivvy, a taste of which I had already had and did not wish to repeat. A job in a reserved occupation would have to be found to save me from such a fate.

Taking my courage in both hands, I inserted an advertisement in the *Daily Telegraph*'s 'Appointments Wanted' column, setting out my age and accomplishments, which by this time included touch-typing, taught to myself with the aid of a secondhand book in my lunch hour, and stating the need for a post in a reserved occupation. Much to my surprise it was answered by a Mr Henry Chwast, who turned out to be a very elegant and polished Pole who had spent the best part of his life in Paris, where he had been married to the daughter of one of France's leading painters of the period. Now he was working for the Merchant Navy Comforts Service with the title 'Information Officer'. I had never heard of this organisation, although I later learned that it was quite a formidable one, akin to the Red Cross and targeted at the British and Allied Merchant Navies. It had been founded by a wealthy shipowner by the name of Watts, whose wife headed the organisation.

It had all begun with the heavy loss of cargo ships, particularly in the Atlantic. When shipwrecked sailors were taken on board by their rescuers, they had to be kitted out in clothes donated by their hosts. While this was sustainable for a short time, a more satisfactory solution had to be

238

found. The women knitters of Great Britain with their skilful fingers provided part of the answer. They would knit the thick seaboot stockings, the mittens, socks and jerseys from wool supplied to them, and the Merchant Navy Comforts Service would see to the rest of the required clothing. It would all be packed into seamen's duffle bags, each containing ten complete outfits, and placed in quantity on each ship of the Naval and Merchant fleets travelling in U-boat-infested waters. To pay for the cost, which was very large, somebody had hit on a brilliant idea. The halfpenny of those days, a common enough copper coin, bore on its reverse side more often than not the image of a sailing ship in full rig. Why not invite the general public to contribute these coins of little individual value in strategically placed collecting tins? The scheme worked. Not only was the amount of money quite considerable, but the propaganda value immense. Mr Kirkland Bridge who, from his church cleaning business, had been recruited as Public Relations Officer, was very good at his job! I thought a little less kindly of him whenever over the years it fell to me to count the contents of tins handed in to us. But I am anticipating.

Henry Chwast, when I first met him, had only a vague idea of what his brief was and how he was going to carry it out, and what my rôle in this should be. It had become clear for some time that merchant seamen, especially those of the Allied Marines, felt in need of advice and guidance in many directions when visiting London, language problems being to the fore with many coming from non-English-speaking countries. The Merchant Navy Comforts Service's Head-quarters (HQ) had been established in the Empire Building in Northumberland Avenue, where stocks were kept and despatched from. Facing Trafalgar Square on the junction with Northumberland Avenue stand Grand Buildings, a massive construction aptly named. Here the Scottish Motor Traction Company in August 1939 had leased shop premises facing the square a week or two before the outbreak of war, which put an immediate end to transport by motor coach, the company's main business. They now offered to lease, or better to sublet, the premises at a peppercorn rent to the Merchant Navy Comforts Service for the duration of the war, to be used as its Information Bureau, headed by Henry Chwast.

We walked along to Trafalgar Square, where we found the shop in a state of hibernation. Its front had been boarded up with large wooden planks, which we carefully removed to reveal a large plate glass window giving on to an attractive interior. Henry offered me the job of secretary, possibly due to my skill in removing nails, second in the ranking after him. At the age of 22, I suppose, it could be looked upon as an achievement. It was of more importance to me that my weekly income was to rise to £4, a good salary indeed, and that, above all, I was safe in a reserved occupation, making a contribution to the general war effort.

It was with great regret on both sides that my warm-hearted Hungarian boss who, with his family, had treated me almost as an additional member of it, and I had to part. But we remained on excellent terms right up to the end of the war.

9

War Work

Henry and I explored our new kingdom. The ground floor, though not very large, was well suited to our purposes. The front door opened on to a spacious carpeted room, with a curved staircase at the back leading to an upper floor. The left side of the shop floor was taken up by a rounded floor-length counter, behind which eventually sat the duty staff, with the business paraphernalia on the top and the telephone, a small radio set and the reserve stock of papers, information sheets, etc. underneath on a shelf. From there another short flight of stairs led to a basement room of the same size as the reception area, containing a couple of tables, two cupboards and a small private telephone exchange.

While Henry took possession of the beautifully furnished, carpeted and light office on the top floor, my realm was to be underground, permanently artificially lit and exposed to the footfalls of the passers-by on the pavement above. It took a little while to get used to, especially the switchboard. Every incoming call went through it and had to be connected to the desired extension, while outgoing calls could be made direct once the outside line had been connected to the extension in question. If the extension was busy, incoming calls had to be put on hold and the caller announced before putting him through. When I first saw this piece of machinery I refused to have anything to do with it, but, of course, in the course of a very short time was forced to learn how to handle it. Being pretty ancient it had its peculiarities, often suffering from a lack of energy, possibly metal fatigue, when certain plugs would not function unless given a rest. Occasionally a service engineer had to be called in, to do I do not know what. The switchboard and I co-existed but never became close friends.

Having completed the comparatively easy task of putting the domestic arrangements in order, the much more difficult one of what our activities should be had to be faced. At the beginning the brief was to attend to the needs of the Allied Merchant Fleets. These required considerable linguistic skills on the part of the staff.

The first to join was Billy Graham, a beautiful but very sad woman in her mid-thirties who, for over ten years, had led the life of a rubber planter's wife in Malaya until the Japanese flood had threatened to overwhelm her like her other compatriots. Her husband, with whom she was very much in love, became a victim of the invaders quite early on. After his capture at the defence of Singapore, he had been taken to Changi Jail and shot. Billy managed to escape to Australia at the last moment, wangled her voyage home and was now anxious to put her office skills and knowledge of Urdu and Malay at the service of her country. This would prove very useful in dealing with the Lascar seamen manning many merchant vessels. We admired her greatly for the way she bore her misfortune.

It was with profound sorrow that I subsequently discovered how badly fate had continued to treat her. One day an American Army Major called at the bureau, introducing himself to her as a friend of somebody she had known in happier times. He took her out, brought a little glamour into her drab existence, courted and finally, when definitive proof of her husband's death had reached her, she consented to marry him. It meant leaving a Britain she only connected with pain, and since her second husband was financially well placed, and in the USA owned a large, superior farm near Boston, she hoped to build a satisfying and contented life. How cruel life can be, though.

During a visit to my parents in New York in the early part of 1948, she invited me for a short stay to her new home. What I found caused me great distress. It was indeed a large farm not far from Boston, at this time the most English of American cities. The house was big, very well furnished and, to my war-weary eyes, even luxurious, with excellent central heating and an electric blanket, unknown to me until then, warming my bed. But it stood quite isolated in the wide open spaces of the American country-side, with no near neighbours or any other manifestations of civilisation within easy reach. The smartly turned-out Army officer had reverted to being a dairy farmer, busy with his animals and agricultural concerns all day long, while his town-bred wife was left to her own devices. To turn a difficult situation into an almost unbearable one was his heavy reliance on the bottle. Cases of Scotch whisky, each holding a dozen of the best export brew, were stacked in the kitchen and disappearing at a rapid rate, for consumption started quite early in the morning. Billy tried to cover up in front of me as well as she could, but with little success. I was glad when my short stay came to an end. We soon afterwards lost touch. Of course, when she joined our staff all this was mercifully hidden in the impenetrable future.

The next to join came from quite a different background. She was a middle-aged lady of about 50 with grey hair, rather plump and indifferently dressed. Her manner was slow and deliberate and sometimes not really quite right for the job. But her antecedents certainly were. She was the daughter of the last British Ambassador to the Russian Imperial Court, spoke perfect French and, not knowing the language, I assume excellent Russian, and blended in well with the grand ladies around the corner at the Merchant Navy Comforts Service's Headquarters. Her tales of life in St Petersburg conjured up foreign and yet fascinating ways of existing.

The third member of our office team was my personal friend Marietta. She got taken on not only for her good French – we all spoke French – but her command, even if rather superficial, of her mother tongue Czech. It could be asked when, in its short existence, Czechoslovakia had had a navy, being completedly land-locked apart from the boats going up and down the Elbe and the Moldava. Stranger things than Czech sailors happened in wartime and, in any event, the size of the staff only gradually increased to its full strength with the demands made on the bureau's services.

We started off by contacting London hotels willing to offer preferential terms to seamen on leave. Lists were kept at the desk and bookings made on behalf of callers. Henry liaised with certain large cinemas and theatres in the West End prepared to donate complimentary tickets for their matinee shows. It became one of my duties to make the round of these establishments once a week to collect whatever was on offer. I particularly remember the pleasant man who was the manager of the Odeon cinema at Marble Arch, with his courteous manner and the inevitable invitation to a cup of tea and a little chat. Perhaps the extraordinary thing is that none of us, myself included, ever took advantage of the largesse so freely given.

Another vital service we offered involved just Henry and myself. British seamen who had been torpedoed could apply in person to HQ for kitting out from top to toe in brand-new clothing. Allied seamen had to come to us for vetting before a chit could be signed entitling them to the same hand-out. Henry, and in his absence myself, was empowered to act and append a valid signature. It was an interesting

244

part of my work, bringing me into contact with men who had been shipwrecked not just once but two or even three times and yet felt much more unsafe in London under bombardment from the sky than they ever did at sea, to which they were longing to get back with all possible speed.

The Merchant Seamen's Union owned a beautiful large house at Limpsfield Chart in Surrey, which was used as a convalescent home for men in need of recuperation. To keep the recovering patients occupied, an entertainments officer by the name of Alistair McLennan had been appointed. He cut an impressive figure. Of medium height in his early forties and as Scottish as they come, he always wore a kilt with the accompanying accoutrements, including tucked into his right knee-length stocking a dirk with a lovely yellow stone set in the hilt. I got to know him well after Henry had made an arrangement with the home's management to invite a party of about 20 men led by our Scotsman once a week to lunch, followed by a theatre matinee. By now the bureau's brief had been extended, as far as information and entertainment were concerned, to include seamen of all nations and not just those of the Allied fleets.

The Shaftsbury Hotel at the top of St Martin's Lane was permanently booked for lunch on a Wednesday, the final number being confirmed by telephone on the morning of that day. It became another one of my duties to take care of the party from the convalescent home from the moment of its arrival until its safe delivery to the door of the theatre. This probably sounds easier than it was, for even Mr McLennan's watchful eyes, firmly fixed on his charges, found keeping them altogether a very taxing business. To get to our lunch we had to walk along the Strand side of Trafalgar Square, up St Martin's Lane, passing several public houses on the way. It was quite a common occurrence to discover that members of the group had disappeared into one of these establishments, bringing the whole procession to a dead stop on the narrow pavement filled with the midday crowd. It would have been asking for further trouble to send another member of the party into the lion's den to retrieve the straying sheep. For a woman on her own, it was not done at that time to enter licensed premises, which excluded action on my part. It had to be Mr McLennan who rounded up the stragglers, while I took the rest on to our destination. It was with a great sigh of relief, in spite of the free and quite good lunch, that I counted them through at the theatre's front door and returned to the office.

My duties, as is already obvious, were many and varied. I took dictation, typed all the correspondence, took a turn at the reception desk if, as sometimes happened, we were short-staffed, and prepared the weekly returns for HQ. A daybook kept by the enquiry clerks had each caller entered according to nationality and request. The latter even included passers-by, intrigued by the beautiful four-foot model of the tea clipper *Cutty Sark* which graced our large shop window and was worth a fortune, lent by a generous shipping line. Every Saturday I had to cast out this information into various categories, giving a total for each day and for the whole week. Since the number of persons making use of our services ran into the hundreds and mechanical aids to calculation were not known, the rapid commercial arithmetic I had once learned stood me in good stead.

It may sound strange today having to work on Sundays. To begin with, we opened seven days a week, but it soon became clear that particularly we women, with our outside commitments, could not work without a day's break. Eventually the working week was reduced to six and then to five and a half days, with staff taking turns to cover Saturday afternoons.

Henry had another splendid idea, good for his image, probably welcomed by the recipients, but another heavy burden for me. The BBC being the voice of Free Europe had substantially increased its foreign-language broadcasts going out on shortwaves. This expansion was accompanied by the publication of special programme notes once a month, listing languages and times of individual pro- grammes. Why, went the argument, should our office not make itself responsible for the dispatch of a copy to every Allied ship of whatever type? The BBC agreed, and a huge stack of programmes appeared in my basement as regular as clockwork. Since there were at least two pages to each copy having to be stapled together before distribution, anybody who had some time to spare, including the young son of Henry's lady friend was roped in to get the job done, with the final responsibility always being mine.

Another of Henry's enterprises concerned the setting up of a loan library for Allied seafarers. There existed a large sea war library service catering for anything afloat, but here again it was felt that foreign-language books would be better in the care of an organisation devoted to the speakers of these languages. It became necessary to rent an additional room on the second floor of Grand Buildings, with a member of staff designated to run the library. Occasionally I had to go up there to check that all was in order, which allowed me to make the acquaintance of the girl in charge of the Russian TASS agency office next door. She did her best to enrol me in the Communist party. Her enticements did not appeal.

10

Beyond the Office

Being in the heart of London had many advantages. There were the lunchtime concerts at the National Gallery given by that great pianist Myra Hess, whose cousin I had got to know at the wine and spirit firm when he called on us as a traveller for German wine wholesalers Sichel & Söhne, himself a refugee from that country. Not only was the music glorious and the setting imposing, but there was also an excellent lunch to be had at a reasonable cost. Society ladies who were still able to employ cooks provided the simple yet extremely well-prepared dishes below cost price.

At the New Theatre a short way up St Martin's Lane, Laurence Olivier and Ralph Richardson performed singly and together with a brilliant company of fellow actors. It was easy to stroll up there during the lunch break to buy tickets for what, surely, must have been one of the greatest periods in modern theatrical history. To see Olivier in Sophocles's *Oedipus Rex* before the interval and in Sheridan's *The Critic* after it was a display of the highest acting skill. My future husband would collect me from the office after finishing his day's work at the Admiralty, a bar snack at the pub on the corner of St Martin's Lane would sustain us for the evening and off we went to be transported away from the bombs, the empty sites where houses and shops used to be, the rationing and the growing anxiety about the progress of the war.

Once a week in my lunch hour I would walk to the street market in Brewer Street to buy, off the ration, the little I needed. It was a red-letter day when cherries appeared on the stalls, Kent Napoleon cherries called 'Naps' by the market traders, even though they were an expensive luxury at the stiff price of 1/6 a pound.

One of the sights Londoners quickly became accustomed to was the nightly invasion of the London underground stations by people of every kind, seeking a safe refuge from the deadly rain descending from the sky above. At first the authorities, fearing for the efficient and safe conduct of their trains, had tried to stem the human flood cascading down onto the platforms, but to no avail, in spite of a rumour which proved to be true when such things could be openly discussed, that a bomb in the East End had hit the entrance to an underground tunnel, blocking the exit and fracturing a water main, leading to the drowning of 400 persons sheltering there. Common sense prevailed and organisation took over. Bed spaces were marked off, halving the width of the platforms for use by the travelling public. Each space was given a number which, in turn, became the 'property' of a refugee from the world above. Whole families lived like that for many months, coming up every morning to carry on with their daily lives and returning before nightfall. It must be the case that thanks to the depth of the London tube tunnels the casualty list among the civilian population was not bigger than it was. This was especially the case when the V1 (*Vergeltungswaffe eins*) was added to the German armoury in 1944.

Travelling by public transport in the dark was of a special nature. To lessen the danger from flying glass bus, tube and train windows were stuck over with a thick yellowish cotton mesh, making it impossible to see out. In order to allow a glimpse to orientate oneself, a diamond shape in the centre of each pane had been left uncovered. The interior lighting, to conform with black-out regulations, had to be the minimum possible, producing a spectral world inhabited by grey, indistinct, ghostly figures. Train travel brought its own hazards. In order to hinder any enemy who might have succeeded in landing somehow in this country, all signs giving an indication of place, county and cross-country roads, in other words identifying an area, were removed and the countryside turned into no-man's-land. This was all right if one knew one's way about. But!

Firmly stuck in my mind is my first trip to Newbury to visit a dear friend from hostel days. After the usual call at the police station to notify them of my travelling plans, stating day, time of departure and return, and of course destination, I caught the stopping train to Reading at Paddington Station. Once the journey had started, the fun began. Every time we halted, passengers not familiar with the route craned their necks to peer through the clear diamond in an endeavour to discover the train's whereabouts. Sometimes we just stopped on the line, sometimes it was in an actual station. It was with the greatest relief that I espied my friend on one of these anonymous platforms. I had arrived! One has to ask oneself how many unnecessary journeys were undertaken to unwanted destinations by people lost in an unfamiliar landscape. Journeying into London was much easier. The train did not go any further.

Time passed, as it will. In March 1944 Tony and I became engaged, with a view to getting married in the autumn. As was only proper, we used a free weekend in that month to travel down to Bath where his widowed mother lived to make it official and obtain her blessing. It was a very cold house we entered, whose garden ran down to the river Avon. Even with the fire blazing away in the living room grate, I never felt warm except in bed with a hot water bottle bringing my toes back to life. And the utter silence at night kept me awake. We returned to London on the Sunday night reasonably early to allow sufficient time for Tony to get back to the Officers' Club in Guilford Street off Russell Square, his home during his Admiralty posting, while I had to get to Notting Hill.

Just as the train was within a quarter of an hour's journey from Paddington Station, it stopped, the lights were dimmed even more than they already were, and the crowded compartments filled with foreboding. I, who had lived through London's trials and tribulations since the beginning of the hot war without much worrying, became agitated. Somehow I was certain that something had happened to the house in which I lodged. Tony, a scientist and not given to feelings caused by a sixth sense, tried to convince me of the unlikelihood of such an occurrence, considering the tens of thousands of dwellings in the urban circumference.

At last we moved again, drawing into a station under a severe air attack. The station floor was covered with several inches of water pouring in a continuous stream from the roof, with firemen doing their utmost to stop it from catching alight, while the neighbouring Great Western Hotel was burning fiercely. We waded to the entrance of the underground. Tony, being newly engaged, thought to humour me by offering to see me home, although this would make his journey back to the club a difficult one. As soon as we left the tube train at Notting Hill Gate we could smell burning. The smell increased frighteningly on turning the corner into Pembridge Square. Its source, only too evident against the night sky were huge flames shooting from the top of 'my' house.

When we got to the front door we found it open, with water cascading down the stairs. The door to my little flat had been broken open and all my possessions removed, the drawers taken out of the chest, the blankets ripped from the bed and used to bundle up my clothes and anything else of a moveable nature. The large walk-in cupboard, my delight for so long, also harboured a waterfall, fortunately by-passing the suitcases I had stored there.

We went in search of my property and did not have far to look. On the lawn covering the centre of the square the police had roped off an area where a miscellaneous assortment of goods had been deposited. There I found all I owned, with the exception of my clothes ration book left in one of the drawers. The sight of such a valuable object had been too tempting for the valiant rescuer of my bits and pieces. It hurt nevertheless.

Having established the fact that I was not quite destitute yet, the question arose of what to do next. It was a fine and dry but cold night, the police were standing guard over the pile of objects on the lawn, but, where were we to go. Tony had by now decided to do the gentlemanly thing and stay with me for the remainder of the hours till daybreak, the situation deteriorating by the minute. The incendiaries were continuing to drop, the United Dairies Depot across the road was also burning well, lighting up the whole neighbourhood. In between, the sound of bombs exploding could be heard. In order to find some sort of cover we re-entered the building which we had left only a few minutes ago and descended to the basement floor, emptied of its contents. We found a vacated furnished room and, fully dressed so as to be able to escape at a moment's notice, made ourselves as comfortable as possible under the circumstances. Thus passed a never-to-be-forgotten night.

Next morning the fires were out, the air was full of the smell of smoke and ash from the conflagration, and I was homeless. Tony left for his club to get ready for another day at the Gunnery Division, and I telephoned Henry to ask for a day's leave to find shelter once again from the hostile outdoors before nightfall. Not far away in Princes

Square a furnished room, the exact opposite to the one I had been forced to vacate, happened to be for rent. The only thing they had in common was their situation on the ground floor.

While my past home had been small and narrow but quiet and enfolding, my new one, in better days, must have been the drawing room of a very large house. The windows, of which there were four reaching from floor to ceiling, were provided with solid wooden shutters and pierced the wall facing the Bayswater Road. These shutters I closed religiously every evening as soon as I got back, not only on account of the strict black-out regulations but also as a precaution against flying glass. The heavy anti-aircraft pompom guns stationed in Hyde Park made the windows rattle with every salvo, making one fear for the safety of the large window panes. The bed was tucked away in a corner well away from the dangerous glass, and with the rest of the sparse furniture appearing lost in that vast space. I felt very unsafe and uncomfortable, but need allows little choice. As luck would have it, I had caught cold traipsing through the icy water at Paddington. In consequence, having spent many hours in wet shoes, I was now confined to bed, feeling wretched and hardly able to speak, looking at the ceiling and wondering about the future.

Tony, who knew a great deal about the war, also knew about the developments in German weaponry. He never told me anything, of course, not even when I described to him with some excitement how I had seen a plane on fire passing my window as I lay in bed. It was a V1, as we all soon learned. This pilotless small plane was nothing but a flying bomb primed for its engine to cut out before descending, giving one about two minutes to find shelter before it hit the ground. The explosion, though considerable, had little penetrating power, making basements and the little brick-and-concrete street shelters into which one could dive give a certain degree of protection from the effects of the blast.

It was the V2 (*Vergeltungswaffe zwei*) which caused the utmost concern. When I heard the first one I thought, as did most of the population, that a gasholder had been hit and exploded. It was nothing of the sort, of course. As everybody today knows, it was a large rocket travelling at such height and speed that the sound of the explosion was the first indication one had of its arrival. It created a large number of casualties and tremendous damage. This outcome was achieved in two ways. On reaching its pre-set target the propulsion section separated from the explosive-filled nose cone, the former dropping to earth a considerable distance from the latter, creating its own havoc. I firmly believe that had this fearful weapon made an earlier appearance on the war scene, the future of London and with it the outcome of the war, might have been in jeopardy.

11

Wedding Without Bells

By the summer we had settled on Saturday 18 November 1944 for our wedding at St Martin in the Fields, the Admiralty church entitled to fly the White Ensign rather than the Union Jack. The man who was to marry us was Chaplain to the Canadian Forces, a friend from Tony's club, and the best man Duncan Bruce, Tony's close companion in his work and play. We booked the reception at the Rembrandt Hotel in South Kensington for 40 people and my old boss from the licensed trade gave us all the wine we needed as a wedding present. We notified my local parish church as to the reading of the banns as required by law, applied for a licence to marry, and looked forward to the great day.

With the air attacks on London intensifying, Tony asked me to move nearer to London House, his home in Guilford Street, and so, yet again, I moved, this time to Mecklenburgh Square, a few minutes walk away. From there we started to search for a small flat for both of us. What we found was just right. No 44 Bramham Gardens, Earls Court, was what today would be called a studio flat in a well-appointed, fully serviced, gracious house. It consisted of a very large, comfortably furnished room with adjoining bathroom, the first private facility of its kind I had known since leaving Vienna. There was no kitchen, but a gas ring next to the gas fire allowed for a certain amount of cooking to be done. We extended our ability to provide hot food

255

thanks to the purchase of a quite ingenious piece of equipment. A large, solidly cast metal dish in the shape of a saucepan lid had been fitted with a circular electric element and a heat-proof handle. When this oven in miniature stood upright, a saucepan or frying pan could be placed on it. Turned upside down, it worked as a grill. I kept it in use long after I owned a proper cooker.

Breakfast, always cooked, was provided by the housekeeper and her female sidekick, who did all the fetching and carrying as well as the cleaning. We had to give up some of our rations, but that did not worry us. Restaurant meals were not rationed, the only restriction being a top charge of 5/- no matter where one ate. For most people such an amount far exceeded what could be afforded on a regular basis, ourselves included. It had to be a special occasion before we would venture out to eat in style.

Having found our new home, I moved again to avoid paying rent in two places. My mother had been assiduous in sending food parcels from New York, full of goodies of limited use to us. How could I cope with a two-pound tin of ham without a refrigerator to store it once it had been opened? Friends with proper homes benefited, nothing was wasted. However, once a one-pound tin of butter was included, a luxury indeed, to be kept for a special treat. My wedding cake was going to be that treat.

Once again my old boss and friend, the Hungarian, came to my aid. He had an extensive acquaintance amongst his countrymen, as was only to be expected. One couple, by the name of Floris, owned a top-class wholesale cake, chocolate and biscuit factory on the second floor of an old house in Brewer Street. Their foremost client was Fortnum & Mason, whose expensive, hand-made chocolates and superior biscuits, sold in special boxes, had here their origin. It had been one of my jobs when working in Bond Street to call on Mrs Floris, who was in charge of the manufacturing side of the business, to collect whatever my boss had ordered, making me a familiar figure to all at the firm. Mrs Floris, an impressive woman always dressed in a spotless white coat, kept an eagle eye on the various processes under her command. The making of the chocolates was what fascinated me in particular. The coating of the various centres and any additional decoration, executed in liquid chocolate, was put on by hand by women operatives at an incredible speed, making it seem a deceptively simple skill which it must have taken a great deal of practice to acquire.

Now, off their own bat these kind-hearted people offered to take the order for my wedding cake using mother's butter. The two patissiers were Swiss nationals and therefore untouched by the call-up regulations affecting everybody's life. Undisturbed and hardly conscious of the exigencies of rationing, they plied their trade. It was going to be just a one-tier cake, but of the best quality, to be collected a couple of days before the event.

Cousin Fritzi and I went to Fenwicks in Bond Street to choose a wedding dress. It was understood that it would be an afternoon dress, white with the normal trimmings being judged unsuitable, not least on account of the cost, for neither Tony nor I had parents who could contribute to the expense of the whole event. After looking long and hard at a blue dress for £12, three weeks' salary for me, I settled on a turquoise dress, cost £8. The shoes and stockings my mother had provided. The latter were one of the first pairs of nylons to be seen in this country, and the former an elegant yet most comfortable pair of peep-toe elasticised shoes. The hat, somewhat in the style of a forage cap, was made of stiff buckram stuck all over with small grey feathers. I bought half a yard of fine grey netting for a small veil to cover my face, which I sewed on with a few stitches, and for my going-away I ordered a tweed suit from the Fifty Shilling Tailor, a well-known tailoring chain, made to measure and of such excellent quality that it was to last me for many years. Those were the days!

The padre who was going to marry us arranged for a rehearsal a couple of days before the date, and my future mother-in-law in Bath was getting the ring, engraved with orange blossoms and of 22-carat quality, from a jeweller of her acquaintance. Officially only 9-carat rings could be sold. To make certain of a good fit I was sent the standard measuring device, found my finger size and returned it to Bath.

Wedding presents started to arrive and, in spite of the wartime difficulties, our friends did their very best to find a welcome gift. Henry, always generous and in the best of taste, gave us a tall, heavily decorated Japanese vase which has stood by the side of our living room fireplace ever since; the Convalescent Home for Merchant Seamen at Limpsfield Chart donated a large assembly of Pyrex ovenproof glass dishes, bowls and plates which, with the exception of three pieces, have survived more than 57 years of constant use; and the good woman who kept our offices spic and span, working hard to keep her very large family, went to Woolworths for a comprehensive assortment of kitchen tools, most of which are still doing duty today.

The stringencies imposed by the war resulted in the most useful and practical presents anyone could wish. There were water glasses, the usual breadboard with accompanying knife, a set of table knives and a large white linen tablecloth, big enough to cover a table seating eight persons. Its edges were raw, which gave me the opportunity of practising my skill at hemstitching. The most valuable and least useful present was that from my dear friend Marietta. It was and is a beautiful long silver tray with a pierced gallery along its sides, part of her family silver. Only rarely does it see the light of day, while everything else is still in constant use.

The summer turned into early autumn, and everything

possible seemed to have been taken care of to make our wedding the successful and enjoyable occasion we wanted it to be. The invitations to the reception had been prepared and were waiting to be posted. The guests, because of the expense, were to be restricted to two personal friends on either side in addition to the actors in the church ceremony, the remainder being a crowd of relatives of my future husband. Most of them I had never met, just as my bridesmaid, chosen on my mother-in-law's insistence, was the young and hardly known to me daughter of one of her close friends.

With the date almost upon us Bath suffered its one and only air raid of the war, not as destructive as the one on Coventry but severe enough to do some serious damage, not only to this beautiful city but also to the psyche of its inhabitants. There is nothing so potent and convincing as living through an experience oneself. The result was that mother-in-law changed her mind about coming to London to attend the wedding for fear of exposing herself to yet another air raid during the two nights she would be staying with her nephew in Beckenham. Tony, if left to himself, might well have given in to her, finding it extremely difficult to gainsay his mother, who had not only lost a husband but also a very much loved daughter, Tony's senior by nine years, anything at all. Being only too aware of the implications of a postponement, I finally had to threaten on getting married without her being present. This did the trick, she was going to make the sacrifice. After all, if we risked our lives every day and had done so for years, it did not seem to be asking a lot.

As arranged, on the morning of Thursday 16th November, I went to collect the cake, beautifully packed in a sturdy box, paid the very modest bill and, in a happy mood, left the Floris premises. It was a drizzly day, and, as I had been accustomed to do since I lived at home, I was wearing

259

rubber overshoes to protect my feet from the damp. Walking down the curving, rather steep stone staircase, I suddenly lost my footing on the wet surface, and with it my balance, falling down a whole flight with only one thought in mind, how to protect my precious cake. Whatever was happening to the rest of me, my right arm held the box with its irreplaceable contents firmly aloft. The cake survived without a scratch, but the same could not be said of my left ankle, which was badly twisted. It continued to swell and stiffen in the course of the day until I could hardly bear to stand on it, let alone walk with it. Now it was my turn to press for a postponement, and now it was Tony's turn to insist on the arrangements being carried out to the letter, for was not his mother prepared to attend at an imagined risk to her life? Cold compresses and sheer determination had to come to my assistance.

On Saturday, the great day, cousin Roddie arrived in good time to accompany me to the church where he was to give me away at the 2 o'clock ceremony in place of my faraway father. Just before leaving the house Barkers of Kensington delivered the wooden clothes horse I had bought, no doubt a pointer to my future rôle as a housewife. Sitting in the taxi with cousin Fritzi making up the party, we discovered to our discomfort that while, indeed, I had my sheaf of pink carnations, nobody had remembered to get a buttonhole for Roddie. We stopped in Piccadilly Circus where the flower sellers were plying their trade on the steps of Eros. A large carnation to match my bouquet was slotted into its appointed hole and on we drove to St Martin's in the Fields.

To walk up to the altar with my badly swollen and very painful ankle required all my concentration although, out of the corner of one eye, I managed to notice how full the church was. Naval uniforms with their gilt braid and buttons lighting up the gloom were much in evidence. All went well until the ring was slipped on my finger, Alas, alack! All the trouble in getting the size right had proved in vain. Mother-in-law, unable to accept that my hands were young and slender, had the ring made to fit her own finger. Still, there was nothing to be done then. Only after returning from our honeymoon did a jeweller properly fit it, which meant my being ringless for ten days, something hard to bear for a new wife. Even after all these years, it is still the same size and easy to wear.

12

The Twosome

We had booked the midnight sleeper, First Class naturally, to Torquay, leaving a considerable time gap between departing from the reception and getting to Paddington Station by 11.30. John Gielgud was having a big success playing Hamlet at the Haymarket Theatre during that season, giving us the opportunity of spending most of the time interval in a riveting if somewhat unusual fashion. However, there was something else to be done first. In order to be allowed to enter the West Country coastal region, I had to notify the police that, thanks to my marriage, my status had changed from 'enemy alien' to 'faithful subject of His Britannic Majesty'. It did not feel any different to me, never having harboured any inimical feelings towards His Majesty or the country which had taken me in when the need was greatest – still bureaucracy had to be satisfied.

The newly joined couple took the bus to Vine Street Police Station, which dealt with 'foreigners', clutching the hardly dry marriage certificate. A few minutes of pleasant conversation and I was free to go where I pleased for the first time in four and a half years. At that moment it meant having tea at the Piccadilly Hotel, almost next door to the police station, from where we walked to the Haymarket.

John Gielgud, tall, slim, fair-haired and dressed in black from top to toe, gave an impressive performance. Still wrapped in its effect on us, we made our way to the station

262

reasonably early for the retrieval of our suitcases booked into the left-luggage office early in the morning – only to discover the office firmly shut with nobody about looking in the least connected to the staff. Fortunately there was over half an hour to spare before the train's departure, offering the possibility of a positive resolution of the situation. With Tony's uniform acting as a spur, a couple of railway employees were eventually run to earth and, after some delay, the keys to the left-luggage office found, as was our baggage. At last we could relax in our small compartment. Although extremely tired, sleep was only intermittent as far as I was concerned. It had been a long, long day, my ankle hurt, the train shuddered, the wheels clicked and clattered, we stopped and started, my thoughts were with my absent family, and I wondered about the major step I had just taken without advice from anybody I had confidence in.

Eventually 7 o'clock came with dawn breaking, and Torquay station loomed into view. We were the only passengers to get off on this grey drizzling morning, with no other living being in sight, with no taxi to take us to our hotel, with no railwayman to give us directions of how to find the town. Tony grabbed hold of the two cases, and we started down the hill towards the sea weary and not exactly in the best of temper.

The hotel was pleasant enough, though not at all like the Imperial, whose name conjured up my spirituous dealings of Old Bond Street. We were the youngest guests among a cast of elderly retired residents who had fled to the Queen of the Cornish Riviera for the duration of the war. Although we tried hard to pretend to be a married couple of long standing, the true state of affairs must have been obvious to the least observant.

After returning to London, life went on much as before, except there were two of us instead of just myself. We entertained our friends, serving meals conjured up from

263

rations and cooked in our primitive kitchen corner, played cards and Monopoly, went to the theatre, saw *Where the Sun Shines*, *Flarepath*, *French without Tears* and other highly patriotic plays, frequented the Music Hall in Golders Green by means of the number 27 bus, laughed at Sid Field 'addressing the ball' at the Prince of Wales Theatre, spent many a happy hour at the Players Club underneath the arches at Charing Cross, in short conducted ourselves as do the young, unencumbered with personal responsibilities, when money is not short and external circumstances too uncertain to make plans for the future.

Our most heartfelt desire was for the cessation of the constant attacks by the German V1 and V2 weapons. The invasion of the Continent by the Allies on 6 June 1944 had given everybody hope that the launch sites situated in the Low Countries would be quickly overrun. It was not to be. The fighting was fierce, raging in a see-saw fashion, while we continued to be at the receiving end of unwanted gifts from abroad. Slowly the news became more encouraging, and the battle for Berlin, with the concomitant suicide of Hitler, at last indicating the approaching end of this drawn-out struggle. 8 May 1945 was a day never to be forgotten. Peace had broken out!

Tony and I joined thousands of others flocking to the Home Office Building in Whitehall to hear and see Winston Churchill proclaim the Armistice from its balcony. The crowd was so dense that I was afraid of being crushed to death. One could only move with one of the several streams of people edging its way through the throng. It took us up to Trafalgar Square and from there through Admiralty Arch down the Mall to Buckingham Palace. All vehicular traffic had been stopped by the mass of humanity pouring down this beautiful avenue. The weather was mild if overcast, just right for the occasion. Up went the cry for the King and Queen who, with members of their family, duly appeared on the Palace balcony, not once, not twice, but many times to join their subjects in one great celebration. However, we all knew that on that day only the first and nearest of our enemies had been defeated, and that the war in the East was being waged and blood was continuing to be spilt.

The lights, absent for almost six years, went on all over the country, the black-out disappeared like magic, and the church bells, silent for all that time, were to be heard again pealing out in joy and not, as had been their wartime role, to announce the invasion of the British Isles by the enemy. Yet the war went on, with nobody having the faintest idea when there would be real peace. The work of the Information Bureau continued, Tony's Admiralty posting continued, and so did the news reports from the Far East. It all implied many more months of hard and bitter fighting. We again went to Torquay for a week's holiday in July, this time looking and acting less newly married than on the previous occasion. Suddenly, without warning the news of the dropping by the United States of two atomic bombs on Japanese towns broke. Events speeded up like a film played at a fast-forward setting. 15 August brought the Japanese surrender, and the war was finally over. That night lying in bed, I listened in the stillness of Bramham Gardens to the familiar hooting of the little owls roosting in the trees in that quiet square, and thought it a good omen for the future.

13

Peace at Last

With the ending of hostilities the release into civilian life of serving personnel could begin. It was an orderly process. Tony's turn came in March 1946. Before the war he had been teaching Physics at Wallasey Grammar School for Boys in the Wirral, the scene of one of my abortive attempts at domestic service, and about three miles from West Kirby, the scene of my unfortunate attempt at finding happiness at the outbreak of the war. What an odd coincidence! His job had been reserved for him as it had for everybody in the services, so Wallasey would be our first proper home. At the beginning of March we travelled by train to the small town on the opposite shore of the Mersey from the great port of Liverpool, in search of something suitable to rent furnished. To buy was not only too expensive but did not fit in with our plans to move as soon as Tony could find an alternative post at a higher level.

The hotel we stayed in was cold and very old-fashioned, with an open, empty fireplace in the bedroom down whose chimney the storm straight off the Irish Sea howled all night, making me fear for its eventual collapse. Next morning, through the local estate agent, we managed to find a small furnished semi-detached house within walking distance of the school at a rent of £30 per month. Since Tony's salary would only be £36 per month, it meant living off our savings. Still, we had to live somewhere. The house belonged to an elderly spinster in her sixties who had been certified as mentally deranged, and whose affairs were in the hands of the Commissioners in Lunacy, with her sister-in-law keeping an eye on the property. Of the three bedrooms the smallest was firmly locked, being used as a storeroom for her personal belongings.

While the house was of an undistinguished, fairly modern design, the furnishings were somewhat unusual and unexpected. On entering by the front door one was faced on the opposite wall of the hall by an almost life-size painting of a colourful pirate pointing his pistol at the caller. In the living room facing the road stood a pianola in full working order with a large stuffed crocodile lying on top of it. The cabinet at its side contained about 80 rolls of music covering the period of popular tunes from the turn of the last century to 1915. What a lot of fun we and our friends had with that wonderful instrument! How many pennies were won and lost when they were placed on the silent keys, with the first one to fall as the music progressed taking the lot.

In the dining room a large stuffed turtle had found a home. Both it and the crocodile were banished to join the treasures in the locked room, but the pirate stayed. The sight of him would have frightened the life out of any burglar.

At the back of the house was the kitchen with a New World Gas cooker which I took to be painted black inside until my first attempt at cleaning revealed it to be really grey. The black colour was just burnt-on fat. It took almost a day to restore it to its original appearance. The back door led from the kitchen to an outhouse containing a gas washboiler. Furlined boots became my normal footwear in the nether regions until spring at last arrived in the North-west. The garden was small, thank goodness, boasting three blackcurrant bushes, much overgrown, and little else. When one stood in it on a clear calm day, soot rained gently down from above, speckling everything with black spots, including the newly washed sheets and pillowcases hung out to dry. One of my new neighbours later consoled me, saying that it was quite normal, that they no longer noticed it and that nobody minded. It was the price to be paid for the ship-building at Rock Ferry and the heavy steamer traffic on the Mersey.

We rented the house from the middle of the month and prepared to leave town, the life and the income so familiar to us. Tony was discharged from the Navy with a gratuity of £200 and a demob suit in grey worsted, a felt hat, white shirt and a pair of brown shoes – black ones he already owned from his service days – all new and of good quality. I cut off the lovely gilt buttons from his naval overcoat and replaced them with dull ordinary blue ones. He wore it for years in the lean times we were now facing, until finally passing it on to a chimney sweep.

The Austrian Youth Association had already dissolved itself, with most of its members dispersing in the country and a few returning to Austria. I gave notice at the Bureau, which was going to continue functioning for a few months more. Then I started to pack. Tony, as a parting gift from a grateful country, was handed a First-Class travel warrant to anywhere in the UK; I, however, was not included. Tony's oldest and closest friend, Tom Demerell, who had been severely wounded by a flying bomb landing almost on top of the gunsite manned by him and his crew, and was responsible for shooting it down, was staying at a convalescent home in Hampstead. Somehow he managed to run a car. Now he offered to take me and my effects together with any overflow from Tony to Wallasey, while my husband would travel in First-Class comfort by train to Liverpool.

We filled the small car as full as it would go, not forgetting the ironing board strapped to the rear of it. The journey took six weary hours, though the traffic was light enough. In the Midlands we drove through a thick blanket of industrial smog worse than the pollution encountered on Merseyside. At last my new home hove into sight, with Tony standing at the front door to welcome us.

Another beginning had begun.